CONVERSATIONS IN THE ABBEY, VOL. II

The Next Generation of Senior Monks of Saint Meinrad
Reflects on Their Lives

D0902082

Ruth Clifford Engs, editor

CONVERSATIONS IN THE ABBEY, VOL. II

Ruth Clifford Engs, editor

Table of Contents

*Profiles of monks, starting with the most senior in monastic profession.
+Members of Alcoholics Anonymous (AA) keep their anonymity at the
level of the press, radio, film etc.

Dedication

Ora et Labora

This work is dedicated to the monks of
Saint Meinrad Archabbey – past, present and future.

Foreword

In the minds of many folks, monks are voiceless medieval figures from the pages of a history book, or occasional dreary characters woven into a novel on The New York Times Best Sellers list. Like some extinct species, they no longer walk the face of the earth. But for some other folks, monks are neighbors who live just over the next hill or friends whose company is always treasured. They live and breathe in the present time, just as surely as a meadowlark welcomes the new day with its morning song.

For 160 years now, the monks of Saint Meinrad have welcomed students, guests and pilgrims to the hill. Those men and women who have been here know that we are indeed flesh and blood, and not merely characters drawn from fiction, although, like every monastery, we have had our share of real characters in the community. They keep our life from being dull.

The alumni of our schools, our many oblates, numerous retreatants, the families and friends of the monks – all of these folks have known Saint Meinrad variously for a day or a month or for many years. They have stayed here and prayed here, they have studied here and visited here, and to varying degrees they have come to know the monks of this house. Each could tell some story of how they see Saint Meinrad.

In her book *Conversations in the Abbey: Senior Monks of St. Meinrad Reflect on Their Lives* (2008), Dr. Ruth Clifford Engs allowed the monks to speak for themselves about their life in the community. This second volume continues her series of interviews and focuses on a relatively younger generation in the community, a group of men whose monastic life began in the decade before Vatican II.

While they knew and lived the life of the house prior to the reforms of the Council, they also were part of that generation of monks who forged those reforms into the customs and practices that came to shape the life of the house, even to the present day. In this sense, they are a unique generation in the history of Saint Meinrad, bridging two very different eras, both of which give witness to the common life of Benedictine monasticism as it is lived in this house.

This second volume in the series allows this generation of monks to speak for themselves. They bring a flesh-and-blood perspective to the story of monastic life at Saint Meinrad and add to the variety of that "multitude of people" in whom the Lord seeks his workmen (*Rule of St. Benedict*, Prologue 14). Their individual stories, while distinctively their own, belong to the larger story of Saint Meinrad, which is still unfolding.

Dr. Engs is herself no stranger to Saint Meinrad. She is a frequent guest, a friend, a collaborator and an oblate of our house, and so she brings a well-trained ear to her task of listening to all our stories and from them being able to tell our story. In the conversations related in these two volumes, Ruth is a definite participant, even if she chooses to mute her own voice so that the others might be heard for what they have to tell.

To all who listen in on these conversations: hear these real monks who speak from the heart about the joys and sorrows, the successes and the failures of their lives. They are men who seek God in the workshop of the monastery where silence is a practice and restraint of speech (*Rule of St. Benedict*, Chapter 6) is a value. But for a moment, they allowed themselves to be coaxed out because "there is a time to keep silence, and a time to speak" (Ecclesiastes 3.7b). While you have the chance, then, listen with the ear of your heart.

Archabbot Justin DuVall, OSB
March 21, 2016
The Passing of our Holy Father Saint Benedict

Preface

Introduction

Like *Conversations in the Abbey: Senior Monks of St. Meinrad Reflect on Their Lives* (2008), this next volume (Volume II) is a collection of oral history biographies that includes the personal reflections of men who have lived through much of the 20th century and the first decade of the 21st century. Unlike the first volume, there are no historical chapters about the work of the monastery, inasmuch as most of the businesses mentioned in those historical chapters no longer exist.

In earlier years, the brothers did most of the physical work in the monastic community. This included a farm with a large garden, pigs, dairy and beef cattle, and a vineyard. Other businesses included a sandstone quarry, coal mine, and a large mail order business with original sculptures and Christmas cards created out of the Abbey Press.

A few of the monks in Volume II mention these agricultural and other businesses, as they were an important part of their lives in their younger years. One monk profiled ran the mail order business. Readers interested in the older monastic industries of the community are referred to the first volume for details.

The monks featured in Volume II are all members of Saint Meinrad Archabbey, a Benedictine community in southern Indiana. Saint Meinrad is approximately halfway between Evansville, Indiana, and Louisville, Kentucky. It is located in a rural area with plentiful rolling hills, agricultural operations, forests and fields.

Employees at the Archabbey are from the surrounding area. While Saint Meinrad has always relied on others for assistance, through the mid- to late-20th century, the monastery was more self-sufficient for its needs. Today, due to changes in society and a decrease in the number of monks in the community due to death and fewer vocations for this way of life, many jobs are now accomplished by lay people.

The primary work of the abbey is the operation of a Seminary and School of Theology to educate and form future priests, permanent deacons and lay ministers. Although they take a vow of stability, many of the monks work outside the community as chaplains, pastors, educators and community outreach workers.

Benedictine monks in their daily lives strive for a balance between prayer and work with the motto, *Ora et Labora* (Pray and Work). The Benedictine monastic tradition and way of life was begun by St. Benedict in Italy in the early sixth century. The Benedictine community has a tradition of hospitality and living a humble life.

Many recent publications concerning monks and nuns have focused on their spiritual and prayer life. However, since the Benedictine lifestyle is a balance of both prayer and work, which are considered essential to the spiritual life, sustenance of the community and growth of the individual, questions about both prayer and work are featured in this volume, as they were in the first book.

The monks included in Volume II were all born between 1930 and 1940. The first volume of *Conversations* featured men primarily born before 1930. Both of these cohorts experienced vast changes in society and the upheaval that has characterized much of the modern history of the Roman Catholic Church.

The men featured in this current work, as they first entered the monastery, would have been at the beginning or in the midst of the changes emerging in the aftermath of Vatican II (the Council that mandated reform in the Church). The traditions, and even relationships within the monastic community, became challenged in the aftermath of the Council. These challenges are discussed by many of the monks.

The monks interviewed for this present book include brothers, priests and a former abbot. Different experiences emerge from the men interviewed in this work, compared to the first volume. In many ways, these experiences reflect the changes in the Church and society. For example, two of the brothers later became priests and were allowed to remain at the monastery, rather than transferring to another monastic community as had been the custom. An African-American monk was the leader of the Civil Rights Movement in Indianapolis during the 1960s and founded a university, and the former abbot left an uncommon legacy.

The lives of these men often interconnect. Several received their Bachelor of Arts degrees from Saint Meinrad College. Two priests were directors of St. Placid Hall – a high school for brothers – and a few of the monks went through this high school. One brother and two priests served at a mission in Peru, and a couple of these monks experienced the devastating 1970 earthquake there. Another monk constructed the guest house at Saint Meinrad and at Prince of Peace Abbey in California without detailed blueprints, and one maintained a large cattle operation in Tennessee.

Enormous talent, inner strength and leadership abilities are found among this cohort. Another difference in the men profiled in this volume, compared to the first, is that this group is more open about stressful personal experiences and "dark nights of the soul." These experiences included being in the middle of an earthquake and seeing a colleague and others die, having a nervous breakdown from work stress, and recovering from alcoholism and illnesses.

Many of the monks interviewed expressed doubt, uncertainty, disappointments and struggles – this is the human condition. On the other hand, perseverance, accomplishments, joy, lessons learned from failures, striving for humility, and resolution of conflicts are found through prayer, the love of God and Benedictine spirituality. Little homilies, embedded in their stories, emerge from these most inspiring and talented men. Their lives serve as positive role models for anyone.

The History and Process of this Project

After the publication of the first volume, I requested, and was given permission, by Archabbot Justin DuVall, OSB, to interview the next generation of senior monks. I gave each monk a list of questions that asked for recollections of childhood, teenage years, early life in the monastic community, career, spiritual life, and reflections on changes in society, the Church and monastic community—pre- and post-Vatican II.

Since I had a career in public health, I asked additional questions from this group to glean some medical care and health information of the 1930s and 1940s common to Indiana, Ohio, Kentucky and Illinois. This Midwest region is where most of these monks spent their childhood years. These new questions included the type of medical care the monk experienced as a child, in addition to their smoking and drinking patterns as teenagers or young adults before they entered the monastery. The monastic community has been "smoke free" since around 2003.

I recorded the interviews on a Sony digital audio recorder. They were transcribed by Ellen McGlothlin. I then greatly condensed and edited these raw transcriptions for this publication. The condensed and edited version of the biographical profile was given back to each monk for his further review, comments and changes. If major changes were made, the manuscript was sent back to the monk for additional comments and approval.

Copyediting was then accomplished by Mary Jeanne Schumacher, the director of communications for Saint Meinrad Archabbey. The whole manuscript was reviewed by a former abbot, Fr. Timothy Sweeny, OSB, a classmate, colleague or superior of this group of monks.

Three monks who were interviewed, and part of this collection, have recently died and did not have a chance to review their condensed biographies. These include Frs. Gregory Chamberlin, OSB, Boniface Hardin, OSB, and Stephen Snoich, OSB. Therefore, any errors in their chapters are mine.

It needs to be kept in mind that the personal opinions of the monks are not necessarily the opinions of Saint Meinrad Archabbey or the Catholic Church. Each monk was free to express his own attitudes or opinions about the questions asked. Like the first volume, all questions were handed out ahead of time. Not all monks chose to answer every question and/or diverged from the questions and added other material that makes for added richness and depth to this volume. Some monks detailed more information than others, thus the length of each of the profiles varies.

Finally, it has again been a privilege and a great honor to be able to interview, and interact with, the senior monks of Saint Meinrad Archabbey. Their lives are an inspiration for anyone.

Ruth Clifford Engs
February 10, 2016
Feast of St. Scholastica

Acknowledgments

Like most publications, this oral history of the senior monks of Saint Meinrad Archabbey could not have been accomplished without the help of many individuals.

First of all, I would like to thank Archabbot Justin DuVall, OSB, for his support and encouragement of the project. I am also grateful to all the monks profiled in this publication for engaging in the interviews and allowing them to be published in this work. Fr. Sean Hoppe, OSB, was most helpful in setting up interview rooms.

Mary Jeanne Schumacher, Tammy Schuetter and Krista Hall, of the Archabbey Communications Office, are commended for their ideas, layout and talent, which made this book an attractive piece of work. I would also like to thank Ellen McGlothlin for her transcription of the oral histories that make up the biographies of each monk.

I am especially indebted to former abbot, Fr. Timothy Sweeny, OSB, who reviewed the whole manuscript. Also Fr. Meinrad Brune, OSB, has always been helpful with specific questions and has supported and encouraged my various publication efforts for the oblate office or monastic community.

Finally, I am especially beholden to my husband, Jeffrey L. Franz, for allowing me the time and space to be creative.

Chapter 1: Br. Maurus Zoeller, OSB

Over a period of 30 years, Br. Maurus worked, and became a manager, at the Abbey Press. After retiring from the Abbey Press, he became a popular guest master, tour and retreat director, and still conducts pilgrimages around the world.

Born on a farm near Tiffin, OH, on June 24, 1932, Br. Maurus attended St. Joseph Grade School and graduated from Calvert High School in 1950. While in high school, he worked for a printing press.

He made his first profession as a monk on August 19, 1952, and perpetual profession on August 10, 1955. Although he began as a baker's assistant, in 1958 Br. Maurus began work at the Abbey Press. He became manager of the printing division (1960-1968), product development director (1968-1978), manager of Abbey Press Gift Shop (1978-1990) and its highly successful former catalog division.

In 1990, Br. Maurus began work as a tour director, retreat director and guest master. From 1997 to the present, he has been busy as a retreat director and pilgrimage guide. He has led pilgrimages all over the world, including northern, southern and eastern Europe; Britain; Ireland; Canada; the Holy Land and around the United States.

Dr. Ruth C. Engs interviewed Br. Maurus Zoeller, OSB, September 1, 2009; additional information from Br. Maurus, August 26, 2015.

Childhood and Early Years as a Monk

Tell me about your childhood and family life.

I was born on a farm about six miles from Tiffin, Ohio, on June the 24th, 1932, at the beginning of the Great Depression. They named me Charles. My father had just bought a 160-acre farm and I was number 12 of 13 children born to Francis Zoeller and Annie Clouse. Both my grandpas and grandmas were basically 100% German. Somehow, through the grace of God, we eked out a living. I don't think any of us 13 children suffered from a lack of food.

Tell me about the farm.

We had a lot of vegetable gardening. We would have corn in season and Mom would gather a couple of big buckets of corn. We ate eight or ten ears of corn for supper and that was our meal. We didn't have meat or anything else. But Mom would always fix a good breakfast in the morning after the boys milked about 25 cows.

How about your early schooling as a child?

In first grade, I went to a little one-room school house about two blocks from my home. It had about 60 kids and one teacher who taught all eight grades. For second grade, they opened a consolidated school called Hopewell-Loudon Consolidated School. It was a brand new school and they had 1st to 12th grades there.

We would be bused about 12 miles from my home into this public school and I went there from the second grade to the sixth grade. Before I began seventh grade, my Dad retired from farming. He turned over the farm to his sons and daughters. When we moved to town, Dad always went back and helped them on the farm.

How about your religious life as a child?

When we moved to Tiffin, Dad became a daily communicant for some 35 years. Every day my father would go to Mass and my

Mom would join him two or times a week. I went to Catholic school, St. Joseph's, in Tiffin, which was about two miles from my home. They had first to the eighth grade there and the first year I learned how to serve a Latin Mass.

I think I was a very good boy in seventh grade and went to daily Mass and communion. In the eighth grade, I served quite a bit and also went to daily Mass. I received a plaque of the Sacred Heart from the pastor because I was not tardy or late or missed any school for the whole year. I still have that plaque and am very proud of it.

When I graduated from eighth grade, I signed up to go to Calvert High School, a Catholic high school in Tiffin. The pastor called me into his office and said, "Charles, I noticed you haven't signed up for Latin at Calvert." I said, "No, Father, I didn't sign up for Latin." He said, "Why? Don't you think you ever want to be a priest?" and I said, "No, Father, I don't think I ever want to be a priest."

Then he said, "Well, how about if you take one year of Latin and after the year is up, if you don't like Latin or if you don't think you want to be a priest later on in life, at least you took one year of Latin for me." So I took one year of Latin in high school.

Did you ever work while still in school?

As a seventh, eighth and ninth grader, I worked after school delivering papers. In the tenth grade, I got a printing job at Haefling Printing Company, a little print shop there in our town. About 10 of us worked in the print shop. I would go down after school and clean up their presses and also make lead for the Linotype machines. I really enjoyed the work and I learned how to run the presses.

So at the end of my junior year, I worked all summer long at the press and really enjoyed it. I was running two automatic Kluge presses and sometimes I would run a hand-fed press. So I kept very busy and enjoyed that. One of the things that really impressed me for all my life was that my boss, Mr. Haefling, never told me to do something, but rather always asked me nicely if I could find the time to do this or that job.

Tell me some more about high school.

I remember one time, as a senior, the boys were misbehaving in the homeroom and Sister David asked the whole class to stay after school. After the bell rang, when school was out, I started walking out and Sister David hollered at me and said, "Charles, come back and sit down. We all have to stay after school for misbehaving." I just kept on walking and went to work.

The next morning, Sister David called me in and said, "You were supposed to stay after school. Why didn't you stay after school?" I said, "Well, I had to go to work. That is my job and I had to go to work." She said, "Well, what is more important, school or work?" I said, "My life's work is more important than school." So she didn't give me a hard time at all. I really enjoyed the work.

Did you drive in high school?

I had a motor scooter in the ninth and tenth grades. I would scoot around to go to work and to school. In the tenth grade, I bought a car, a '36 Chevy. My friend Dave Klupp had a big old-time Ford. One time we were playing follow the leader on the way to school and he drove down into the shallow part of the Sandusky River. We had about five kids in each of our cars and my car got a flat tire in the middle of the river. So we got it to the side of the river and changed the tire.

We got back about two hours late to school. The principal called my Dad and said that I was misbehaving, as I got everybody late for school. I think the Monsignor was about ready to kick me out of school, but Dad talked him into being patient with me. Anyway, I had a great time in high school.

What were some of your hobbies, activities and interests when you were in school?

I didn't take any football, basketball, baseball or any after-school sports because I was working after school every day. I would also work on Saturdays. So through my grade school and high school, I never entered any sports. My younger brother, Bernard, and I would play softball, but I didn't have any extra hobbies as my hobby was kind of my work, which I enjoyed so much.

Did you drink or smoke when you were in high school?

We drank a little bit.

What did you drink?

Beer, we drank beer in high school when we would have a party. On my 18th birthday, on June 24, when I was a senior in high school, I drank a little too much beer and one of my classmates ended up driving my car home.

Did you smoke in high school?

No, I never smoked at all in high school. My Dad and Mom told all their children, if we lasted until we were 21 years old without smoking, we would get $100. When I was in the monastery, I did get the $100 because I hadn't smoked. At about 25, when I was in the bakery, I started smoking because you got free cigarettes. I smoked for 25 years. I used to smoke sometimes at the Abbey Press a pack and a half a day. I was a heavy chain smoker.

How did you stop?

Fr. Eric [Lies] and I use to go vacationing in Florida to spend a week together on Palmer's Golf Course. His uncle, Arnie Lies, had a condo down there and he let us use it and play free golf at this famous golf club, and we would drive back and forth to it. One time when we came back, Fr. Eric said he didn't want to ride with me anymore because I was smoking and the smoke bothered him too much.

This was around 1985 and it was at the beginning of Lent, so I went to Br. Daniel [*Linskens, the monastery's physician's assistant*] and said, "I would like to give up smoking, but I don't know how." I was too much addicted to it. So he gave me Nicorette gum and I went through quite a few packs of Nicorette a day. After six months, Br. Daniel said, "You are becoming addicted to that now instead of smoking."

He had me cut down to about six Nicorette a day and, after about nine months, I got down to three and finally I could stop the Nicorette. Br. Daniel told me that I got asthma from smoking. And in March of 2013, I developed lung cancer and I was told it was probably due to my 25 years of heavy smoking. So I am still suffering from the smoking that I did.

As a child at home, what kind of health care did you have? Did a doctor come to your farm?

We were all born on the farm. I don't even know if a doctor came out to take care of Mom. I guess there was a doctor, but I am not sure. When we moved to town, we didn't have any health issues.

What did you do after you graduated from high school?

When I graduated, Mr. Haefling – I worked at Haefling Printing Company – offered me a fulltime job there. My folks told me if I saved enough money, I could buy a new car. So about three months after I had been working at the printing press, I had $1,100 saved and bought a 1950 Studebaker for just $2,200 – that was a wonderful car.

One time I had it up to about 105 miles an hour on the highway. It got about 35 miles to the gallon and had a stick with an overdrive on it – and it would really go. I really loved the Studebaker and I thought it was a car for the future!

And how did you become interested in the religious life?

When I got the car, I used to double date with a classmate with these wonderful young ladies from neighboring towns. We would go square dancing once or twice a week. One of my classmates and buddy, Francis Lucius, one time after a double date instead of talking about the girls, started telling me about going to Gethsemane and becoming a monk and so on.

Francis told me that he had started to go to daily Mass before he went to work. I got to thinking I rarely went

Br. Maurus, as a young monk

to Mass except on Sunday and I thought, "He is no better Catholic than I am. If he could go to daily Mass before he goes to work, I could too." So I started going to daily Mass.

About two months later, I got serious about life. I realized that if I got married and had a bunch of kids, I wouldn't be serving others or helping others. I really got to thinking if I'm a good person and live a good life, that would be a reward in itself. So I decided if there is a hereafter, I better do something about it.

So seven months after I graduated from high school, I went to Monsignor Gobel and talked to him about the possibility of being a brother. I said, "I'm thinking of joining the Navy or becoming a brother. What do you think?" He said, "Well, if you join the Navy, you're stuck for four years. And if you become a brother, you've got four or five years to decide whether you really want that life. Try out to be a brother and, if you don't like it, go join the Navy."

He also said, "Why don't you talk to Tom Kuhn, who is studying for the priesthood at Saint Meinrad? He will be home in a couple of weeks at Christmas." I knew Tom Kuhn, as he was a grade ahead of me. So I talked to Tom when he got home. Tom told me that they had a group of young brothers at Saint Meinrad and suggested that I visit the place.

So January the 14th, 1951, I got in my new car to go. Mom and Dad also wanted to go with me. But I said, "It is my vocation. If I want to stay, I will stay. It's my life and I would just like to check it out. And if I want to sign up, I don't want anybody to try to pressure me." So I drove down here and spent two days.

I remember walking around on the second day with Br. Macarius [*Jakious*]. I thought he was an old man, but he was only about 39 years old at the time. He met a dog and, instead of giving the dog a kick, he started petting the dog and making a big fuss over it. It dawned on me that these guys are very friendly, kind, loving and caring.

The last day I was at the abbey, I went to Fr. Claude [*Ehringer*], the novice master, and said, "Hey, what's it take to join the monastery?" He looks at me kind of seriously and walked over to his desk and opened the desk drawer and pulled out a paper and said, "You can have your pastor sign this, fill it out and send it in. We are starting a group of young brothers here February 7th. So, if you want to come back here February 7th and try it out, fine. If not, it's okay."

So I thought, "I might as well give this a try." So I got back in my new Studebaker and headed home. In Seymour, Indiana, I was passing a farm truck and the guy turned left into the farm lane. I can remember bouncing along in the ditch and I actually looked up and said, "Lord, here I come and I have my application to the monastery."

When I came to a stop, I realized I was still alive, just all shook up and pretty well banged up. The car was pretty bad. There was a doctor who had been following me fairly close, and he told the sheriff that it was the farmer's fault because he didn't signal he was turning. So his insurance company paid for everything.

I got a bus ride home to Tiffin and I was telling my brother, Junior, about joining the monastery. He said, "Well, God sure doesn't want you in that place. You smashed up your brand new car." I said, "Now wait a minute. I will let you guys get the car fixed up and I will try out to be a monk for a couple of months." I only had 551 miles on it when I smashed it up. So Mom and Dad dropped me down here February 7th, 1951.

Was there a particular person who influenced you to consider a religious vocation?

My father, Francis, who went to daily Mass for some 35 years. He lived to be 92 and was a daily communicant. My Dad, Mom, my younger brother Bernard and I spent many evenings kneeling on the floor as we recited the rosary. I did this not because I wanted to, but out of obedience.

What was your parents' reaction to you trying out a religious vocation?

Mom and Dad would have liked me to be a priest, but basically they were very pleased. I was 12th of 13 kids; I was a very spoiled kid in high school and in grade school. Mom and Dad kind of left me to do my things. I really enjoyed printing throughout my high school days and I really didn't like schooling.

I preferred to work and help my brothers on the farm in the summertime when I was in the seventh and eighth grade and the ninth and tenth grade. I really enjoyed farming, but I enjoyed printing much more.

So when my Mom and Dad brought me down here, I really had intended to only try it out for a couple of months just to check out the life and see what it was about. Well, it was kind of a different change. The first four weeks they had me in the church cleaning – dusting the pews, cleaning the altars and adding the water, wine, and hosts for all the priests.

Mom could never get me to dust at home, but they got me in a monastery to do dusting. Well, after about four weeks of that, they needed somebody in the bakery, so they sent me up to the bakery. I was a baker from March of 1951 to 1958. I really didn't enjoy the bakery; it was a job that I did.

Why did you stay if you didn't like dusting and the bakery?
It was only by the grace of God and the many prayers of my family and friends that I persevered as a brother monk. We had a very good time playing volleyball many evenings, and in the winter months I picked up and enjoyed playing chess. I still play chess about three or five times a week.

We had about 40 brothers in the 1950s, ranging from 18 to 30 years old. All the brothers were a very happy and fun group to recreate with. So with the grace of God, I never found anything better than being a brother monk. God's blessings have been with me in my daily prayer and work during my entire religious life! I confess I really have enjoyed my prayer and work in the monastery all these years!

What was your daily life when you first entered the community and were a novice?
For us brothers, we would have Morning Prayer at 4 a.m. in the Brothers' Oratory. There were about 40 young brothers in the community at the time. Then Fr. Claude usually had Mass for us

from 4:15 until about 5:00. Three or four mornings a week, I would go to work at 5:00 and then went to novice classes about 11:30 in the morning.

I would get to class after working from 5:00 until 11:15. Sometimes I would doze off, because I was just completely exhausted. Fr. Claude was very understanding and empathetic with me. He told me one time, "You know, when you are sleeping, at least you are not committing any sins." I really got a big kick out of that. Anyway, I got through my novitiate okay and made my three-year vows.

Every other week or so, we would serve the priests for their Masses. Sometimes we would come up from the crypt [*Masses were offered in the basement crypt individually by the priests at this time*] from serving one Mass and we would sometimes get caught by another priest to serve at his Mass. Through the novitiate and our juniorate, we went to conventual Mass at 7:30 every morning. So sometimes I would attend two, three, four Masses a day.

Then we would go to work from 7:30 to about 11:30 or so and then we would work from 1:30 to 4:30. At noon we would have *sext* and *none* prayers [*Liturgy of the Hours*]. After that, we had the main meal, and afternoons we would work. At around 5:00, we would have Vespers and then recreation.

A lot of times we would play volleyball and I enjoyed playing volleyball or handball. We would play these also on Saturdays and Sundays. We played volleyball spring, summer and fall. The community gathered together after supper and we walked around, sat on a bench or played volleyball. In the wintertime, many of us, about 16 of us monks, would play chess.

What has changed?

We used to have supper from 6 to about 6:30 and then we had recreation from 6:30 to 7. Then from 7 to 7:15, we had individual *compline* – night prayers – and that was it for the evening. In late

1995, Abbot Lambert Reilly tried community *compline*, but it was optional.

When it was optional, only a few of the older monks would go. The younger monks, including myself, decided if they went it would become a permanent thing. But it was suggested that we get back to having community *compline* again. This time it was not optional. Compline is now a part of our schedule and it is at 7 each evening.

Describe silence when you were young compared to now.

Oh gosh, we probably had a day silence approaching the night silence of today. Night silence was from 6 p.m. until after breakfast, around 8 in the morning. It was a longer period of silence.

Now we have silence from 10 p.m. until 8:30 after Mass as sort of a quiet time. If you need to take care of something, you do it. You are not going to commit a sin if you talk to somebody or ask somebody a question. If you need something taken care of, you talk to take care of the situation or problem.

What type of clothes did you wear then compared to now?

We wore habits. In the bakery, we had a little white apron with sort of a white capuche [*hood*] on it. You didn't wear black in the bakery or you would have flour all over you. In fact, we would play volleyball in our habits through the summer most of the time. We would just tuck our tunic and scapular up in our belt.

What were your living quarters back then?

Well, I spent about the first eight years above the bakery and we didn't have air conditioning. It was pretty hot in the summertime, so we would open up the windows. After that, I was in the basement of the monastery and it was hot down there in the wintertime. We had pipes running through for heat in the church and it would get hotter than heck. I would need to open up the windows about two inches or so.

In the summertime, we would bake down there. In fact, it would get so hot I had a fan put in at one point. I tried to sleep outside but the mosquitoes would bother me so much, so I would come inside and try to get a bit of sleep. We had a hard time sleeping through much of the summertime.

Did you have your own room?

From the novitiate on, we always had a private room with a bed, a desk, a chair and a wardrobe. During the novitiate, we had a curtain on our door, but we always had a private room and we always had a door after the novitiate.

Was there a bathroom in it?

No. We had a common bathroom and common showers. We didn't even have a sink in our rooms at any time until we came to the new monastery. We moved into our new monastery in 1982. Abbot Timothy Sweeney asked the community what they would like to have in it. We said, "We sure would like to have a sink in the rooms."

Well, after Fr. Abbot Timothy talked to several other monasteries, he decided to put a shower, a toilet and a sink in each monastery room. Of course, the novitiate had common toilets, showers and sinks in them. However, in 2013, all the novitiate rooms had toilets, showers and sinks added to each of these rooms.

It is really wonderful. As you get older, you appreciate having a toilet so that you don't have to go down the corridor to use one. It has been wonderful having them. It was a tough life without them, but we just did it. We didn't have air conditioning or good heating and all these kind of things until we moved into the new monastery.

Did you have visits from family or friends when you were here as a novice or junior?

Yes, my Mom and Dad came over 30 times here to visit me. And many of my brothers and sisters with their children visited me occasionally. Several friends and classmates from Tiffin visited me over the years and I really enjoyed visits, as they were all very supportive of my vocation.

What helped you in your formation when you were young monk?

The help of my confreres kept me appreciating monastic life. Just the camaraderie of the community has always been a great help to me and supportive. My family, Mom and Dad – she lived to be 75 and my Dad lived to be 92 – and my brothers and sisters have been very supportive and enjoy coming to visit.

Every other year, I go home and spend vacation time with my brothers and sisters and many of my nieces, nephews, friends and classmates. And every other year, I spend vacation time visiting my family and friends in Florida.

Do you have an interesting story from early years in the community?

Well, I was very happy to get out of dusting the church. The bakery was a secondary thing, but I survived and found it was helpful in taking care of the needs of the students we had here. Br. Fidelis Benkert at the bakery always told me, "You work faithfully eight hours a day and have no worries, and then someday you will become boss and you will work 16 hours a day and have all the worries."

That has stuck with me through life. As I managed at the Abbey Press, I realized you do work harder when you are in charge of something and you do have a lot of worries with a lot of things to take care of.

Are there other differences between monastic life then and now?

In the past, it was more you had to do this and now you have more freedom to do it, or not do it. We didn't travel in the old days. As brothers, we would get two weeks' vacation after our final vows, and thereafter two weeks' vacation every 25 years or for a 25th or 50th wedding anniversary of our parents or death of a family member. Now Father Abbot allows us monks two weeks' vacation every year. I went to many Abbey Press conventions and to Christian bookstore conventions. Also I do pilgrimages and take people along – it's a free trip for me.

In my early days, we would make a commitment to this way of life; it was a lot like marriage. Today 50% of people can't survive a marriage and some young men don't have the spirit of commitment, like we did back in the 1950s or '60s. We believed in making a choice for life, no matter if it was a marriage or a religious life. I think it has now become a "me generation," rather than helping and serving others. I think we want all the pleasures in life and we want to do our own thing. We don't want to be tied down.

Back then, you decided what you wanted to do in life and stuck with it. I never dreamt I would spend over four months or six months in a monastery, but the commitment was there. The grace of God to survive was there and you go through tough times and hard times, but we would realize this is what we wanted in life.

I have never regretted being a monk because there is a joy in serving the Lord and the Lord says, "Come follow me and I will give you a hundredfold." I think that is a fantastic deal. That is what has kept me in the monastery all these years, because it has been a life of a thousandfold instead of a hundredfold in my life as a monk here for 63 years. I enjoy life and God has been very good to me and I have really enjoyed being a monk.

Work

Tell me about your work experiences.

I didn't get into printing at all in the beginning. I had brought tools along and my aprons. I thought I would be put in the Abbey Press, as I knew they had a press here. But for seven years I was in the bakery. Toward the end of my seven years in the bakery, I was pretty exhausted. Fr. Robert Woerdeman was in charge of the Abbey Press printing operation and he asked for some help down there. So Fr. Abbot Bonaventure Knaebel asked me to go down and help him in the office at the Abbey Press in August of 1958.

I would really have liked to run the presses, but they needed help in the office. In August of 1960, we were out to Camp St. Benedict, a campsite on the Blue River where we would spend a week of vacation in the summer. One day Fr. Abbot Bonaventure called me aside and said, "You know you are awful young, you are only 28 years old, but I need a new manager for the Abbey Press printing division to take over Fr. Robert's job as printing manager. Would you accept this?" I said, "Yeah, I would try it out." So I was appointed Abbey Press printing manager then.[1]

Then what happened?

I think about a year or so after I was appointed printing manager, I examined our bookkeeping system and found out that after the equipment was completely depreciated it was still fairly good, so the bookkeeper would add another 20 years for additional depreciation. When the extra depreciation costs were dropped, costs of operating became reasonable and much less.

---

[1] For detailed information on the history of the Abbey Press, see Chapter 13 of Engs, Ruth Clifford, editor, *Conversations in the Abbey: Senior Monks of Saint Meinrad Reflect on their Lives* (2008) and transcription of Br. Maurus Zoeller's interview with Ruth C. Engs, September 20, 2005, Saint Meinrad Archabbey Archives.

We had quite a bit of repairs on the machines, because they were 20, 30, 40 years old. I started sending letters out to publishers of magazines and I ended up getting about 12 monthly magazines to print. So in 1962, the printing started taking off once we got the costs down.

In 1962, when I was putting out catalogs for seminaries for their deacons to purchase their ordination invitations and imprinted holy cards, I wrote to Clement Schmidt, a famous calligrapher designer in Germany, and I asked him to do 50 designs for holy cards for little scriptures and inspirational texts. These texts were put onto the holy cards with Schmidt's designs. One night I woke and I was kind of dreaming of the possibility of taking those holy cards and putting them on a little more paper and making note cards out of them.

A couple of weeks later, we started making note cards. So now we had holy cards and note cards and envelopes. Fr. Eric designed a little brochure advertising these and we mailed it to about 25,000 priests and sisters around the country. We got about a 30% mail order return – 5% is normal. I really got fired up spreading God's message of peace, love and joy, and I came up with all kinds of the Lord's words on printed material, prayer cards and notes.

You also started to make other items at Abbey Press?
I heard that Huntingburg Hi Plex Company in Huntingburg, Indiana, could laminate boards, so we went over there and talked to them. I took our holy cards over to them and they made little 3x5 plaques out of them. Next we had them make 7x10 plaques. Then we started putting out all kind of cards, posters, banners and scrolls.

Then what happened?
Around 1964, I had lots of products and hired the first trade sales manager, John Hounsel, out of New York. He would go around the country to the large Catholic bookstores and gift shops writing orders for our Abbey Press products. So in 1964, we started

the Abbey Press Trade Sales Department of selling products to stores. We would go to the National Catholic Education conventions and sold a lot of holy cards, notes and plaques to the sisters at these shows. Later, we also went to the Christian bookstore conventions.

However, an attorney from Berlinger & McGinnis, a religious card company, wrote and said, "We are going to sue you if you don't stop printing those designs, because your designs by Clement Schmidt are very close to the ones he did for us and we have a copyright on them." I ended up talking to him and Fr. Eric and I bought out the McGinnis line of holy cards and also greeting cards. It was at this point that I really got involved in publishing, as I saw a tremendous market for these types of religious or semi-religious products.

What did you next do at the Press?

Ned Watts was hired by Fr. Eric to start the Abbey Press catalog in 1963. They started putting our products in the Abbey Press catalog, a retail catalog and wholesale catalog. We bought out Grailville for their religious statuary and started a sculpture shop down in the old chicken house. We got into plastics in the little building next to it. We would make paperweights and all kinds of plastic see-through things and put paper notes and holy cards in them. Then we went on making all kinds of religious statues in WEP materials, which is water extended polyester material. That was a little more durable and didn't break up as much in mailing these statues.

In 1968, I took over as product development director for Abbey Press and hired many people. I was spending about 90% of my time buying art and developing products. So I ended up turning the printing operation over to Mike Franchville, my assistant in the office.

At one point through the years, I had up to 48 pages of Abbey Press products in the catalog that we produced here. We had all kinds of paper products, things that hung on the walls and polyester material. Jerry Knoll was a genius at putting texts out. I asked him one time to do some texts for our products and about a week later he gave me a whole book of texts – scripture text and religious inspirational text to put on new products.

In 1978, after 10 years in product development from 1968 to 1978, Gerald Wilhite, general manager, asked me if I wanted to start an Abbey Press Gift Shop down at the bottom of the hill where they had phased out the farming operation. We fixed up the milk parlor and had a gift shop in there and we had a pretty good business.

Also, we used to have yard sales. The first yard sale we had, we just said, "Make an offer for the product." We found out that this didn't work too well. We had a $10 product and somebody would try to buy it for a quarter. So from then on, we started pricing the yard sale gift items and then putting them outside a pretty good distance from the gift shop. My brothers and sisters from Tiffin, Ohio, would come down and help me get the yard sale ready to sell the gift items.

These yard sales became a great way to get rid of samples and products that were left over from selling them in the Abbey Press catalog. Many weekends, we sold up to $100,000 at the gift shop and on the yard sales. In 1985, the community gave me permission to build a nice big building, a metal building out in the field, next to the old gift shop. We would put tents up in the back of the gift shop for yard sales.

Did you ever get any time off?

Yes, when I took my three-year vows and final vows, all the monks could go to our Camp Benedict for a week's vacation. After Vatican II, we then could take two weeks' vacation as long as the cost for the vacation was fairly reasonable.

In 1990, Fr. Abbot Timothy [Sweeney] gave me permission to take a sabbatical and I went to Rome for four months. I took a

19

theological course at Sant' Anselmo monastery in Rome and traveled around Rome and also some of the country's sites. I did get a railroad pass for three weeks and traveled by myself through 13 countries and put on some 14,000 traveling miles by railroad. It was a very exciting and wonderful time visiting all these countries. I'd spend two or three nights traveling on the train and then I'd spend a night in a *pensione,* which only cost about $5 per night's stay.

Fr. Abbot Timothy also gave me permission to go on pilgrimage to the Holy Land. So I went to the Holy Land for two weeks. This was the second of my now 12 pilgrimages to the Holy Land. I really have enjoyed pilgrimages to the Holy Land and having lots of folks join me (so I get a free pilgrimage). Walking in the footsteps of Jesus, visiting Jerusalem, Bethlehem, Nazareth, Mt. of Beatitudes, etc. brings the Old and New Testament alive, so pilgrims really appreciate reading Scripture.

Toward the end of my sabbatical, Fr. Abbot Timothy wrote that he needed a new tour director and would I accept this job? He said I should let him know before I got back if I would accept it or not. I thought and prayed about it and wrote back and said, "Thanks, Fr. Abbot, for the offer; I'd rather stay where I'm at. I enjoy the Abbey Press and the work. Why don't you get one of the young brothers to give tours and leave me where I am?" But I also said, "I don't have any major objections. I'd just rather stay working at the Abbey Press."

When I got back to Saint Meinrad in August of 1990, Fr. Abbot Timothy had worked out a job description for me to be tour director of the Abbey. So I switched from the gift shop up to the Abbey. I was taking care of the tours around the abbey, and two years later, Fr. Abbot appointed me as retreat director and guest master. So as retreat director, tour director and guest master until the present day, I take care of the retreat programs.

I ask monks to give conferences on scripture, on religious life, on the holy *Rule* and many other religious themes. It has been wonderful cooperation from many of the monks who give midweek and weekend retreats, and I am very grateful for their help and kindness. Most retreatants really appreciate that monks give them retreats.

I added it up a couple of months ago [2015] and I am up to 76,000 people to whom I have given tours around the abbey. For these tours, I spend at least an hour to an hour and a half. I really enjoy taking grade school, high school and college kids on tours. It's kind of hope for the future.

When I worked at the Abbey Press, it was stressful in a lot of ways. Up on the hill giving tours, giving and handling retreats has been very relaxing. If I have time, I give a tour; if I don't have time, I don't do it. So it is not as stressful as when I had to put out all these pages in the catalog that had to pay for itself. It had to be a profitable occupation. We could do a lot of good, but you couldn't do good or do a lot of advertising if you lost money.

So changing from the Abbey Press to doing tours and retreats has been a wonderful blessing for me and for my health. I jogged for three times a week for about a half hour for the past 25 years. However, since my very early cancer in my upper left lung, I don't jog anymore. But I had a serendipity miracle.

What was that?
In early March of 2013, I tried to get out of bed, but my legs could not hold my body. It seemed like I went from 60 to 80 years young during the night. I called the monastery infirmary and they had a monk help me to get to the infirmary. After an EKG test, they sent me to Jasper Memorial Hospital. After MRIs and PET scans, they discovered a lump in my upper left lung and thought this might be cancer. So they planned on doing a biopsy to check if it could be cancer.

However, the day I was supposed to have the biopsy, the doctor called and cancelled the operation. The doctor had lined me up to go to the Indianapolis Cancer Hospital. The doctor thought they should also check my legs as I couldn't walk without a cane.

After doing all kind of tests on my legs, they could not find a reason for weakness in my legs. However, they found I did have the beginnings of cancer in the biopsy. You see, without my weakness in my legs, my lung cancer would not be discovered perhaps for years. So they operated and removed the upper part of my cancerous lung and checked nine lymph nodes in the lower left lung and found no traces of cancer.

After the operation, I came down with double pneumonia and was in a coma for six days. The nurse called Fr. Abbot Justin and told him they didn't think Br. Maurus would come out alive. So Fr. Abbot had Fr. Noah Casey come to the hospital and anoint me.

However, I came out of the coma as I sure wasn't ready to meet my Maker yet. So after 10 days, I was released from the hospital. I was told by the doctor that I need *not* go through chemo or radiation, as the beginning of cancer was completely removed. When my friends, Pat and Barbara Phillips, brought me back to the Abbey, they told me I just had a "serendipity miracle."

The strange part of the problem with my legs (which was why I went to the hospital) cleared up to normal after three weeks at the Abbey with no medication. I really and truly believed that all the prayers from the monks, co-workers, my family and friends created this serendipity miracle for me. My doctor said, "Walking a half hour per day is the best medicine I could recommend for your health." So I switched from jogging to walking a half hour each day. I'm very grateful for all the prayers for my recuperation and grateful to God for letting me live a bit longer.

Do you have any more work stories?
I started Trade Sales back in 1964 and [*years later*] they asked me to be the model for a bobblehead figure. I thought it was kind of silly. I didn't even know what a bobblehead was. So anyway, I asked

Fr. Prior Tobias [*Colgan*] if a monk could be a bobblehead. He looked me in the eye and said, "Okay, provided you give me one!"

It's been fun giving them out to folks buying our products at the Christian bookstore conventions and signing my name in gold print on the back with, "From your monk friend, Brother Maurus." We did sell many of them through the Abbey Press Gift Shop and to retreatants and friends visiting the Abbey. The whole deal for me was a lot of fun! We got 700 of them and all of them are gone.

Prayer

In terms of your prayer and spiritual life, what would you like to convey to younger confreres or even the laity?

Through prayer, you become a happy person. You are living and loving and caring for God. Praying means that God will take care of the world and all its problems. Prayer is so important to our life until we rest in God. St. Augustine says, "Our hearts are restless until they rest in God." This is where you will find peace, joy and happiness serving the Lord.

God expects us to be the best person we can be. It makes you love others, care for others and help others. This takes you out of the "me, me" outlook on life. Joy that you get in life is by helping others. I think that is what kept me as a monk all these years – loving and caring for others, and God blessed me by my having a lot of friends and joy in my work and prayer life.

You have to devote a certain amount of time for prayer. It is like eating. If you don't eat, you are going to starve. If you don't pray, how do you expect to be a better person? How do you expect to know what is best for you in life and how to go about that? Through prayer, God gives you the grace and the strength to do what is best in life so we can enjoy all of eternity with him.

It is following our holy *Rule* – and the holy *Rule* is not just for monks. It can be applied to all people at all times. One of my favorite quotes is from Fr. Eric's retreat topic, "Pray Your Way to Happiness." And since my very good monk friend, Fr. Eric Lies, died January 20, 2012, he gave me his notes for this retreat and I've given it four times at our Guest House and Retreat Center.

What is your favorite part of the Rule of St. Benedict?

Well, the part that impresses me most is that our hearts become enlarged and we run with unspeakable love in the way of God's commands after we persevere through this life. I think the holy *Rule* to me is a concise way of living life and giving a purpose and wonderful meaning to life. Pray your way to happiness and living and serving and helping others is a joy that is inexpressible.

This leads into the next question. What is your key to living Benedictine spirituality?

Living in community – helping where you can help, giving tours, planning and handling retreats and socials for retreatants, doing the dishes or serving wine to guests and being as helpful a person as you can. Finding meaning in your life – I find great meaning in what I do in loving and caring for others. That is what life is about. And the more you love others, the more you care for others, the happier person you will be. Blessed Marmion says, "Joy is the echo of God's life in us." If we don't have joy, we ought not to be in the monastery.

I pray every morning that my day will be filled with loving and caring for others. I pray to be the best person I can possibly be. I thank God for another day to serve him and to serve others and I'm grateful for God's blessing. God has been very good to me and blessed me in countless ways. I am trying to be a very grateful, joyful, kind and caring person.

What has been your most difficult time in your life?

While I was in the Abbey Press. In March of '64, my mother died, *[President John]* Kennedy had been assassinated, and it was a very depressing and stressful time for me at the Press. I was doing all kinds of things there. Fr. Martin Dusseau, the business manager, had some efficiency people come to the Abbey Press to evaluate our production system to see if we couldn't cut costs.

We had to fill out forms for each press and other equipment on how fast it would go, how long it would take for every job, and they would evaluate the work. As this continued, the quality of work started going downhill. Fr. Martin and the consultants suggested I get rid of at least three people. So I let go three of the bindery workers. I was really becoming very, very frustrated and stressed out with the whole deal.

I remember at nights I would go down and work. Then I got from Br. Daniel some Valium for the stress. I also started drinking a little on the heavy side. One morning I woke up at the Abbey Guest House. I don't know what happened earlier, because I had blacked out. I remember looking into the ashtray and it had about two packs of cigarettes that I had smoked through the night somehow. I had a nervous breakdown from the stress.

I spent about six weeks at Our Lady of Peace in Louisville under a doctor's supervision. In those days, they gave you shock treatments. I played chess, but I couldn't remember what was happening from day to day. After about six weeks, they released me and I remembered that I was supposed to be a monk and came back to the Abbey.

Br. Daniel told me that I should only work a half day down at the Abbey Press. The doctor told Fr. Abbot Bonaventure that he should be responsible for my work and either pull me out of the Abbey Press or not let me have anything to do with the consultants and the business manager anymore because it was driving me up a wall.

So I was under Abbot Bonaventure from then on. I remember getting rid of the efficiency forms and going back to just respecting what we had and the quality started picking up. At times, I really had a hard time remembering. The treatment basically wiped out my present memory. I could remember the past way back, but I couldn't remember what happened with some of the things I was doing at the Abbey Press.

After a couple of months, which I found really amazing, my memory kept coming back more and more and most of my forgotten memory finally returned. It really was unbelievable to me what doctors can do for a person. I stopped taking Valium and I haven't been drinking so much since then, but I still enjoy my wine and, once in a while, a highball. Since then, I have never seen a psychiatrist.

One really funny part happened when the doctor came for his Christmas visit to the Abbey with other doctors. We had a meal in appreciation for their help and good work. I can still remember the doctor asking me, "Why have you not come back to see me?" I told him, "I didn't think you asked me to come back." "Yes," he said, "I did ask you to see me again, but I guess you forgot!"

This difficult time sounds like a positive growth experience for you.
Yes, I realized if you run across a big problem that you can't take care of, instead of banging your head against it – that is what I was doing at the Abbey Press – that either I should go over it, under it or around it. If I can't get out of it, I will turn around and run the other direction.

But since then, I have never gotten into a situation where I started banging my head against the problem. I realized if you need help, doctors can help you. This happened lately when I got into an asthma problem from smoking. The allergy doctors gave me special medicine and it pretty well cleared up.

What has been your happiest time or experience?

When I made my final profession as a monk of Saint Meinrad Archabbey, I was very happy and looked forward to being a monk. My family was very proud of me. I had a lot of good times celebrating my 40th and 50th and 60 years of profession jubilee. I even gave a homily for each of these occasions at my St. Joseph Parish in Tiffin, Ohio, and my family provided a wonderful banquet for my many relatives and friends.

My profession was probably the happiest time in my life, but I also enjoyed working at the Abbey Press. The people I worked with were very helpful and cooperative and we had a lot of fun over the years. I also really enjoy meeting people and the lots and lots of benefactors and friends who come to the Abbey Guest House and Retreat Center. I enjoy helping them. When I am home, I usually serve wine at supper at the Guest House for all of our retreatants and they really enjoy the option to have a little wine.

Any other joyful experiences?

I have enjoyed monastic life and I tell people that, after 63 years, I haven't found anything better in life than being a monk of Saint Meinrad Archabbey. It has been a wonderful life; God has been very good to me. I am probably what you would call a spoiled monk. I also enjoy taking people on pilgrimages because it gives them, and me, a new insight into the various aspects of the world, their lifestyles, the beautiful scenes we visit and especially the Holy Land.

I hate to get up in the morning and I hate to go to bed at night. But I tell people, "After 63 years you don't think about it, you just do it." You get up and meet the day and enjoy what you are doing. So that is kind of where I am at this time in my life.

Changing from the Abbey Press to giving tours and retreats has been a wonderful blessing for me and for my health. At 83, I now walk daily for about a half hour.

Changes in the Church

As you know, St. Benedict became discouraged with society's general disregard for spirituality in his time, and that is one of the reasons he developed a theory and practice for living. Today some observers are of the opinion that society is once again falling back into indifference in leading a virtuous life and a lack of spirituality. How has this affected Benedictine spirituality found within the Abbey or within the Church?

Well, I think that is why our retreats are becoming so popular and why more people are coming, because they realize that the world and America is going down the tubes fast. In the monastery, we seek God and we seek to help others. The holy *Rule* gives us the framework to help others.

By giving retreats on scripture, on the holy *Rule* and on prayer, the monks are passing on to the people who come to Saint Meinrad ideas to improve their purpose in life and suggest how to live their life. We talk about scripture or how to apply scripture to our life, how to pray, how to live life and how to be happy in life, rather than being concerned about all the problems that each of us must face throughout life.

We have better than 1,200 oblates who are associated with Saint Meinrad who are trying to live a more Benedictine life of loving and caring for others, seeking God and having more of a prayer life. If we don't pray, how do we expect to go to heaven?

There have been changes that have affected the contemporary Church and some Catholics think that Pope John XXIII was overly optimistic and that ever since Vatican II the Church has been paying a heavy price for his initiatives; many others applaud his gestures. What has this all meant to you in terms of the monastery and the Church? What changes have you seen?

Thank God for Pope John XXIII! He opened up the doors and helped people understand a little better what the faith is about and that we can hear the scriptures read in English in church and that we can talk with Protestants. We have a lot of Protestant folks and ministers coming to our retreats because they are on prayer and scripture. Before Vatican II, the Protestants felt the Catholics were way out in left field, but now I think that many Protestants coming to our retreats feel they are very welcome here. They can pray in English with us and, before Vatican II, that was impossible.

I think Vatican II was a wonderful thing for the Church. Because we have fewer vocations isn't because of Vatican II. I think it is because people have difficulty in committing themselves to a purpose and staying with that commitment, whether it is marriage or religious life or whatever. We are becoming more of a selfish generation. We are looking for everything television can offer us and becoming a people who don't believe in prayer and seeking God as we used to. So I think we need to get back to that structure. That is my humble opinion.

How different is the Church today compared to when you were young?

Well, it is more accessible to everyone – to Catholics as well as everyone else. Anyone is welcome to come to our services. Some of our retreatants really appreciate being able to come to our daily Mass, Morning Prayer, Midday Prayer, Vespers and Compline because they are now in English. We are welcoming them and helping them find God where they are and uplifting them to have a more peaceful and meaningful life.

Looking at the monastery today, compare the morale of the monastery as it was 30, 40, 50 years ago.

Well 30, 40, 50 years ago, the abbot was the superior. You did what the abbot wanted and asked you to do. For example, when I was sent to the bakery, I didn't ask; I was just sent to the bakery. I was sent to the Abbey Press and we didn't even discuss other possibilities.

Now people can discuss with Father Abbot what they are interested in doing and also what the community needs, so you kind of balance that. There is now more freedom to discuss and to be open and to share. I think Fr. Abbot Justin DuVall is doing a fantastic job communicating with the community what the situation could, should and ought to be – also how we should help each other along and live a life of prayer and working and praying for the Church and the world.

Even though the Mass is celebrated in English, was eliminating Latin from the academic curriculum a good idea?

Having the Mass in English, the liturgy in English and the Divine Office in English has really been a breakthrough. But it has presented a problem for a lot of people who would like to go back to where they were before Vatican II. It is impossible to go back; we have to go forward and live with the times and try to help people the best we can with living in the present and toward the future.

In our seminary, they should be teaching Spanish, I think, because there are so many Spanish-speaking people coming to this country and they, in the near future, will probably become a high percentage of Americans. This is because they have four, six or eight kids and we, as Americans, are lucky to have two or three. In 20 or 40 years from now, we will probably have more Spanish-speaking people and I don't know how many of them will learn English.

When I first came here, we had German brothers here and some of them spoke only a couple of words in English. Now so many people only speak Spanish. So I think Spanish would be more important than Latin. I don't think we will ever see the Latin Mass come back. For those who dream about the past and think that we have ruined the future, I think they are on the wrong train and are going down the wrong track.

There have been many changes in the liturgy since the days of the Council. Can you comment on positive and negative changes that you have seen in the Church?

Well, the positive change is that we have English for the whole Mass, the sermons and the gospel. The negative would be that we don't have the Latin chant that we used to have, but even the Latin chant was sometimes too long. English, to me, is a very positive and good move and shows that we are moving forward.

The priests are doing more preaching and teaching, rather than running the whole parish like they used to do. I think that is a big improvement. We are turning more over to the laity to help run the parishes, and even at Saint Meinrad we are having more laity help us. I think we should rejoice that Vatican II took place and that we have more freedom now than we ever had as monks, or priests, or brothers or sisters, or lay folks.

What has been lost or what has been gained since the Council in the monastery? The Church?

I guess the old way of looking at things has been lost, and we are probably not as disciplined as we used to be and that probably is a loss. The good part is that community prayer is in English and we can understand, can communicate better, and better appreciate the Mass and the Divine Office.

The number of religious vocations has declined and the number of retirements and deaths are increasing in this population. What is the meaning of these changing patterns to the monastery and the Church at large?

When I came, we had about 60 brothers here and we did a lot of the work. Now we are down to about 20 brothers. We did farming, we had a chicken house, a bakery, and we took care of everything. We had a landscaping crew, a vineyard, hogs, pigs, and cows for milk and so on.

31

We did most of the work. But now we don't have many brothers to do the work we would like to do. And it especially is a big problem for the Abbey Press. We are turning these jobs over to co-workers. It's kind of tough to realize we can't do all we used to do and it's hard not to have monks to take care of the things, whether it is teaching, preaching, nursing or all the jobs we have around here.

Fewer vocations and fewer people to do the work of God – that is now life as it is. We must live in the present and look toward the future. We can't look at the past; the past is over and gone. We can't recoup it, and vocations are a matter of the Lord calling people. But I don't think a lot of people are answering the call to dedicate themselves to the priesthood, brotherhood or sisterhood.

Why is that, do you think?

I don't think a lot of parents are supporting the youth like they used to do. My parents were gung ho about me becoming a religious. They would have liked me to become a priest, but they really supported my choice, and I wonder how many parents in today's society would support a vocation. Many parents have only two or three children and it is hard to get parents to see that one of their children could be a priest, a sister or a brother. If they became a religious, then they would not have grandchildren.

I think the country needs to wake up and realize that children need to be taught virtue, taught the Ten Commandments, how to pray and how to live a dedicated life. That is a big reason why we don't have many vocations.

Hasn't there been a slight increase in vocations here in the past few years?

Yes, but we used to have 30 fraters in the juniorate studying for the priesthood and they were in a group by themselves. We would have 8, 10, 15 brothers. Now we are lucky to have four or five juniors studying for priesthood and maybe two or three brothers in the novitiate, so it has changed tremendously.

Back then, we had 100 and some priests here. We had a lot of juniors coming up for final vows, and now we only have one or two for final vows, maybe two or three in the novitiate, and maybe five or six juniors. But we are getting some really good young people here, and they are talented and well educated.

When I entered, I just had a high school education. They asked me if I went to college and I said, "Yeah, I went to the college of hard knocks. I never really wanted to go to college, but I enjoy working." I did take many courses at Evansville College for art and accounting and management that I needed for my work. I have enjoyed what I have done.

Where do you see the Church in 25 years, 50 years from now?

The Church is going to be here, but it may be a little different from what it is now. It probably will be operated mostly by lay people if we still have fewer priests. I don't know; I can't predict the future.

The future of the monastery – I think there will be a monastery here, but how many people I have no idea. It is slowly declining and we are getting older, but my hope for the future is that it will pick up. We have survived 1,500 years and I don't think 50 years is going to make much difference. We might have fewer vocations or it might be flowering.

What are your hopes for the future of the monastery and the Church?

The monastery should be more of a center of helping people to seek God, to find God, to find more peace, happiness, joy, and love in their life and to help them become a more loving person. That is what the retreat program is trying to do. The future is in God's hands and we just need to pray for the future of the Abbey, pray for the future of the Church and hope for the best. Let go and let God take care of things.

Profile based upon: Br. Maurus Zoeller to Prof. Ruth C. Engs, September 1, 2009, Interview Transcriptions, Saint Meinrad Archabbey Archives, St. Meinrad, IN; additional comments by Br. Maurus, August 26, 2015.

Chapter 2: Fr. Augustine Davis, OSB

Fr. Augustine Davis, OSB, is an outdoor enthusiast who likes to work with his hands. He served in a number of positions, including at missions in Peru, Tennessee and Mexico.

Born September 21, 1930, in Cedar Rapids, Iowa, he was given the name Claire. Fr. Augustine graduated from St. Patrick's Catholic High School in Cedar Rapids (1949). He received a bachelor of arts in philosophy from Saint Meinrad College (1956).

On July 31, 1954, he made his profession as a monk and then made his solemn profession August 15, 1957. He graduated from Saint Meinrad School of Theology with a degree in theology (1959) and was ordained a priest May 11, 1959. He then earned a master's degree in industrial arts from Indiana State University (1966).

Fr. Augustine served as assistant director at St. Placid Hall (1959-66), a boarding school for high school boys who were considering becoming brothers, until it closed. Subsequently, he was appointed to San Benito Priory, Huaraz, Peru (1967-79). After the 1970 devastating earthquake in this community, he directed the reconstruction of the priory. He was recalled to Saint Meinrad and was appointed physical plant director and liaison between the monastery and contractors for a new monastery and library (1979-86).

Fr. Augustine then served as pastor to a South Pittsburgh, TN, Marian mission and as overseer of a 600-acre beef farm until its closure (1986-96). He then briefly served at Priorato An Benito Abad, Morelia,

Mexico. In 1997, he was recalled to Saint Meinrad as director of Spanish ministry and delivery, and in 2005, he was appointed to the physical plant office. He is now retired.

Dr. Ruth C. Engs interviewed Fr. Augustine on July 29, 2009; additional material from Fr. Augustine, April 2, 2013.

Childhood and Early Years as a Monk

Tell me about your childhood and early schooling.

I was born in Cedar Rapids, Iowa, in Mercy Hospital. We lived on a farm that is now the Cedar Rapids Airport. The farm was taken over by the government to make an airport during the Second World War. We lived there until I was ready for school and we moved to another farm by Solon.

I started grade school in a one-room school that included eight grades. So there were, I think, 17 students for the eight grades. We only went there two years and then moved to near Swisher, Iowa, and [*they had a*] two-room school. I continued there through half of the seventh year of grade school. Once again, my dad moved.

We moved to Cedar Rapids, but did live on a farm. The farm was just a pastime, kind of a hobby [*for my dad*]. The last half of seventh grade through eighth grade, [*I was at a grade school*] called St. Ludmila.

What type of a school was it?

It was a Czech school, or Bohemian, same thing. Then I graduated [*from*] eighth grade at that school. It didn't have a high school, so we had to go across the city to high school. St. Patrick's High School [*a Catholic high school*] was about 3½ miles from our home. We rode bicycles to school. Then … in the later part of my sophomore year, I worked at an A&P grocery store. I made enough money, so I bought a car.

What kind of car?

A '37 Ford Coupe – a business coupe it was called. The former owners put a back seat in it. It wasn't made that way, but it had a back seat in it. We had an awful lot of fun with that car, because we could have as many as six people [*in it*] even though it was a coupe. I graduated in 1949 from St. Patrick's High School.

What kind of hobbies, activities and interests did you have as a child or in high school?

Well, mostly outdoor. I rode a bicycle all the time for entertainment besides going to school. And living on a farm, we had chores we had to do. There were five boys and one girl in our family. My next younger brother always helped my mother, but I was always outside helping my dad. I harnessed the horses and drove a team of horses when I was about 7 or 8 years old.

What kind of work did you do with your team of horses?

Work in the fields. We used the team to harrow [*break up clods of dirt*] the fields. We also used them for making hay. The horses pulled a hay wagon. My father pitched the hay up on the wagon and I then drove the horses to the barn. The hay was hoisted up on an elevator into the top of the barn. It was a pulley system. Then Dad pitched the hay in piles in the top of the barn.

However, I remember one time we had a tractor and I loaded on a binder and my brother Joe drove the tractor.

What's a binder?

It was a [*machine used for cutting the oats and putting them*] into bundles. Then the bundles would be put into shocks in the field. A bunch of these bundles [*were put*] together with one placed on top to shed the rain. Later on, they would [*put*] these in threshing machines that separated the oats from the straw. We fed the oats to the horses and we sold some of them.

Tell me more about you and your brother as children working with a tractor.

[*Some days*] the two of us were out in the field cutting oats. Neighbors would [*drive by*] on the road and they would stop and marvel at the two of us young fellows – younger than teenagers – working on the farm.

Did you and all your brothers and sisters work on the farm as children?

Right, and enjoyed it. I always enjoyed the work we were given, except for cleaning out the chicken house. We had a couple of hundred chickens; they were mainly for laying and we sold the eggs.

What other animals did you have?

About 10 or 12 head of dairy cattle, and we did all the milking by hand. I started when I was about 6 years old milking cows.

Did your father own the farms?

He was renting. We lived on a small 80-acre farm when I was born. Then he moved to a bigger one each time he moved. He was always asked to come to a larger farm. He never had to try to find one, because he was a good farmer.

Let's look at some of the things you might have done in high school. Before you came to Saint Meinrad, for example, did you smoke or drink?

I smoked in high school. We, the family, always had beer and some wine or something in the refrigerator, and we as children participated in the family festivities so I never had any desire to drink outside of the family.

So drinking wine or beer was a part of the meal?

Yeah, it was a very good system, I think, being raised this way.

What kind of health care did you have when you were young?

Mostly just our mother. The first doctor I can remember going to was a doctor at one of the Amana Colonies in Iowa. They had a registered doctor and we used to go there for minor things. We never had any major medical needs. In all six children in the family, there was never one broken bone. It was a very healthy childhood.

Who or what influenced you to decide on a religious vocation?

In grade school, St. Ludmila, the teacher [*who was a nun*] would read to us on Friday afternoon from some book. She read *Hero of the Hills*, which was a biography of St. Benedict written by Mary Windeatt. I became interested in St. Benedict. [*The author of this book*] lived up at Monte Cassino [*about two miles from the monastery*] in a small house.

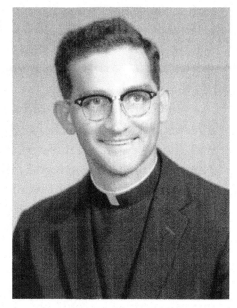

Were you an altar boy?

No, never until I was in the seminary. I never served.

Fr. Augustine, as a young monk

Were their other factors that led to a religious vocation and why did you choose Saint Meinrad?

Before I graduated from high school, I had been thinking about the religious life. When I was a sophomore in high school, the teacher was very lenient. Instead of making us read books and make book reports, we could read pamphlets and make a report on the pamphlet. I read from a pamphlet on vocations and the last chapter of the pamphlet was about Saint Meinrad.

At the end of the article, there was an address and I wrote to Saint Meinrad saying I was interested in the monastic life. I received a personal letter from Father Abbot Ignatius [*Esser*] and that made a very good impression. But, I promptly forgot about the vocation until I was in my senior year of high school.

Another teacher, who was a sister, asked me what I was going to do after high school. I said, "I really didn't know," and that, "I was somewhat interested in monastic life." I had thought about it earlier. She said I should have a spiritual director. She said any priest that I chose [*could be*] a spiritual director. Well, it happened that the priest, Monsignor Kearn, who had married my mother and dad, was now pastor in one of the parishes in Cedar Rapids – St. Matthew's.

So I went to him and said I wanted him to be my spiritual director and that the teacher in the high school had suggested this with the view of a vocation. So, after a number of sessions with Monsignor Kearn, he agreed I probably had a vocation and he wanted to know whether I would be interested in the diocesan priesthood or the religious priesthood. I said, "Definitely the religious," even though my mother's brother was a diocesan priest in the Dubuque archdiocese.

So, my spiritual director said I should write to five different monasteries. [*Since*] I was only acquainted with the Benedictines, all five monasteries I wrote to were Benedictine. From two of them, I didn't receive any response. Another one or two, I received a form letter from the vocation director.

However, I received another personal letter from Abbot Ignatius. The two letters coming from the abbot himself made such an impression on me that this was the only one of the five places that I considered. So after graduation, I got in my car and drove from Cedar Rapids, Iowa, to St. Meinrad, Indiana, and visited here for three days.

Father Marion [*Walsh*], the guest master, talked with me during these three days. Then he said, "Now that you are about ready to leave, are you coming back this fall for classes?" I said I wanted to go home and think about it and pray about it some before I would decide. He said, "Well, you are going to have to have a cassock if you come back for classes."

All the students were expected to wear the cassock at church and at meals and in the classrooms. So I said, "Well, I don't know if I am coming back." He said, "That's okay. There is a lady down at the foot of the hill that takes old cassocks and remodels them for anyone who needs a cassock." He said, "I think you should go down there and have her get a cassock for you so that if you do come back, you will have a cassock to wear."

I reluctantly agreed to go ahead and do that. Then after I got home, knowing that that cassock was waiting for me, it seemed to have more influence on me than practically anything else. So, I came back in the fall as a student.

How did your family feel when you decided to become a monk?
My mother was rather against it because her own blood brother [*was*] a diocesan priest. She thought I should follow in his footsteps. So she was not real favorable of me being a monk and especially living so far away. My dad was favorable. He thought I made a good choice and my mother did, too, later on. They were both very encouraging as far as the priesthood and ordination was concerned. In fact, they bought me the chalice for ordination, so I always figured that was a good sign they were in favor [*of it*].

Discuss what happened when you came here for college.
In those days, you had to finish minor seminary before you could join the monastery. Minor seminary included high school and two years of college – six years. So, I needed two years of college. I expected to get into college when I came here, but the high school

students [*who*] were here already had four years of Latin and two years of Greek. I had to have four years of Latin and two years of Greek before I could start college.

So, it took me two years to make up the four years of Latin and the two years of Greek before I could start my college years. So, I went to Saint Meinrad two years without making any advancement in my education. Then the third year, I started my first year of college and then second year of college. After that, I entered the monastery and became a novice.

This was after your second year of college?

Yes, I had been at Saint Meinrad four years before I could become a monk. You don't make any advancement in your schooling [*when you become a novice*]. After the [*year of being a novice*], we made simple vows and continued studies up until ordination.

Explain what you did when you were a novice.

Well, we had housekeeping chores and then we had classes in Benedictine history and liturgy – that was the main part of the day. Our monastic chores [*included*] cleaning bathrooms, other rooms and public rooms in the monastery. We were working all the time.

Father Placidus [*Kempf*] was our novice master who spent all his time teaching us. He was a great person and I have many fond memories of him. The novice master was the center of our formation and he was a very dignified and a learned man. He was a Latin scholar and wrote poetry in Latin, and in class he would quote from his own poetry. The class was very interesting and enjoyable.

Describe something of the tone and the nature of the discipline that you were under as a young novice and how is that different from today?

Well, in those days, the discipline was much stricter. As novices, and as young monks, we were not allowed to go home to visit. We had no vacation whatever except for a camp on the Blue

River, which is about 30 miles from here. It was called Camp Benedict. We used to have a week that we spent there [*in the summer*] and I enjoyed very, very much being outdoors. I liked to go spelunking in local wild caves.

The discipline was very strict. We wore our habit almost all the time, even during recreation time. We played football in our habit. We played volleyball in our habit, and so the habit was our normal dress that we wore all the time.

There was one thing that is very different from what it is now and that's our mail. All the mail that came to the monastery was always opened, and the superiors had the privilege and the right to read any mail that came in for the monks. As far as how many they read, or what, I have no idea; probably very little.

But if there was some reason they were suspicious of something, they had the privilege of reading the mail. All the outgoing mail, the letters to our relatives and friends and whatnot, were always open, not sealed. The superiors did the sealing and if they wanted to read it before they sealed it, of course, they could.

When did that change?
I have no idea, but it was a long time ago.

When you were here as a young monk, you mentioned that you weren't allowed to go home. Were your family or friends allowed to visit you?
Yes, on a restricted basis. My folks usually came to see me once a year and that's all. At that time, there was no guest house, so any relatives that came stayed at private homes downtown. They would be able to come up and visit with me during the day, but they, of course, went to the place they were staying and I stayed here at the monastery.

What were your assignments when you were a young monk and are they different from today?

Not that much different really. In our formation years, we had a lot of house work and duties in the kitchen and serving meals and the like. That pretty much continues [*today*]. As a student, during the years I was studying for the priesthood, a person's time was taken up by studying, of course, and in those years we were in the church at 4 [*a.m.*]. We got up about 3:45 and so you couldn't stay up late at night to study. You had to get your studying in between things. Our time was really a premium in those days, but I am sure that is true today for those in the formation years.

Describe differences in formation when you were young compared to today.

[*We were*] always together. The fraters [*those studying for the priesthood*] were not allowed to visit, or mix with, the students of the schools. And we were not allowed to mingle with the brothers or the fathers. There was separation between [*these groups*]. So we did everything together. Our recreation was always together, our work was always together and it was very closed. We were a group into ourselves. [*Today there is no separation.*]

How about recreation?

In those days, the winters were colder and there was considerable ice on the lakes here and we used to ice skate. I ice skated all winter at home in Iowa; we had wonderful facilities for ice skating. So I enjoyed this very much when I came here. I brought my ice skates with me not knowing [*if this was*] an ice skating area. We did have some real cold winters and I was able to skate a couple of times, no more than that, a few times.

Do you have any amusing stories from your early years in the community?

Well, one about Fr. Placidus, the novice master, comes to mind. We used to have urinals in the monastery and Fr. Placidus would go at night from his room to the bathroom, barefooted and with his robe on. He was very particular. He put up a sign, "Please stand at the urinal close enough and long enough because the next person may be barefooted," which was himself.

Another story. If we had any reason to go to a dentist, or anything, we had to get permission, of course, and they usually grouped us together. They would postpone the dentist appointment until there was a group of us to go and Father John [*Thuis*] was the chauffeur. He always drove us and it was an experience to ride with him. His foot on the [*gas pedal*] would go up and down all the way and so you were always going faster, slower, faster, slower.

We always had a lot of jokes about that. Even in Louisville, where we usually went for any doctor or dentist appointment, we always went as a group. We very seldom ate a meal outside of the monastery. We usually figured our trip so that we didn't have to stop for a meal outside the monastery, which is recommended by our rules and regulations.

Does that still happen today or do monks eat outside the monastery?

In fact, they look for a reason to go somewhere so they can have a meal outside.

In terms of your ordination, is there anything you would like to discuss?

Yes, I had the privilege of being able to design my own chalice. I liked to work with my hands and so I made on a wood lathe a model of a chalice I wanted to have made for me. I made two or three of them before I got the one I really liked and I wanted it in enamel. I had a devotion to our Blessed Mother and I wanted blue enamel in honor of her.

Then I wanted the symbols of the trinity on the base. On the cup, I had stars representing each member of my family. Two large stars for my parents and six little ones for each of their children, so anytime I use the chalice I am reminded to pray for my family.

Work

Tell me about your work and career path.

The novice master, Fr. Placidus, prepared us for teaching and to expect to be teachers. So that is what I, more or less, expected to do. Actually, it worked out that way. Before I was ordained, I was [*told*] that I would probably be teaching industrial arts, such as woodworking, drafting, ceramics, electricity and internal combustion machines. Before, or just after I was ordained, I was sent to Indiana State University for industrial art courses and I actually ended up with a master's in industrial arts.

Before I got my master's, I was assigned to St. Placid Hall. I lived with the students as disciplinarian and taught them industrial arts courses. We had about 40 students. I was at St. Placid Hall until they closed it in 1966.

The year before, Abbot Bonaventure [*had*] asked for volunteers to start a new monastery in Peru. I volunteered the very day that we had the meeting [*where he announced this*]. I had a conviction that I would like to work in a foreign country. But as long as St. Placid Hall was open, there was no way I was going to be sent because they had sent me to get my master's degree in industrial arts, which was specifically for St. Placid Hall.

But then they decided to close [*St. Placid Hall*]. When that happened, we had a new abbot, Gabriel [*Verkamp*]. So I went to see him and asked him if he knew that I had volunteered for Peru. Anyhow, he thought at first that I was asking to go to California, because at the same time we had a [*new*] place in California. I said, "No, no, no. I want to go to Peru," and he said, "Oh, okay, we will consider that." So it wasn't long after that he called me [*into his office*] and appointed me to Peru. So actually before they closed the doors of St. Placid Hall, I got to go to Peru.

What did you do in Peru?

I was teaching industrial arts again – courses in mechanical drawing, ceramics, woodwork. I think those are the main ones. The kids liked to work with their hands. Within a year after I got there, the school administration in Lima discontinued manual arts courses for high school. So then I taught religion and [*was the*] disciplinarian at the school.

How many students did you have?

We averaged 30 students, all boarding school students, and I lived in the building with [*them*].

I understand that you were there during the 1970 earthquake. Can you tell me about this?

Yes, I was. There was a family in the town of Huaraz. The children used to come up and see me, two girls and a boy. One Sunday, just before they were going to go back home, they noticed in my room a Chinese checkerboard and they wanted to know what it was. I told them it was a game with marbles that you played and they wanted me to teach them how. I said, "No, we haven't got enough time now, but the next time you come, I will teach you."

So the very next weekend, on Sunday, they came up and wanted to learn how to play. I was just getting the Chinese checkerboard off the shelf when the earthquake started. I had eaten a meal at their home a week or two before, and I knew the house was completely adobe. It was a two-story building and I knew the place would be rubble. There is no way that the house could withstand an earthquake as strong as it was.

I figured the mother – she was a single mother – would have been in the home and probably the other brothers and sisters of these three children [*who*] were visiting me. So I figured I was stuck with three orphans. After things settled at the monastery, I took the three children down the hill to the town and we got within a short distance of where the house was. But there were no buildings standing at all in that area.

I knew that their mother worked at the hospital and I figured after this earthquake she might be [*there*]. So I [*took*] the three children with me to the hospital [*and on the way*] I met an engineer who was from Germany that I knew. He wanted me to go with him. He said that he had a Jeep and he could go around the outside area of the town and haul the wounded to the hospital.

I said, "Well, I've got these three children," and he said, "Let them come with us." The first trip we took some injured to the hospital. Then I left [*the three children*] off at the hospital and I said, "Now if you see your mother, you can go with her; otherwise, stay at the hospital and I will pick you up later on and take you to the monastery," so they would have some place to sleep.

Then we went again and got another Jeep load of wounded and, when we got back, the children were gone and I knew that they had found their mother. Then we worked that [*whole night*]. I would ride on the front bumper of the Jeep and holler *heridos*, which means "wounded" in Spanish, and [*relatives and neighbors*] would bring the injured to the road and we would haul them [*to the hospital*]. We did that from about 5:00 in the afternoon until 1:00 or 1:30 in the morning. Then finally there weren't any more injured to haul, so we quit.

In the monastery when you were reaching for the Chinese checkerboard, describe what happened and what you did.

Well, it was a prefab building that we lived in. It just rocked with the motion [*of the quake*], but the motion was so great that the three children and I got out of the door of the building. However, because of the shaking of the ground, we couldn't walk or run. We just stood and waited and it seemed like five minutes or more, but it was only a few seconds. I think it was 37 seconds that the earthquake lasted. After the earthquake stopped, I said I wanted to find out if the rest of the monastery members were okay. I did that and then I took the children downtown.

Down in the town, Fr. Bede [*Jamison*] died in the earthquake protecting two children. They were at a party at the elementary school. Their mother later came up to the monastery to thank us for saving their lives. Fr. Pius [*Klein*], who was also there, crawled under a piano and led people to safety. Many people died in this quake.

What did you do after the earthquake?

During that time, I was put in charge of reconstruction to reconstruct the monastery and patch up everything. I was there three years after the earthquake. I came back [*to Saint Meinrad*] unwillingly. I was content in Peru and we had just finished our construction. I felt attached to the place so I was reluctant to come back, as I was happy there, but obedience is obedience.

Why were you called back?

Br. Luke [*Hodde*] was physical plant director. Father Abbot appointed him treasurer, so he had to have a replacement for the physical plant director. There was no one at the monastery that he could appoint to that position. He knew that I had farm experience and liked to work with my hands and that I had been [*working*] for three years doing reconstruction down in Peru. So he brought me back to make me physical plant director. Also at that time we were [*planning*] a new monastery.

Describe what you did when you got back here.

Soon after I got back, we started the plans for the new monastery and library. I was involved in all of that. We were in meetings and meetings and meetings with contractors and with architects of all kinds. We represented the architects to the monastery and we had to represent the monastery to the [*architects*], so we were in meetings all the time. The monastery got built and, after seven years as physical plant director, something happened.

While I was in Peru, I was on a motorcycle every day – once or twice a day – for over 10 years. Br. Angelo [*Vitale*] had been given a motorcycle to use. So I asked him if I could ride it. I rode it around the [*Saint Meinrad*] grounds a little bit a few times.

One Saturday I was doing some painting of lines for parking. Br. Angelo saw me and he says, "The motorcycle is not working right. Could you come over for a few minutes and see if you can figure out what is the matter with it?" So I said, "I will meet you down at the shop. We have to have some tools before we can do anything."

So I went down with my pickup to the shop buildings and he coasted downhill on the motorcycle. When he got down at the bottom of the hill, the motorcycle started working right. So he said, "Forget about it. The motorcycle is working okay." That is the last I remember. I am told that I asked him, "Are you sure it is working all right? Let me try it." Anyhow, I got on the motorcycle and started going up the hill back up to the monastery.

Apparently – I don't remember anything – the brakes were starting to stick. I put on the brakes and they wouldn't let loose, so I probably gave it a little more gas and all at once it let loose. The bike went out from under me and I hit the asphalt and injured [*my right*] ear and was knocked unconscious. Anyhow, within a few minutes, they had me on the way to Jasper in the ambulance. That was in the morning.

In the afternoon, I woke up in the hospital. There was a nurse in the room and I asked her what was going on, why was I there. She said, "You had an accident." I asked, "What kind of an accident?" She said, "You were on a motorcycle." And I said, "I don't remember any accident," and I had no recollection of the accident at all. There was a bad injury to this ear. To this day, I can't walk a straight line. My balance is off and I have no sense of taste or smell.

So then what happened when you got out of the hospital?
Although I was director of the physical plant and in charge of housekeeping and security, Br. Luke, the one who [*had been*] the physical plant director and went to the Business Office, realized that he was going to have to get a replacement for me. He needed someone with degrees and experience in industrial arts or construction. So he hired two laymen. One man was hired for housekeeping and security, and another man was hired for the physical plant.

What did you do after this?
I wasn't assigned to anything, as it took about two years to recuperate from the accident. I also had to leave the volunteer fire department because I couldn't smell or taste much.

So after your recuperation, what was your next assignment?
About two years after the accident, Father Abbot Timothy [*Sweeney*] called me in and said he had another job for me. He said, "We have a mission in Tennessee and Father Basil [*Mattingly*] who is down there has asked to go to Africa to teach." The abbot said yes, so they needed someone to take his place in Tennessee. I was the only one that had any farm experience. I didn't like the idea of going

down there, as I really wanted to live at the monastery. But I went and was there for 10 years.

What did you do on this assignment?

Farm work and parish work on weekends. [*We had*] cattle, beef cattle, and when I started, there were hogs, too, but I got rid of them. In the week from Monday until Friday, I worked on the farm doing farm work. We had a big tractor and all the implements. I made hay and then fed the hay to the cattle in the wintertime.

Did you have anyone helping you?

There was a layman that helped to some extent. He didn't have any farm experience, but he was a good man. So he helped me for the first seven years. Father Abbot Lambert [*Reilly*] was elected in 1995. One of the first things he did was ask me if I wanted to stay there or come back to the monastery. I said, "Back to the monastery." So he brought me back within a year and the place was closed.

But [*the abbot*] didn't let me stay. He asked me to go to Mexico. So I was in Mexico for a year in Morelia, Mexico, a city with over 1.5 million people. They [*had*] a shortage of members in the monastery. There were only six monks besides myself. I said, "Well, Father Abbot, I am willing to go, but I don't want to be in a situation where it is being terminated." I had closed St. Placid Hall, and also the mission.

He said, "If they decide or are intending to close the place, just ask and I will bring you back." So within the year after I was there, we had a meeting and the monks, six of us or seven, decided to close the place. After the meeting, I telephoned Father Abbot Lambert and said I wanted to come home and he said, "Okay." Then I got another telephone call a day or so later saying that he was asking me to stay on for another year, so I did.

Did it close then?

It closed afterward. Yeah, it is no longer in existence.

So you came back here and then what did you do?

Well, I wasn't assigned to anything and so I started helping Br. Augustine [*Schmidt*], who was the electrician at that time. I started helping him with electrical problems. Then the abbot assigned me to the physical plant office – the job I've got now [*2009*]. I am an assistant to Janet Braunecker, who is the head secretary to Pat Clark, the director of the physical plant.

What kind of work do you do now?

Mostly computer work and filing and whatever. If she has something that she has to send, they gave me a car and I do her running around. Actually, I don't have a tight schedule.

I have always, since grade school, been interested in stamps and stamp collecting. So I have all the letters that come in to the Abbey Press. The empty envelopes are put in a box with my name on it, so I get all the envelopes from the Abbey Press. I go through them and pick out stamps.

From all over the world?

Yeah, there [*are*] a lot of foreign stamps. It's kind of crazy, but I figure if a stamp has the value of only four cents, for example, if you only had one of each stamp, then you've only got four cents in a collection for this stamp. But if you have a hundred of the same stamp, you have 100 times its value. So I keep [*many*] stamps of all kinds. I have probably thousands and thousands. Someday, they may be valuable to the monastery.

Is there anything more about your work you want to mention before we get into prayer and spiritual life?

Well, I have always considered St. Benedict was very, very interested in, and specified things, for work. He saw the value of work. Our model is: work and pray, or pray and work, whichever. So I have always valued work as part of my Benedictine monastic vocation.

Prayer

Can you tell me something about prayer?

Prayer is union with Christ, union with God. We can't spend all of our time in prayer and so St. Benedict joins the two, work and prayer. Each fortifies the other; your spiritual life gives value to your work and your work, as a means of livelihood, supports the time for prayer. I always valued these kinds of ideas. You can't have pure prayer; you can't have pure work, but the combination of the two supplements each other.

In terms of the Rule of St. Benedict, *what is your favorite part of this book?*

I think humility. The chapter on humility is so important and I value it very, very much. I have always used part of my time for meditation and humility.

What is your key to living Benedictine spirituality?

I would say, "Love your neighbor." We live a close-knit family type of life, and love of each other is very important.

What has been the most difficult time in your life?

The most difficult [times] were to accept obedience in changing [geographic locations]. I [like] routine. Anytime I am in one place, it becomes a routine for me. If I have to go to someplace else, it is destructive to the whole routine; it takes time to build up a whole new routine. So my [*most difficult times*] have been in changing from place to place. I could have spent all my life in Peru. I could have spent all my life in Mexico. I enjoyed it once I got settled and in a routine, but I prefer Saint Meinrad.

So it was going from one place to another that was difficult for you?
Yeah, that was the difficult thing.

What has been your happiest or most joyful experience in your lifetime?
Well, it is the priesthood. [*It is*] working as a priest with people in the confessional and giving advice when they come for spiritual direction; the whole idea of the priesthood is wonderful.

Changes in the Church

Today some observers are of the opinion that we are similar to the times when St. Benedict lived and society is once again falling into indifference in terms of the meaning of a virtuous life and the lack of spirituality. How has this affected the Benedictine community?
We have to be vigilant against the influence of the outside on our monastic life. If we let the ways of the world influence us, it takes away from the religious life, the Benedictine life. So we have to be constantly on the alert and diligent [*and not let*] the worldly ways creep in.

Is that difficult?
Yes, very difficult, because we are very much engaged with our educational pursuits and going to parishes and the like. The influence of the outside can creep in very easily, and does.

That leads to the next question. Some Catholics think that Pope John XXIII was overly optimistic and that ever since Vatican II the Church has been paying a heavy price for his initiatives, where others applaud his gestures. What changes have occurred and how is the Church different today from pre-Vatican II?

[*In the pre-councilor days*], there had been great devotion [*in*] the Catholic Church – private devotions and liturgical devotions. I think a lot of that has been lost. The changes in the liturgy and the Mass, especially, were brought about in the wrong way, without enough preparation and education [*of the laity*], and it led to disrespect for a lot of the things of the past. I would say it is only in the last year or two, maybe three, that some of those things have begun to come back.

Can you give me an example?

Devotion to the Blessed Mother. I think there were a number of years it was looked down upon and not considered necessary at all. The last two or three years … [*this devotion*] has come back.

Is there anything else that you have seen?

Off the top of my head, I think confession. The sacrament of confession for a number of years was neglected. At least in some areas [*of the country*], it has come back. Not as much as I think it should, but it has [*returned*] somewhat.

Compare the morale of the monastery today with that of 30, 40, 50 years ago. Is there a difference in morale and to what extent has the decline in vocations had an impact on the Church and the monastery community?

I think the morale is quite good. Some [*men*] come to monasteries that don't have the right motives so their morale is not good, but they are usually weeded out.

Are they the ones who usually leave?

Yes, and those who come with good intentions of sacrifice ... and are willing to make [*it*], their morale is good. So, as a whole, I would say the morale is good. There are always a few that can't take it and they grumble and eventually leave.

This next question has to do with Latin. Even though the Mass is celebrated in English, was eliminating Latin from the academic curriculum a good idea?

[*Latin*] is required for one year and then it is offered other years. I think it is a mistake to disinherit so much of the Church history, which is in Latin. I am not a linguist and I always had a problem with Latin, so I am very pleased with being able to say Mass and the Divine Office in English. But I respect the history of Latin and think the writings of the Fathers of the Church must be studied in the native language, which is Latin. I respect those who have the ability to do that very much.

Should more than one year be taught to seminarians?

I would have to think about that more. A pharmacist has to have some Latin and I think a priest has to have some Latin. The pharmacist doesn't speak Latin and, at least today, priests don't speak Latin. I don't think there is any problem with that, except there is a tremendous amount of material in Latin [*and*] if we only speak English, we lose.

There have been many changes made since the days of the Council. Please comment on what you think are the positive and negative changes that have occurred in the last 50 years.

I am very much of the opinion that we, in general, don't understand the Vatican Council's writings and teaching. In other words, a lot of the devotion to the Blessed Mother that I mentioned, and its decline, was considered part of the Vatican Council, which is not true. If we read the documents of the Church and the Council, we can find that the devotion to the Blessed Mother was, and is, promoted.

The same thing has happened in a number of fields in the Church. [*For example*], architecture changed drastically after the Vatican Council. [*These changes*] were the result of those in opposition to the Church and they saw their chance [*through*] the Council to have a big influence, and they did. Many today feel that [*people*] are ignorant of the facts of what the Vatican Council actually promulgated.

What has been lost and what has been gained since the Council?

There has been a lot gained, but there has been an awful lot lost. Let me give one example: the receiving of the Eucharist in the hands. Historically speaking, the Vatican never intended to give permission to receive [*it*] in the hands. There was a special group, and I can't say where or why, but the Vatican made an exception and gave this particular group permission to receive in the hands. Like wildfire, it spread all over the world, but it was not the intention of the Vatican [*for it*] to be given generally in the hands.

So you see that as a loss?
Yes.

Is there anything else you see as a loss because of the Council?

[*The same thing happened to*] devotion, whether it was a devotion to some saint or devotion to the Blessed Sacrament or devotion in general. [*This*] was looked down upon after the Vatican Council. I think that is a great loss in our spiritual life and in our human life, [*as*] we need this devotion. I have thought about that many, many times. We had a great loss when we lost real devotion.

Is that now changing?

Yes. One place I see it is in the seminary. The students are requesting devotion, like 40 Hours exposition of the Blessed Sacrament. This didn't come from the director and governing body of the seminary; it came from the students.

What has been gained since the Council?

Well, we gained a lot so far as Church law. [*They are not*] as repressive. The Vatican Council opened all the laws you were under and give liberty and freedom of choice; although there is always the danger of misconception. Let me give you an example: [*not*] eating meat on Friday was a law of the Church and every Catholic was expected to abide by it.

After the Vatican Council, the law was opened or lifted, but not done away with. In other words, when it came out that we could eat meat on Friday, the law [*required*] if you ate meat on Friday, you had to give some other act of mortification to take its place. Now that part has been completely forgotten, but that was the law.

With the idea of abstaining from meat, we gained our freedom to choose what mortification we want and to make the mortification something that we ourselves are offering to God. What did it mean to the people? It really wasn't meaning much. It wasn't the spiritual act it should have been. We were given the freedom to choose and, in choosing, we [*should*] have had a better idea of mortification, but it didn't work out that way.

Have there been other gains since the Council?

Yes, the Mass in English.

The number of religious vocations has declined, although recently they have begun to creep up a bit and, of course, the number of retirements and deaths has meant a drastic decrease in religious vocations. What is the meaning of these changing patterns to the monastery and the Church at large?

I think before the Vatican Council, the Church and monasteries were spoiled with all the vocations they had. In other words, it is difficult for us today because of the past. We look back at the past the way things were and it is not that way today, so we think we are suffering. Actually, we still have Mass, and Mass is available to those who want it and are willing to go a little ways. Our mode of transportation has increased tremendously, so that we can go 50 miles to Mass if we have to.

[*This*] is the same with the other sacraments such as confession. There are enough priests to go around to hear the confessions of the people, if the people will come [*and*] if priests will sacrifice themselves to spend time with the people. So the Church, in a way, benefited by the smaller number of priests and religious insofar as it has brought us back to appreciating what we have, because we may have had too much before.

Where do you see the Church in the future? What changes do you see happening?

There will be fewer parishes. In some of the bigger cities, there [*were*] two or three churches within three or four blocks. That was not necessary and will probably not be in the future. That's not a bad thing, and could be a good thing, as a lot of parishes were very small. I think parishes can function well, not gigantic parishes, but medium in-between [*ones*]. So it is a matter of adjustment; we have to make adjustments for what we have [*in terms of the*] number of religious and the number of priests. I don't think the Lord is going to allow the number of priests to get too low, nor the number of religious either. He has more at stake in it than we do.

What are your hopes for the future for the Archabbey and the Church?

I hope the Abbey does have enough vocations to carry out at least some of the things it has been [*doing*]. The more monks that you have, the more activities there are going to be. Is that always good? Not necessarily. If we have fewer monks, we should reign in and have fewer activities, but that doesn't spoil the monastery. If the monastery is doing a good job with the personnel they have, they can do a lot of good for the people. So I am not pessimistic about the future of either the Church or the monastery. I think God will provide.

Do you have any final thoughts?

I would just like to mention my great gratitude, both to the monastery and to the Church at large. I appreciate having lived in a pre-Vatican monastery and a pre-Vatican Church, and I appreciate living in the post-Vatican Church and monastery. So I think if we can keep an attitude of appreciation, there is great hope for all of us.

Profile based upon: Fr. Augustine Davis, OSB, to Prof. Ruth C. Engs, July 29, 2009, Interview Transcriptions, Saint Meinrad Archabbey Archives, St. Meinrad, IN; additional comments from Fr. Augustine, July 2015.

Chapter 3: Fr. Boniface Hardin, OSB

Fr. Boniface, known as "Father" in the Afro-American (his term) community of Indianapolis, IN, was a community leader during the Civil Rights Movement era and beyond. He founded the Martin Center and Martin University – an adult learning institution – for minority students, and was awarded many honorary degrees.

Born in Bardstown, Kentucky, on November 18, 1933, Fr. Boniface was given the name Dwight Randolph. At his baptism, James was added to his name. After completing elementary school at St. Monica School in Bardstown and St. Peter Claver School in Louisville, he enrolled in Saint Meinrad Minor Seminary in 1947. Fr. Boniface professed his simple vows on July 31, 1954, solemn vows in 1957, and was ordained to the priesthood on May 11, 1959.

After his ordination, he served as assistant treasurer of the Archabbey (1959-65). He became associate pastor at Holy Angels Church, Indianapolis, (1965-69) in an African-American neighborhood. In his first years, social tensions were high and the threat of violence was imminent and he became a calming influence in the black community. In his parish and within the wider community of Indianapolis, he evolved into a wise leader.

In 1969, Fr. Boniface founded the Martin Center, an Institute of Afro-American Studies; the Indianapolis sickle cell center (1971), and co-founded with an associate, Sr. Jane Schilling, Martin University (1977), whose mission was to serve low-income, minority adult learners. He was president of the university for many years (1977-2007).

Fr. Boniface performed as Frederick Douglass beginning in 1990 for a number of years in plays he produced. He suffered a stroke in August 2011 and died March 24, 2012.

Dr. Ruth C. Engs interviewed Fr. Boniface Hardin, OSB, April 27, 2010, at his home in Indianapolis amidst numerous clocks, religious statues and African artifacts given to him by friends.

Childhood and Early Years as a Monk

Tell me something about your childhood — where you were born, etc.

I was born November the 18th, 1933, at the general hospital in Louisville, KY; however, my family lived in New Haven, KY, at the time, which is near Bardstown. I am the second of six children; the firstborn died at birth. I am the second born. There are three other brothers and there is one girl, Elizabeth Anne, who died also at birth.

I was baptized on December the 16th, 1933, and my mother named me Dwight Randolph Hardin after Dwight Eisenhower and a Phillip Randolph, who was a friend of her family. He was part of the march on Washington, DC, in the 1920s – the Pullman Porters protest. So I claim Phillip Randolph. When I was baptized, the pastor said, "They are not Catholic names." So he gave me the name of James, and I became James Dwight Randolph Hardin.

When it came time to make solemn vows, the monastery had a hard time finding my baptismal certificate. I gave them all the names and they finally found it and put it down as Dwight Randolph Hardin. James was not there.

My mother was not Catholic at the time, so I always tell people I was born a Baptist, and less than a month later I became a Catholic. That was when my father had me baptized. Later she became the best Catholic in the whole family. She was very devoted to the Church.

Tell me about your parents.

My parents met at Kentucky State. They got certifications to be teachers, but my father waited tables at old Topper [*Talbot*] Tavern, which is where Jesse James stayed in Bardstown. He didn't teach school, as such, at that time, and that is how he was able to make money for the family. We also had a little store in Hickmantown near Fairfield. It wasn't a town; it was a section of the town.

He was a very smart man and well read. He read the paper every day all his life. My father was very much like his father. He was very exact, very proper and you always knew ahead of time what you were supposed to do. And if you didn't know and couldn't explain yourself, you got punched or socked or something. I only got one whipping from him in my life and it wasn't because I did something bad; it was because I did something dumb.

My mother taught school in New Haven, KY. It was a one-room schoolhouse. One year there was a flood in Louisville and the children came out to New Haven. She taught school many years, even after we moved to Louisville, KY. Notice we say Louvill, not Louisville, not Louieville, but Louvill. You know someone is from Louisville when they say it that way. If they don't say it that way, they don't know a thing about where I came from.

Bardstown is a historical town. It had the first cathedral west of the Alleghenies [*St. Joseph Proto-Cathedral*]. When Pope Benedict came to the United States, he mentioned Bardstown on a list of his cathedrals. I made my First Communion there at the cathedral and I was confirmed by the bishop.

Bardstown was very important in my life and my family's life because my great-grandfather and my grandfather were slaves in Bardstown. My great-grandfather helped build that church.

As a slave?

Yes, he was in bondage. This is my family heritage and we talk about this even today. We talk about how we deal with slavery in our family as a part of our heritage, and we survived it. Now Bardstown is a very Catholic town. Everybody knows about Stephen Foster and the song "My Old Kentucky Home."

This house wasn't very far from Papa Hardin's home; it was just a holler and a throw from it. A judge lived there and was buried there and around his grave are little pointed plates to show where the slaves were buried around him. So slavery was a part of Bardstown, Kentucky.

Until about 20 years ago, they had a slave block at the courthouse, the Nelson County Courthouse. They tore it down during the '60s because people had them tear it down. It was inscribed telling people that slaves were sold at this place.

So my grandfather, when he was a young man, was a child of a slave. So I am the grandson of a slave child. In my family, slavery is alive and we still have to deal with it. There was a seminary there in Bardstown and they had a slave that worked in the house.

My early family life was very simple. We lived in different places; we lived in New Haven, KY, for a number of years, moved to Fairfield also near Bardstown, and then to Louisville. My father didn't go into WWII, as he worked in Jeffersonville in the depot there so he got exempted. During WWII, we moved there. We were in Louisville when the war ended.

How about your schooling as a child?

We had our own school; it was down the street, because it was against Kentucky law to teach colored children and white children in the same building.

Was this a Catholic school?

It was definitely a Catholic school run by the Sisters of the Charity of Nazareth. They had a motherhouse – and they still do – outside of Bardstown. They wore little bonnets; it was a little Catholic school [*St. Monica*] and the Church established it. My father went there and my uncles did, too. We only had two rooms in the school; it was a mansion of some sort and was given, I guess, to the Church.

I remember my first day in school in first grade. My mother left me off at the school and I went in and cried. I also remember the first grade teacher made me write my name wrong on the board. I told her my name was Randolph Hardin and I did not have a "g" in my name, and she made me write it a hundred times "H-a-r-d-i-n-g" – Randolph Harding.

I argued with her and she thumped my head on the blackboard. So that is my memory of first grade. Other than that, the teachers were good teachers and they loved us. I just ran into the wrong one that day, but we all have our stories about the nuns. I got mine, too.

Did any of those nuns influence you to go into the religious life?

Sr. Mary Felix, probably. She had a wonderful smile and I liked her – you imitate people you like. I am sure, way deep down inside of me, her smile and her happiness probably helped me. The parish priest was also very sensitive to us.

How about your religious life as a child?

We lived the way a lot of southern towns lived; you didn't cross the line. When you went to the theater, you sat upstairs. When you went to church, you sat in back. And in this Catholic church, the colored people had their pews in the back of the church. Now on Sunday afternoon, you could go to benediction [*of the Blessed Sacrament*] and you could kneel anywhere, but not during Mass. The priest was nice. Father Louie was very nice. He probably was an inspiration to me, my first inspiration [*to become a priest*].

The bishop decided there should be a Catholic church for colored people. My father objected to building a new church for the colored people. He would say, "St. Joe is our church." The proto-cathedral still exists. It is a beautiful church; they renovated it and one of my classmates in the seminary ended up being the pastor there. So anyway, St. Monica's Church was started and I served [*as an altar boy*]. So, anyways, those were good days in Bardstown.

And this was an all-black church?
Colored, we used the word colored. At this time, we were colored.

So there was a colored Catholic church and a white Catholic church?
Yeah.

Are there other family stories of your slave great-grandfather?
It is something that he really didn't talk about. Now, we know that the secretary of state in Kentucky, at that time, looks just exactly like my grandfather on my daddy's side, spitting image. My Papa Hardin didn't have a lot of hair like myself. He was thin and he was very, very light skinned. He was close to my father; he looked also like a white man, my grandfather did. He never acted like, and he didn't say, that he was white. He was always colored.

Almost all blacks have white ancestors from slavery, but we don't talk about it. Another train or line of heritage, the Bricks family, is part of my family. The Hardins came from England, we know that, and they settled there in Bardstown. My youngest brother is a historian. He has a doctorate in history from Western [*Kentucky University*], Bowling Green. He has been doing research on our family. So that is all I know now.

Do you have other information about religious life as a child?

We moved to Louisville and we joined the colored church called St. Peter Claver, as we still had segregation of the church. St. Peter Claver was a patron of Negros in the 16th century and that was fine. Our pastor was a Franciscan, Fr. Simon Gresham. He was a wonderful man and came from Jasper, Indiana.

Was he colored?

No, he was white. I think he may have gone to Saint Meinrad. He knew about Saint Meinrad, because he took me there one time fishing. At St. Peter Claver, we had a drum and bugle corps. Fr. Simon was very erect and he wore a straw hat. We would march down Broadway, the main street in Louisville, and he marched with us. Our drum and bugle corps was very famous, and people always cheered us because we were the colored children and we played very well.

We didn't have a bus, but a U-Haul would come and get the band and carry us all, wherever. We would play inside the senior citizens home and march in parades and everything. We didn't have uniforms. The drum and bugle corps did at one time, but we didn't at that time. So, Fr. Simon would have a chair and he would sit on the back end of the truck. We would be back in there and we played as we were going along. He probably had a lot to do with me being a priest.

He taught us discipline and always loved us, and we loved him. He is gone to God now. He was a good man. He was hard of hearing, so whenever we would go to confession with him it was really something. Saturday afternoon you went to confession and told him you disobeyed your parents, hit your brother and all these big sins.

He would chase us out of the confessional and would say, "Go back out there and examine your conscience." So we would go get our books and look up all the sins – and here we are 7 years of age –

and we would go into confession and he would say, "Now that's better." Bless his heart. We knew we had to give him something that he could hold on to. That was the way it was, but we loved him.

Do you have other amusing stories about school?

As children, we heard stories from Protestant kids, such as if you see a nun you were supposed to put your hand over your mouth. We didn't know what they were talking about, because we saw nuns every day and we never put our hand over our mouth.

The Franciscans [*at the school*] came from St. Boniface [*Church in Louisville*]. They would come down and take care of us, but Fr. Simon lived right next door to the church. Sr. Inez and Sr. Sirella were Ursuline sisters who lived in Louisville. They loved us, too, and taught the whole time I was there until I went to the seminary, which was in 1947.

Do you have any other stories from when you were young?

Well, I'll tell you one of my terrible experiences. We lived in Fairfield at the time. My father started a restaurant and my mother wasn't teaching then. My mother was hanging up clothes one day in the yard, and two men held a third man and another man shot the man they held.

The hard part about it was that the man who did this used to drive me around in his open-seated car. My mother knew what was going to happen, so she told me to get in the house. I don't know how old I was, I don't know if I was 5 or 6, but I was around that age and I will never forget that.

Was it mobsters?

No, it was just one human being shooting another human being. Later on, that human being – the one that was shot – lived and came to talk to me when I was a small child in Louisville. I think this experience impacted me about how cruel human beings could be to other human beings. That impact on a child's memory was so great that I am talking to you about it today. So that is one sad moment in my life that I will never forget.

What was health care like when you were a child?
Oh, I don't know, I guess my mother and father took care of me. My mother was kind of like the matriarch of the family, my father's family and her family. We had measles and chicken pox.

Did you go to the doctor or did the doctor come to you?
No doctors; I don't remember going to doctors.

Did doctors come visit you?
I don't remember a doctor at all. We were cared for by our parents. They took care of us and that was it.

What led you to Saint Meinrad?
Fr. Simon would come to our classes and say, "We need more colored boys to be priests." Sr. Inez, our teacher, and Sr. Sirella also said we need more colored boys to be priests. That was going on all the time. Once there was a priest from SVD [*Divine Word Missionaries*] who came and talked to us. That was the only colored priest I had ever met in my life.

Did you go directly to Saint Meinrad after grade school?
I was 13 years of age when I went to Saint Meinrad. I came here when it was called Saint Meinrad High School and College [*also the minor seminary*]. Fr. Herman Romoser was the rector. On September the 9th, 1947, we got on a bus in Louisville and the bus that took us all to Saint Meinrad. The bus was filled with Louisville boys. So it was a good time.

Fr. Abbot Ignatius [*Esser*] received my mother and father and talked to them about how much they could pay for tuition. May God rest him; a wonderful man. My father told him how much he made and said, "This is how much I can send every month." I think my father sent him like $10 a month. Then we had an angel from Louisville who sent money for my schooling. We had been chosen by her. Later on, when I became an assistant treasurer, I saw her name and I saw what she did.

When you went here at the age of 13, were you thinking of becoming a priest or did your parents think this was a good education opportunity?

Yes, I was going to become a priest. I was faithful about serving Mass, summertime and wintertime. I wasn't the only one, but I was always there.

Were your parents supportive of you going to be a priest?

Yes, oh yes. When my mother was in New Haven, back in the '30s, she would teach catechism to the colored children in her one-room schoolhouse before she was a Catholic. She took instruction from the pastor at St. Catherine's there in New Haven. When we moved to Louisville in 1945, my mother made her First Communion, so she was Catholic when I went out to the seminary.

She wanted me to be a diocesan priest because she thought they were cute with the sash down the cassock. I said, "Momma, that is not the reason." You know mothers have different ideas about things. She didn't know the difference in the types of priests, and that was alright.

There were four of us colored boys who went to the high school seminary and they were all connected to me. One was a classmate in Bardstown. His name was Jesse Cotton and he was in the seminary with me at the same time. He stayed about a year and a half. Then there were two others who went to the oblate house, Saint Placid Hall. They were going to study to be brothers and they stayed a couple of years. One was a cousin. They were all in the same class and they have all gone to God except myself.

Tell me about your years at the minor seminary.

I guess my grades were not all that good. I guess I was satisfactory. I got a 100 in grade school, and when I came to the seminary I got a C. Everybody said you got to be smart to go to the seminary. I wasn't used to getting Cs; I was used to getting 100s, because I was the smartest kid in St. Peter Claver. Then I would get a C, and I did not particularly like that. It was just a miracle that I was able to learn anything.

What courses did you take?

I took all the courses in Latin and Greek. When I went through the high school and college, I took German I and II, because at the time the monks spoke German in recreation.

Do you have other experiences when you were in the high school seminary?

When you are in the seminary, the "spiritual guardian" comes out every morning and tells you about being close to God and this and that, and you think about trying to be perfect. My biggest struggle from the time I was in the second year of high school until the first year of college was that I was scrupulous. Do you understand scrupulosity?

Does that mean always being on time and ...?

No, no, no. That is what the common explanation is. No, when you are scrupulous as a seminarian, it means you see sin where there is no sin. So if you are eating food, you are worried about gluttony. If I had a temptation at that time, I would shake my head – that was another side effect. There were others in my class that went through that.

When you took a shower, you were very afraid to look at your own body. You washed your body and closed your eyes like it was somebody else's body. When I went home, if I saw a girl walking down the street in shorts, I would get up and go in the house because I didn't want to be tempted. It would be a sin just to be tempted.

When we got the newspaper, I would tear out all the things that had ads for ladies' bras and all of that stuff. I would tear it all out because I didn't want my dad to have temptations. He would read the newspaper with these holes in them. So my mom took me to the doctor and they x-rayed my head to see if there was something wrong. They said, "No, we can't see anything, so it's okay."

The thing I want to share with you is that it was okay; lots of my classmates went through this. When I was in the third year of high school, I was in the dormitory. I was pounding on the floor and I said, "Lord, take me away. I can't handle it any longer." I wanted to die because I didn't see any light down the road.

Fortunately, I had a good spiritual director. My spiritual director was Fr. Adelbert Buscher. He said, "Now, you cannot confess anything unless you can swear that it is a mortal sin." Well, then I was trapped because if I confessed something that I couldn't swear to, then I would be committing a sin.

So that helped me and he helped me to come out of that. Many of us went through this experience. We knew the signs and saw that others were having that same problem. It was a terrible experience for a young child to have.

I know the pain of it still remains with me, and that is why I am lots more sensitive, I think. Fr. Adelbert told me, "Someday you will be very sensitive to people." That is why I understand people in pain, because as a child I had a mental health problem.

The seminary didn't know what to do with it, as my confessor couldn't go out and say, "Well, guess what I got? I got one crazy guy right here." He couldn't do that, as it would have violated his vow of the sacrament [*of reconciliation or penance*] and his priesthood.

They don't have the high school seminary now, so that children can learn to grow up with their parents.

So this experience was very traumatic?
Yes, it was.

You obviously graduated from the high school seminary and then you went into the theological seminary.
Yes, I went through high school during that period of time I have been talking about to you. We had high school and then the last two years of minor seminary were the first two years of college. I had declared myself to be a monk way at the beginning with Abbot Ignatius. Then I was at the regular seminary.

When did you become a novice?
At the end of the second year in college, July 9th, 1953, we were invested with a habit. Then I had another name change. I wasn't James Dwight Randolph Hardin. Fr. Placid Kempf was my novice master. He was a loyal holy man and he said, "Randolph is not a Catholic name, Novice James." So there was another name change for me.

Okay, Novice James; I had to get used to the name. I was going to be the perfect monk and if you kept all the rules, then your salvation was

Fr. Boniface, as a young monk

secured. So I tried to be the perfect monk. I don't know if I was, but I sure caused a lot of strife with other people. I learned to be a good monk, I think. Then July 31, 1954, is when I got the name of Boniface.

Abbot Ignatius gave me the name of Boniface. Boniface was comfortable for me because the Franciscans came and took care of our little church, St. Peter Claver, from St. Boniface Church. Boniface was my first choice. Second choice was Meinrad; my third choice was Gregory.

Then I moved on through the monastery and made my solemn vows, I think in 1957. I know the first vows July 31st, 1954, so it would be three years. Then I was ordained on a Monday, May 11th, 1959, and Fr. Abbot Bonaventure [*Knaebel*] was abbot at the time. He assigned me to the treasury office with Fr. Rupert Ostdick and I was there for seven years.

During that time, the Civil Rights thing was going on with Dr. King down in Selma. I didn't get permission to go down there. I asked, but you know I was kind of hyper at the time. I was emotional, and it was probably a good thing that I didn't go. But I did have permission to meet Cardinal Rugambwa from Uganda.

He came to Saint Meinrad. He wanted me to get involved with the Civil Rights Movement. The only thing I could do was talk to the CSMC, the Catholic Students Mission Crusade. I was at the church in Jasper and one of the people kind of got carried away about me being there.

Why was that?

I was a Negro at the time. We went from being colored to Negro. I made some remark at the CSMC and they reported me. It was considered imprudent, but it was okay. I learned something from that. I wasn't happy that I didn't get to go to Selma. I wanted to go to Selma, but I could not get permission. Other monks including Cyprian [*Davis, Fr.*] and Camillus [*Ellspermann, Fr.*] did go.

Work

Tell me about your work career.

As mentioned, when I was ordained, Fr. Abbot Bonaventure put me in the treasury office.

How did you feel about that?

Well, the first two days I didn't feel very good, because all I did was file blue copies of checks –the third copy of checks. Here I have this great education and I am doing this. So anyway, I ended up with a desk and I didn't know anything about business and wasn't very good in algebra.

In 1963, Notre Dame offered a special program for religious on business debit and credit. So I went to Notre Dame for two summers and I learned all about debit and credit and the balance sheet. I was on cloud nine, because now I knew what all this meant. There is a reason why I was put into the treasury office; it was to prepare me for what I was to do later in life.

But I didn't know it at the time. Later in life, I was going to deal with millions and millions and millions of dollars. After taking the classes, I asked Fr. Abbot Bonaventure if I could work with colored people – Negros. I told him, "I would like to do that because there are not that many of us."

I was permitted to go Holy Angels Church in Indianapolis August 20, 1965. I just wanted to serve Negro people and that is how I got to Indianapolis.

Was this a Negro church?

Yes, it was predominantly black, but at one time it was white. There were whites, colored people, Negros, blacks; Fr. Alexius

Mosier was pastor. He had asked for a colored priest, and I was the only one that was available. Fr. Cyprian was in Belgium studying. This appointment [*assistant pastor*] came at the right time. I was supposed to save all the colored, bring them into the Church. I don't know what I did; I had a presence.

All of a sudden, my life changed. There was not somebody to tell me what to do, so I had to go to the door and answer the door: Can I help you? And you didn't know if it was somebody from the street or somebody from the parish. I didn't know the parishioners. I had to be careful of my hygiene, because I was around people.

In the monastery back then, we only were allowed to take one shower a week. You could bathe, but otherwise you weren't allowed to do all the hygienic things. So there were a lot of things I had to learn as a human being. I was a young priest and I always tried to be proper. Then I got involved in the problems of the community.

What were these?

I was in charge of the CYO [*Catholic Youth Organization*] and things like that, and I got involved because people were getting shot. It's like things you see right now. We didn't have as many [*incidents*], but police would beat up on people. I got involved in that and then I got involved with the highway. That was my first real public involvement.

I fought I-65. I tried to get it moved, because otherwise it would be right smack dab through our parish [*and a black neighborhood*]. At first, they were going to take I-65 through Crown Hill Cemetery, which is in our parish, too. John Dillinger and James Whitcomb Riley are buried there and all kinds of other famous people. So then they went through Riverside and people over there didn't like it. So they came through our neighborhood and on the west side.

I got involved with protesting the highway, and on Sunday mornings I preached about blackness, and some of them didn't want to hear this on a Sunday morning. They wanted to go to church, go to Mass. Fr. Athanasius was the liturgist in the Archdiocese of Indianapolis, so I was already in trouble because everything had to be perfect.

I did get some attention about the highway. There were a lot of things that were done to the highway because of my involvement. You know for a priest to be involved and telling the city, the mayor and the governor what to do…. We had marchers from Chicago and Dr. [*Martin Luther*] King came to town – in the early days, I did not meet him. Jesse Jackson came and I got to meet him. He got to know me because of the Civil Rights Movement and my involvement in the highway.

I was just trying to do what Jesus would do. He came and dwelled amongst his people and here I am. I stopped wearing a collar, because it turned people off. I pitched my tent and if I saw something wrong, I was going to try to deal with it. Well, that didn't always go over with my pastor, because I didn't always ask permission from my pastor if I could do something. I did it because it was the right thing to do.

Well, I got in trouble. There was a meeting of the parish committee and I was supposed to be sent away or whatever, because I had become involved in the Civil Rights Movement and was fighting the highway. I had written an article and I had criticized the Church – that was my problem, a big mouth. I was being critical of the archdiocese and that is a no-no.

Because you were talking about involvement in the Civil Rights Movement?

Yes. The Civil Rights Movement is not a static thing, you have to understand. For some people, the Civil Rights Movement is over; it was over when Dr. King died. That is not true; it took on different aspects, but at the time it was marches and protests. I got people at Holy Angels, where I was, to protest the highway.

The mayor of the city was a Catholic and had gone to Holy Angels. He was very upset with me. We protested Dick Lugar – who later was senator – when he became mayor and we tried to convince him to stop the highway [*going through our neighborhood*]. The federal government came and they brought their people. We did save some houses.

So I was very righteous about the problem and, of course, colored people like that. They like somebody to stand up and would say, "Fr. Hardin is confronting the mayor, the governor and the national government and everybody." So I was their hero in the highway fight. I didn't win, of course, because the highway people went ahead and took down the houses except a few. We saved some houses and my parish.

When the police were beating up on colored people, what do you think I did? I would wear the dashiki [*African tunic*] and the kufis, which went all the way down to the ankles like you see some of the Arabs wear. So I would wear these. I also had a staff – very carved and the bugs had eaten into it.

I was at a church one day where we were having a meeting, and I learned afterwards that Dr. Andrew J. Brown and Dr. King were sitting in the back of the church. Dr. King said to Dr. Brown, "What is that?" He said, "Oh, that is Father." I didn't even have a first name. I was walking down the hall like Moses going across the sea. I was in the church going around up to the front.

Did you know King was there?

No, I didn't know he was there until later when he came up and introduced himself. That is how I met him at the Mt. Zion Church. I learned about Dr. King through Dr. Brown. Dr. Brown has gone to God; he was my mentor.

Tell me more about Dr. Martin Luther King.

Well, you know when you stand in front of somebody like that, you are in awe. You don't question him; you just say small talk because other people are around.

What did you talk about?

We were talking about the community and the necessity of people to stand up and this was a part of God's plan that we should not be oppressed. That is always the message and some people did not want to disturb anything – that was the old way. The mission of the Civil Rights Movement was not to change anything, but to make things right. That is all we were about.

The ministers were the people in charge of the community. We had Fr. [*Bernard*] Strange at St. Rita's – he is gone – and he was wonderful. He did things for colored people – Negros – and helped me a lot. He brought black missions here and brought Bishop Fulton Sheen here. You took a risk, as you don't know whether somebody will hurt you or not.

Tell me more about this.

Your name gets attached to an issue and my name was attached to the police. I was the enemy of the police. It wasn't because I had policemen in my parish. It was because I was fighting against the issue of police brutality. So my name became kind of negative at that point, in some ways, and in other ways I was a hero. At the time, I was bulletproof. But if you talk to me now, I would say, "Let's do it a little differently."

You learn some wisdom and you don't always take it to the press. At the time, that was the modus operandi, so to speak. You used the media to get your cause across. We don't do that anymore. Well, some of us still do that, but that is not the way you really should do it. If you really want to make some change, you work behind the scenes. A lot of people were killed.

What year was this?

Oh, I guess we are talking about the late '60s. Dr. King had died in 1968 and people were angry with that. Over on the west side, where I was at Holy Angels, the people rioted. I never understood rioting; it was just an outlet, a venting. They would start fires. So I would grab my dashiki and get in my car and ride off into the sunset. I would say to them, "What are you doing? Put that down." I would confront them.

So you actually went to where they were rioting?

Oh yeah, oh yeah. During that time, too, even in Louisville, there were tanks right down the street from where my mother and father lived. I visited Detroit after they had a riot. You could smell the flesh where people were killed and you could see where bullets had penetrated the stone buildings. So the Civil Rights Movement has a plus-minus to it.

A lot of people didn't understand that the rioting was not what the Civil Rights Movement was about. It was about change and getting people their rights. Some understood it and some did not understand it, and that was the struggle. This was as much a struggle within the black community as the white community.

During that time in the '60s, we became black and beautiful. *Nigra sum sed formosa* from the Canticle of Canticles, *Nigra sum sed formosa filiae vos Hierusalem.* "I am black but beautiful, O ye daughters of Jerusalem," and so we began to sense that. Many of my colleagues, such as William Crawford, the oldest state representative, was a leader [*in the movement*].

His brother [*Fred*] was head of the Black Panther Party in Indianapolis. They had breakfast for children on Saturdays and stuff like that. Other times, they had their guns out and I would say to them, "Put that thing down," and they knew who I was. "That's Father." They didn't call me Fr. Hardin, just Father, like I was the only one. I wasn't the only one in town, but to them I was.

Tell me some more about this time.

Bobby Kennedy came to a park that is not so far from here [*his house in Indianapolis*]. I wasn't there that night. He came the night Dr. King was killed. I was in the parish house that night, but I did see Bobby during that time. He had some courage, he was running for office and I did meet him several times. People learned from him that Dr. King had been killed and because Bobby said what he said that night, he kept this city from burning down. Our people can be really crazy sometimes.

Much later, I watched a film of Kennedy at Madam Walker's Auditorium in Indianapolis. I was on a panel discussion. He quoted Aeschylus, he quoted Christ and he said, "I feel what you feel and I think that sometimes we have to remember the bad times so we can relate to them." The pain that I had as a child, seeing somebody getting shot, helps me understand when somebody down the street at the drugstore or at the hardware store gets shot. I understand that, and that our children have guns.

What happened next?

It was during these times that I became involved with the National Black Clergy Caucus. I went to Archbishop [*Paul*] Schulte, who ordained me, and I asked him if I could start the Martin Center. This was 1969. He wanted to know more and I said, "Well, the National Black Clergy Caucus was going to try and do something to train priests who worked in the black community."

He said, "I see no reason why you can't do this." So I started Martin Center, but it wasn't just for priests. It was for teachers, people who worked in the black community, and social workers, and it was over on College Avenue.

At the Martin Center, Sr. Jane [*Schilling*] and I developed a thing called ethno-therapy. "Ethnos" is street for race, nationality, and "therapy" means to heal – the healing of one's own racial feelings. We developed it and we had priests who came – white priests, black priests, and some priests became bishops. Probably if I had behaved myself, I might have been pushed that way.

To become a bishop?

Bishop, but I was a troublemaker. I wasn't acceptable in the church – an Indiana Catholic. There were editorials about me and some of my parishioners would go – when they thought they were going to lose me – and picket some of the white Catholic churches. So there was hub-bub about it. Then I started Martin Center and ethno-therapy. It kind of took away the animosity that they began to realize I didn't hate white people. There is white in my family. I am white, I am black and I am Indian. So which part of me am I supposed to hate?

Dr. Raymond Pierce, an orthopedic surgeon in my parish, and I would talk every week. We started the sickle cell center. [*It became the Martin Center Sickle Cell Initiative (MCSCI) in September 2012*]. I almost devoted my whole life to sickle cell disease. We got a grant from the federal government to start the sickle cell center. We haven't found a cure for it and we still have our meetings.

The Martin Center College was associated with Indiana University-Purdue University in Indianapolis, IUPUI. It was getting started back in those days. I worked with Dr. Doris Merritt, who worked with us on sickle cell. She is the one who got the money from the federal government and her husband was a geneticist. So I learned all about genetics through that whole operation.

At that time, we were a part of IU school of genetics. I found out I was getting grants for this thing and that thing and Martin Center. I said, "We've got to stop; we have to be more basic." They wanted me to be a branch of IUPUI. It would be the colored school with IUPUI, but we didn't want to be hitched up with them.

I said, "No, we are going to be a liberal arts school and we are going to do it ourselves." We have to do a school, as education is not happening. I saw the need for education. Something had to happen with the colored people, the Negro people, the black people. I named them "Afro-Americans," not African-American, Afro-American.

Why is that?

Fredrick Douglass, in the documents that we have about him, said there was a Miss Afro-American of 1892. It was a Miss Afro-American, so that was the word I thought would take hold because that was something we had in history. Well it didn't. Some people in Washington, DC, declared one day that we were African-Americans. Well, fine. I am not sure what the next name is going to be. We are God's child and that is the main thing. I am all of the above. So I started an institute of Afro-American study. So there was now Martin Center Institute, sickle cell and Afro-American study.

Then what happened?

We had a piece of land on College Avenue. It took a little while to figure out there was a national organization that helps develop schools. They help people who wanted to have a kind of step-school. It wasn't really a full-blown school; it was a school with a focus on the poor people. I joined up with them – Martin Center did – and so we got permission and got incorporated in the state as Martin Center College, which started officially August 9th, 1977. [*Martin College evolved into Martin University in 1990.*]

I was a traditionalist. I came out of Saint Meinrad and I was well educated. Nobody told me that I was going to start a school. I didn't get to go to IU [*Indiana University*] Bloomington. I didn't get to go to Catholic University or any other school and get a degree, as many of my colleagues did. I was a worker priest, I was a missionary. I came to help save the colored people. I didn't know that at first. I learned that when I was doing the school.

We went through the process of accreditation. While doing this, I realized, for the first time, I knew that the minds of the people would never be free until they were able to learn their ABCs and 123s, and learn to be able to speak and present themselves and not reach for a handout.

They had to become free. We were still in bondage as long as they allowed people to do stuff to us. They have to be able to stand on their own feet, and that is what Martin University was supposed to be. We were going to be a liberal arts school to serve low-income minorities – adult learners in a healing and freedom-minded environment. That was the mission of Martin University.

Now truly going for accreditation is a terrible thing. Whoever invented accreditation really ought to be strung up by their toes and hung out over the nearest river, because all they do is come in and say, "What are you trying to do?" You say, "This is what we want to do." Then they say, "Are you doing it?"

They pass judgment on whether or not you are doing what you say you want to do. I guess this is okay. I mean it has been helpful, but sometimes it gets to be awful. So we went through that the first time and we got candidacy status and that precedes accreditation. That meant we could have Pell state funds and the students could borrow. We finally got everything that an accredited institution has to have.

What did the abbot or the bishop think of your starting a college?

I was known to be the troublemaker and here, all of a sudden, here I am in education. They saw me as sickle cell [*educator*] and that helped temper the perception of me. Then when I started the college, I was a whole different person and, all of a sudden, I was a human being again. A real live human being that didn't want to beat up white people.

I think I can say this, this may be jumping it a little bit, but in the beginning, I was the most unlikely person to start a school. Everybody figured it was going to fall on its face. I wasn't used to falling on my face. I was used to starting something and finishing it.

I had wonderful people around me. I had people from all over the country on my first board. I had former presidents, I had a young Hispanic or Latino from Houston, and there was a former priest. I just had a lot of people, and Fr. Cyprian, in the early days, was on the board, too. After a couple of years, St. Francis de Sales [*church*] was closed and Archbishop [*Edward*] O'Meara from Indianapolis offered me the old church that was sitting there. That is where Martin University is now.

Let me tell you one of the things I have done for 15 years. Fr. Cyprian was a part of getting it started. Some of the theology seminarians [*studying for the priesthood*] wanted to know about working in the black community. These young men are white mostly and they would come to Martin University. I would talk to them about being a priest of Jesus Christ and serving the poor.

The first thing I would say is, "Who in the hell do you think you are that you want to be a priest of Jesus Christ? Tell me now." That was the first thing I asked them. They thought they were going to hear all about blackness and what the problems are. No, I dealt with their priesthood.

Then I said, "If you want to be a servant, you have to be like Jesus. You are going to suffer and you are going to die and you are not going to be loved." This is during J-term in the middle of January. They used to spend three weeks with me and I would put them in a home of a black family.

So with the center, the university and programs like this you established, you got back in the good graces of the Church?

I was considered okay, because I was doing something positive. The whole thing about Martin is that it reached out to people. At first, I had more whites than blacks. It took a while to convince blacks.

Whenever there was a new Fr. Abbot, I'd asked him if I could continue to do the work with my people. So I see myself as a representative of Saint Meinrad Archabbey. That is my vow of stability; it is where I am. Wherever I am, that is where Saint Meinrad is. So I live right here. This is my home, but this is where Saint Meinrad is.

People know that I am a monk and I tell them and explain it to them whenever I get a chance – that OSB is always there. I don't put my honors or degrees or earned degrees behind my name. My monastic jurisdiction is behind my name. That is the way I see what I do. I belong to a religious community and my community has been supportive to me.

I was there at Martin University 30 years. Three years ago, I said it is time to step aside. I don't use retirement, because when you retire, people throw rocks on you and they figure you are either dead or you don't do anything. Well, that is not the truth. I am busier than ever.

Prayer

What is your favorite part of the Rule of St. Benedict*?*
Just one sentence: "to prefer nothing to the love of Christ." Prefer nothing to the love of Christ.

What is your key to living a Benedictine spirituality?
I always preach on the gospel when I preach. I always preach on what Jesus said; that is my theology. I believe that our spirituality is that Jesus is still with us, sits with us, talks to us, walks the street, heals people and is still here. He has risen from the dead; he is alive! That is what I believe. That is my whole message anytime I preach, and that is what I am all about.

What has been your most difficult time or experience in your life?

Well, I don't know I have had a lot of difficulties. I am still dealing with slavery and I am disappointed when people don't understand who I am. That time as a child was difficult. It is very hard to talk about my life since 1947. 1933 is when I was born and for 63 years I was in, or a part of, the Church following rules and things. Because I have been out of the monastery, people don't see me as a monk. Some do, but I am one, and I have vows.

How about happy times in your life?

I am happy when I am at Mass; being a priest is overwhelming. When you really think about this bread, it becomes the body and blood of Jesus Christ and this wine becomes the body and blood of Jesus Christ. When I say the words, it is pretty overwhelming when you really think about it, and it is really important to me. Happiness is also seeing people heal.

Changes in the Church

There are many changes that affected the contemporary Church. Some Catholics feel that Pope John XXIII was overly optimistic and that ever since Vatican II the Church has been paying a heavy price, where others applaud his gestures. What is your opinion on this?

I think he was progressive somewhat, but not nearly enough concerning women. Women still don't quite make it yet. This probably may not be acceptable, but I believe Eve was made first, then Adam, because women have more parts than men. I tell people where I preach – now this may be heresy, but I don't think it is; it is pre-Vatican I – that Mary is the "mediatrix of all graces."

After Jesus, after God, Mary is number two and you notice I have all kinds of preponderance or statuaries about Mary [*in this house*]. Mary is number two after Jesus. That is pretty cool, that is good. The Protestants accuse us of worshiping Mary – and that is probably what we do – and that is okay. I think we should worship her.

John XXIII was a good guy. I'm just telling you that you are hearing the voice of someone who is in the diaspora for the Church. The Church and some priests still haven't quite figured that out. The Boniface syndrome is that we need to be where the people are, like Jesus was – that is what it is.

Should Latin still be part of the academic curriculum even though the Mass is in the vernacular?

The Latin Mass is good and we still have places here in town where the Latin Mass is said. Latin is a good background for other languages – for Spanish, for Italian and for French. They are easy to read after you learn the [*Latin*] language.

Striking changes have been made in liturgy and parish organizations. What do you see as positive and negative changes that have occurred in your parish experiences?

Well, the Eucharistic ministers in the parishes are good because we were becoming fossils. Priests were becoming fossils. I have a brother who is a priest, but he is not ordained. I mean he does everything that I do, except say the consecration. I was there with him one weekend.

He has taken over things when the priest is not there, because in the west end of Louisville they have lost all of their priests. This is a Catholic town, and they only have one or two priests in the west end, so he is basically the priest. More men and women have become a part of the Eucharist. They take the Eucharist to the sick.

My brother has anointed people because there were no priests. They call and ask for him, and he has helped bury them because there were no priests. This is 2010! They have an assigned parish pastor, but he is somewhere else. So all they have is this lay person who has all the energy and all the spirituality that I feel that I, as a priest, have. He is just not ordained, but he is a lay priest. I don't like the word lay, but he is a priest.

Is he a deacon?

No, he is not an ordained deacon. What I am saying is there are people, people who are not ordained, men and women who want to be one with Christ. The apostles didn't have an ordination ceremony. Jesus just called them. My brother received a call and he is serving that church. He is black and he is serving that church.

What has been lost and what has been gained over the last 40 years in the Church since the Council?

I don't think there is one Church. I think the Church is divided up into many different aspects. You can go to one place and the Church will do this. You go to another place and the Church will do that. They have different things, and they have more leadership who are not ordained like my brother. I think that is what has been lost.

I think some priests have a fear of being close to people. Some people have priests that are not close, because the priests now are going to two and three parishes. They are pastor of this one and this one, so they lose the closeness with their people. They can't possibly learn a thousand names and a thousand families. So that is loss and there has to be a change.

The Church has always gone back to a medieval concept. But we need to go back to the time of Jesus and do what Jesus did. Jesus said, "There are some who hear my voice that are not of my flock but they are mine." We have to understand what Jesus did in the scriptures. We have to be converted to Jesus Christ in the Church.

The priests need to go out and let the people come in. Let women do things because Jesus had women around him, and He loved them and worshiped them and honored them.

What are your hopes for the future of the Church and the Archabbey?

Well, Saint Meinrad has alumni gatherings and I try to go to them because I see some old friends. They are mostly seminarians – some priests – but I would like for us to welcome the ones who, for some reason, got dismissed from the active priesthood. At ordination, there is a saying, "Thou art a priest forever."

We can't take the priesthood out of the seminarians that are there at the reunions. They are there because they had never given up being a seminarian. They had left the seminary to marry and had a dozen kids. Some of the priests had left the active priesthood – got dismissed because they got married and maybe had a couple of kids. These men are still priests of Jesus Christ. I would like the Church to reclaim those who we have ordained and let them come back in and be something special.

You go down to South America and the pastor is sitting up in front and there is the wife and five kids. They are up in the mountaintops and they are not approved, of course, I understand that. But I am saying there is something that we can do. You see there are men who spent their lives being dedicated to this. So, I am looking forward to the day when people like my brother can be ordained.

I am hopeful someday that we will have married clergy, because I think Peter was married. Jesus visited his mother-in-law. I don't know if his wife was there or not. I know this is not doctrine of the Church. But for somebody who has lived a long time and seen the vacuum and seen the negligence and seen the unwillingness of priests to deal with my people, I think Jesus would understand.

Any other hopes for the future of the Church?

I am giving you a prophecy. Above all, we need to prepare for nuclear catastrophe that we are going to experience. We will experience one in America and there may not be a bishop or a priest like me around. There may be someone like yourself that has to lead the people in prayer and worship and say, "I can remember when I used to speak to the priests of Saint Meinrad." You never know when it is going to happen and it can happen.

How about the Archabbey?

I like what the Archabbey has done with educating people and giving them lay degrees. You get a master's degree in theology. I like the adjustment, but there will be other adjustments and I think Saint Meinrad will do that. I want to do one other thing if we are at the end of the interview.

You can go as long as you want.

I want to sing to you. This is a song which I sang in our beloved community, which we did every Wednesday in our school. It is dedicated to St. Mark, of course, St. Mark the teacher.

Oh freedom, oh freedom, oh freedom over me.
And before I will be a slave I will be buried in my grave
And go home to my Lord and be free.
No more hurting, no more hurting, no more hurting over me.
And before I will be a slave I will be buried in my grave
And go home to my Lord and be free.
And if I do God's will no more weeping, no more weeping, no more weeping over me.
And before I will be a slave I will be buried in my grave
And go home to my Lord and be free.

We have to seek the freedom of Jesus Christ and cast all those old hatreds and all those old hanging on that I got and cast it off and help other people to be free. That is who I am and I thank you very much to take the time to listen to an old man. Amen.

Profile based upon: Fr. Boniface Hardin, OSB, to Prof. Ruth C. Engs, April 27, 2010, Interview Transcriptions, Saint Meinrad Archabbey Archives, St. Meinrad, IN.

Chapter 4: Fr. Meinrad Brune, OSB

Fr. Meinrad has served as the oblate director since 1995 and under his tutelage expanded the program and publications for use by oblates. He also taught at the Saint Meinrad High School and College, served in several administrative positions and as pastor at two parishes.

Fr. Meinrad was born in Indianapolis, IN, on April 14, 1934, and given the name Richard Leo. He attended St. Catherine Elementary School and Cathedral High School in Indianapolis, came to Saint Meinrad High School (1952) and graduated from Saint Meinrad College with a Bachelor of Arts degree in 1958. He attended Saint Meinrad Seminary (1958-1962) and received a baccalaureate in sacred theology from Catholic University of America (1962) and a Master of Arts from Butler University (1968). He took various continuing education courses over the ensuing years.

He made his first profession August 15, 1956, solemn profession August 15, 1959, and was ordained to the priesthood May 7, 1961. From 1962 to 1967, he taught at Saint Meinrad High School and subsequently was an associate professor at Saint Meinrad College (1968-1977). Fr. Meinrad served as pastor at St. Meinrad Parish and at St. Mary's Parish, Huntingburg, IN (1977-1984). He worked in the Development Office (1984-1994), much of that time as alumni director. Over the years, he has given many retreats. In 1995, he became the oblate director, a position he retains to this day.

Prof. Ruth C. Engs interviewed Fr. Meinrad Brune, OSB, October 13, 2009.

Childhood and Early Years as a Monk

Tell me where you were born, your childhood, family life and early schooling.

I was born in the city of Indianapolis at St. Vincent's Hospital, the old St. Vincent's Hospital in the northern part of the city. My dad was Thomas Brune and my mother Frances Brune. Dad was a printer of schoolbook covers at Bookwalter and Ball at 16th Street and Capital Avenue. He was there for almost 49 years until he retired. My mother was a secretary at the state house in Indianapolis until she got married. Then she left her job and was a stay-at-home mother and raised her kids.

I was born on April 14, 1934. I had two older brothers. My oldest brother, Thomas, was also a Benedictine monk. His name was Br. Theodore and he was a brother for 25 years in the monastery and then he became a priest in 1975. My next brother was Bob, Robert Brune. He went on to college and was an officer in the Navy – an engineer. He held several jobs until he became president of the Dayton newspapers.

So there were three of us boys. I was the youngest. We were raised during the Depression, though as small kids we really did not know there was a depression. We had plenty of good food on the table, we had a warm house, and Mother and Dad certainly gave us a lot of security. We did eat a lot of potato soup, I remember, and we got so tired of it, but it was very rich and heavy.

Also, I think of Christmastimes and how beautiful it was. My uncle was a professional photographer and we have pictures of us around the tree with toys. Yet, you would notice that under the tree Mother and Dad had nothing, because they had spent it all on us boys. Mom would go all out with baking fruitcake and cookies and having very good things to enjoy and eat during those Christmas holidays.

How about your religious life as a child?

In those early years, I do remember we were very active in the parish. Mother went to Mass frequently and Dad also. Prayer was very important to my dad, though he enjoyed his cigars and beers and he could cuss a lot, but still prayer was very important to him.

I was an altar boy all through grade school. We had Mass every morning and we began school with Mass. I remember I went to Communion and, of course, we couldn't eat before Communion in those days. Mom would have an egg sandwich and a little pint jar of hot chocolate for me to eat after Mass.

By the time I got to the classroom, it was kind of warm. The sister would let me eat in the back of the classroom and then I could join the class. I did go to Communion almost every day when I was in grade school.

Tell me about your schooling.

I went to a public school one year for kindergarten. One thing I remember about that is I was healthy. My parents were able to feed me well and it was only the unhealthy kids who got graham crackers and milk at school. We had to sit there and watch them eat, and that was so hard because we were too healthy. We were well taken care of, but these other kids needed it. Then I went to St. Catherine's of Siena, which was about five blocks away from our home, for grade school for first through eighth grade.

Did nuns teach you?

We had the Sisters of Providence from West Terre Haute, Indiana. They were the teachers. And in our days, it was sisters who taught all the grades. They were good teachers and very good religious. They were very inspirational to us.

Was there any one particular sister that you remember who might have inspired you?

Our eighth-grade teacher, Sister St. Gertrude. She was short and we thought she was very old. When she first came into the classroom, we thought she would be a pushover. She started out by saying, "My name is Sister St. Gertrude and don't you forget the saint. You go 100% the way I want to go in this classroom."

She was an excellent teacher and prepared us well for high school. At the same time, she was very supportive of us, defended us and really was very fair in her discipline in the classroom. We really came to love her very dearly in the eighth grade because she was such a fine person.

The other sisters were very fine. It is hard to believe my first grade teacher Sr. Mary Terence is still living [2009]. She must be close to 100 years old and must have been 18 or 19 years old when she started to teach in the grade school. They started teaching very early then.

How about high school?

Well, in 1948, we had to take a test and Monsignor Downey, who was the pastor, would always give out four scholarships, two for the girls and two for the boys high school. For the boys, it was either Sacred Heart or Cathedral. Most of us went to Cathedral, the all-boys high school. Sacred Heart was co-ed.

We had the test and I was one of the two boys that got the scholarship. It was only $50 a year to go to Cathedral High School, but that was a big help to have that paid by Monsignor. And if you kept your grades up to B's and A's, he would give it to you your sophomore year. So I, of course, kept my grades up and I got it the second year and I felt very good about it.

The old Holy Cross Brothers Cathedral High School was at 14th and North Meridian streets. There must have been about 750 boys there at the time. The brothers were excellent teachers and I thought very highly of them. They were very firm and disciplined, and I always felt they were very fair in treating discipline problems.

There were only two lay teachers there. One was the football coach. He taught me government and health and safety and was a fine example of a father, husband and a wonderful coach and had winning teams in Indianapolis. I played no sports; all I played was handball.

What were your activities or hobbies in high school?
At Cathedral High School, I was on the stage crew for four years. So I worked the four years behind the scenes – never an actor, but behind the scenes. Then my senior year, I became the head crew member and had all the others under me. I was very active in science club and, of course, did very well in my studies all during high school.

I had a deep respect for all the Holy Cross Brothers. There were certain ones who really stood out – Br. Mathew and Br. Joseph and the principal, Br. Regis. They were just top-notch men. They were good religious and gave us wonderful examples. All through high school, I only missed one day and that was the sophomore year. I came to Saint Meinrad to be with my brother and my parents when Br. Theodore made his final vows as a Benedictine brother. I just really enjoyed my days at Cathedral High School.

Did you have a job when you were in school?
All of us boys had paper routes. I would help my brothers in the first through the fifth grade and then in the fifth grade I got my own paper route. I carried *The Indianapolis News* until the eighth grade. Then when I got into high school, I started to carry the morning paper, *The Indianapolis Star*.

I would each week collect the money for the newspaper. Mother would stay in the kitchen and watch me count the money. She was very good at figures and secretarial work. I would count my money to see what I had to pay for that week's papers. Then if I didn't have enough, she would loan me the money so I could pay off the bill. Then I had to make sure I collected the rest of it to pay her back, and then everything else leftover I could do with what I wanted.

How about in college?

When I was at the minor seminary, during the summer I worked at the United States Post Office for two summers and made good money to help pay for the education. It was right next to the Union Station and everything went by trains. We had to fill bags with parcel post. This was really a big help to my parents. Even for temporary help, you made good money at the Post Office in those days. So I did this for two different summers.

For the third summer, I taught the black children at St. Bridget's School for summer school in Indianapolis. I taught with the Daughters of Charity who ran St. Vincent's Hospital. I did that for a whole month, and that was a wonderful experience working with the kids. I had the sixth-, seventh- and eighth-grade boys.

And after that, the sisters said, "Would you like to finish the summer off working at the hospital?" I said, "Oh yeah, I would," because that was paid; the other was volunteer work. So I worked in the x-ray department cutting x-rays and delivering them to different departments.

As a youngster, what kind of health care did you have? Did you go to a clinic or did the doctor come to see you?

When kids started to come, Mother and Dad went to a baby doctor called Dr. Carter, and he was the doctor who would come to the house to visit when we came down with measles, mumps and all those other things that kids got. We were always quarantined, and we had a big sign on the door. But he would come to the house to take care of us.

The health department from the city would come out and put the signs up and then they would come and check on you and see if you were there. Then when Dr. Carter said that it was all clear, they would come and take the sign down. Quite often, he would come to check on us in the morning before he would go into his office.

We were so appreciative of Dr. Carter, and my parents just had great confidence in him. Even as we grew up, Dr. Carter remained our family doctor. He stayed our doctor until he gave up practice. When we got older, we would go to him and we were so embarrassed because there were just babies and mothers in the waiting room.

Bob and I would stand out in the hallway because we didn't want to go into that office. When it was our turn to go in, Mother would come out and grab us. And, boy, we would run through the waiting room to get into his office. He had a little burner in the corner. As long as he didn't go near that, we felt okay. But as soon as he got up and started for it, we knew we were going to receive a needle and we were petrified by that.

Were these immunizations?
Yes. Every once in a while, he had to give us a shot for something, but not too often.

When you were in high school, did you smoke or drink as a high school student?
No, never did smoke or drink. We would drink some at home. Dad would let us drink a little beer or wine, but on dates we never did. The group that I ran around with, we just didn't do that. I had a certain group of guys that I ran around with and when we had dates – we had no cars – we sat together and had a lot of fun.

Cigarettes, no. I tried it in my senior year. Four of us guys went to New York City and we got some cigarettes and we started experimenting with cigarettes. I would smoke some cigars when I was in the college here at the seminary.

What did you do after high school?

In high school, the vocation director of the Holy Cross Brothers would always meet with me and want me to become a Holy Cross Brother. I really thought about it for a while. Then the vocation director of the Marianist Brothers, from Dayton, would also approach me. I gave some thought to that, but I decided no.

I was offered a four-year scholarship to the Holy Cross Brothers' university in San Antonio, Texas, St. Edward's University. However, I decided to go to Xavier University in Cincinnati, Ohio. I didn't think I was going to stay four years, as I wasn't too sure what I had in mind. I talked with Mom and Dad and they said, "Why deprive another boy of a scholarship who might really need it, when you are not sure what you really want to do?" So I decided I would go to Xavier.

At that point in your life, what were you thinking you wanted to do?

At that time, I wanted to major in Spanish and go to South America and teach English. So I took Spanish at Xavier. I was going to major in that, but when I started out, they put me in Latin. The Jesuits wanted me for an honors course at Xavier, but I didn't want that. They wanted me to take Greek and Latin.

I did take Latin and Spanish, world history and English. I had only one lay teacher and all the rest were Jesuits. That was unusual even then that you would have so many Jesuits teaching. I had great admiration for them. I really thought highly of John Wenzel, SJ, who taught me moral theology.

The Jesuits wanted me to join the Sodality of Mary [*a pious religious association*]. This was kind of like an introduction to becoming a Jesuit, so I went to the Milford Retreat House outside of Cincinnati and had a retreat concerning this. While I was there on retreat, I wrote a letter to Fr. Abbot Ignatius [*Esser*], here at Saint Meinrad, and told him I would like to come to the monastery the next year.

Why did you write to Saint Meinrad?
My oldest brother, Theodore, joined the oblate house – St. Placid Hall – right from grade school. Every summer he came home for a one-month vacation in July. I would come here a week before he came back to Indianapolis for his vacation and would stay with the oblates. So I got to know all the oblates, got to know a good number of the brothers, and even some of the fraters [*monks studying for the priesthood*].

In high school, I would come down for Holy Week at Easter. I would live in the guest room in the monastery, because my brother was already out of St. Placid Hall and now in the monastery.

Is this why you decided to become a religious?
My mom and dad were very spiritual people so I had a lot of good influence there, but no one put pressure on me. On my mother's side of the family, there were several religious. Two of my mother's brothers were Franciscan brothers, one of my cousins was a Franciscan priest, another very close friend of our family was a Franciscan priest, and two aunts were nuns. Because mother was the oldest of the family, she would host all

Fr. Meinrad, as a young monk

these aunts and uncles who had their vacations with us and they would spend time at our house.

After you wrote the abbot, what happened?

Abbot Ignatius wrote back right away and said, "Don't wait until next year because you may not have a vocation by next year." He also said, "I am not letting you come to the monastery to see if you want to be a brother. I am going to put you in the minor seminary [*for the first two years of college*]. After you finish there, then you can come to the monastery and start as a frater. But during that time, if you think you still want to be a brother, then we can make the proper change. Right now I want you to try out the priesthood." And so I did that.

Then I went to the Jesuit priest, Fr. Wenzel, and showed him the letter from Abbot Ignatius. I didn't know what to do, because I was already three months into classes. So he said, "Do you know Abbot Ignatius?" I said, "Yes, I do. In fact, he has been to our home for supper at times and, of course, I have a brother there at Saint Meinrad." He said, "So you really know the place then?" I said, "Oh yeah, I know a lot about it." And he said, "No problem, you should go right now and I will take care of transferring everything."

So I came home for about four days and then some friends of ours drove me down here to the seminary to get into the seminary classes. The president of Xavier, at that time, wrote a beautiful letter to my parents. He said how proud they were that I was going to the seminary and then join the monastery. They refunded my parents' money for the semester.

When I came here, they put me into different classes. I know Fr. Eric [*Lies*] taught one and Fr. Raban [*Hathorn*] another. Fr. Pius [*Fleming*] was the Latin teacher. Even though I had three years of Latin, that wasn't enough for what they demanded here. He was tough, but he was good.

After a week's time, I wanted to get out of his Latin class. So I went in to Fr. Bartholomew[1] and said, "I got to get out of this class; he is so demanding in all that he expects." Fr. Bartholomew spoke to him and, after class the next day, Fr. Pius wanted to see me. He said, "No one ever leaves my class and I will take you one hour a day, separately, to help you catch up for the end-of-the-semester test and then you will be up with the class."

I used to dread it. But when you think of it, that was very kind of him to do that for me and he really was a big help and an excellent Latin teacher. There were many fine monks who were teachers in the minor seminary. I really enjoyed it.

When did you decide to become a monk?

I decided when I came to the minor seminary I wanted to be a monk. That was my sophomore year in college. There were six years in the minor seminary and six in the major seminary. The first two years of college were in the minor seminary.

There were eight of us who applied to come to the seminary and into the monastery. Our names went to chapter under Fr. Abbot Ignatius. They voted on us and accepted us to enter into the novitiate. Then there was an election. Abbot Ignatius resigned and Abbot Bonaventure [*Knaebel*] was elected in June of 1955.

So we came to the monastery under Fr. Archabbot Bonaventure. He wrote to us right after he was elected and gave us two extra weeks of vacation and then we came back. So that last summer, my folks said, "Don't work, just enjoy it," because we came in July to the monastery.

How did your parents feel about you becoming a monk?

When I came to join the monastery in the summer of 1955, my mom and dad came down with me. I thought that was going to be

---

[1] Later left the community

hard. So I took my suitcases out and went upstairs and they waited for me, because all they did was come and then turn around and drove back to Indianapolis.

So when I went back to say goodbye to them, my dad said, "You know your mother and I are very proud of you for joining the monastery. But if you decide it is not your vocation, the door is always open at home for you to return." I thought that was a wonderful way to give me all the support, but also let me know they would never be disappointed if it wasn't for me and I came home.

Tell me about your novice years.

I learned very quickly that you do what you are told to do. When I first came to the monastery, we had a temporary *socius* [*assistant junior master*] for the summer, Fr. Martin [*Dusseau*]. In our first recreation period, we were going to play softball and I told him, "I never was good at sports and I don't care for softball, so I think I will take a nap." Well, I was out in centerfield playing softball. That was my first experience that you don't have your own will.

Fr. Gavin [*Barnes*] said shortly after I was a novice, "I am going to put you on the flower committee for decorating the church for all the big feast days." I said, "Oh Father, you got me mixed up with Theodore, my brother. He is real good at that. I am not good at that and I don't want that job." He said. "Well, frater, there are a lot of things we don't like, but we are asked to do it." He was very nice about it, but said, "You will be on the committee." And I had the job for six years.

Do you have another amusing story from your early years?

We had 12 little cells [*monks' rooms*], just sheets around it for privacy. Abbot Timothy [*Sweeney*] and Abbot Lambert [*Reilly*] were also novices then. The first night in the novitiate, Novice Lambert started eating an apple. And every time he would crunch, we would start laughing, as we just found that hilarious.

We were all laughing and carrying on. It was supposed to be the great silence, and the senior deacon came in and yelled, "Shut up! It is night silence, now be quiet!" I think we all thought we were all going to be kicked out of here tomorrow, but the novice master never said anything about it.

Tell me more about the novitiate.

The novice year was all work, a lot of work and a lot of studies on Benedictine formation. We had chant, Benedictine history, of course, the holy *Rule*. I know we had Fr. Ambrose[2] for chant and Fr. Bernadine [*Shine*] for the *Rule* and Fr. Gavin [*Barnes*] for the Benedictine history.

When it came to first vows, I was so excited the night before. I was in the church after Compline [*night prayer*] and Fr. Bernadine came up to me and said, "I want you to come up to my office." Well, my heavens, I wondered what was wrong.

So I went up there and he said, "I know you are keyed up, but remember that tonight you will put your pajamas on like you do every night. You will go to bed like every night and not be all upset and excited. Get a good night's sleep and make your promises and vows tomorrow." This was very helpful, because he knew I was so excited and nervous about it.

Of course, at my vows, my name Meinrad was given to me at that time. We had three names we'd choose. My first choice was Matthias, my second choice was Aquinas, and I got my third choice, Meinrad. I remember my folks and a lot of the relatives came for the profession.

Afterward, my brother was out in front of church with Mom and Dad and I could hear him. His words were just a little bit hot. He said, "Did you hear that? He got Meinrad, he took Meinrad," and he didn't like it. Mom said, "I like the name," and that stopped all discussion. No more was said, as Mom liked it.

---

[2] Later left the community

After these first vows, we went back to studies and the seminary. It was first philosophy and I was a junior in college. We had Fr. Basil[3] [*Mattingly*] for logic, Fr. Mark [*Toon*] and Fr. Adelbert [*Buscher*].

I waited a year and then I finished my BA. It took me a while to do it because we had to take a break because of the novice year. My BA dissertation was on "The Beauty of God in St. Thomas Aquinas." Fr. Basil directed that. After two years of philosophy, then we went into theology.

In theology, we had Fr. Kieran [*Conley*], who just came back with his doctorate from Rome, and he had all the new teachings on dogma and his classes were excellent. For moral theology and Hebrew, we had Fr. Bernard [*Beck*] and I really liked him. He was down to earth and very practical and kind. We had Fr. Adelbert for some moral theology and he was good, too. Fr. Prosper [*Lindauer*], Fr. Bartholomew [*Fuerst*] and Fr. Gerard [*Ellspermann*] taught Greek. These teachers were just very, very good. We got a good education.

Was your formation different compared to today?

Well, when we came, it was certainly very structured. As fraters, junior monks and novices, you weren't invited to express your opinion. I mean you listened to the seniors and, of course, we weren't chapter members. I never remember ever as juniors or novices sitting down with the junior/novice master to express our opinions.

You might go to the senior deacon and say something or to the senior of our class of novices when we thought we were having a lot of work. We started out with eight of us and the first ones to leave were Paul, then Patrick and then William. So we were down to five. When the three left, we had to do all their work. It was really becoming a little hard and then we went to Fr. Alan, who was the

---

[3] Transferred to Prince of Peace Abbey

senior of the class, and we all talked to him – we did that on our own.

Fr. Alan then talked to Fr. Gavin. We didn't do it as a group. Fr. Gavin did listen and he did try to make changes and even it out a little more, which was very kind of him to do that. But you just did not go in and tell the novice master or the *socius*, for the most part, what you thought or express your opinion.

How about today?

Oh, today I am sure they are much freer in expressing things. This was true when I was later on the *socius* for nine years – two different times. Even in our days under Fr. Timothy, Fr. Vincent and I began to have meetings with the fraters and the novices where they could express themselves. Also, we never questioned the fact we had so little time to study and they didn't take the work away. We had free afternoons on Tuesday and Thursday, but Thursday wasn't really a free afternoon – that was hobby time.

We had to spend the whole afternoon in hobby time, so when you had time to study, you just really used your time well because you had so little time to do it for exams and the like. Then on Sunday afternoons, we all had to go out for recreation, but then you could come in after it. Some took naps, but many times I just started studying because I needed that. So we were very limited on enough time, but it was surprising how well we used our time whenever we had a chance to study.

Did you study in the library?

We were never allowed to go to the library unless we had permission back during those days. The wonderful library was right off the fratery, but we couldn't go in there unless we had permission. That eventually changed. We could start using the library all the time.

Did things change after ordination?

After I was ordained, I got four big jobs. If we were given a job, you just did it. I thought I would explain to the abbot it was too much work. He just said, "I hope it won't be so much work for you." Well, that took care of that. And what could I do, as he thought I could do the work.

How about recreation in your younger days?

After supper we would have common recreation. We would all go out to Paradise right out here [*open space next to the current monastery building*] and walked with the monk you walked out of church with. So many times I walked with Fr. Timothy night after night, because we just came out together and then walked in a circle.

You had to walk so many times in a circle and then you could sit down on the benches out there. Then you came back into the courtyard and would line up and go to spiritual reading and examination of conscience in the Chapter Room; then we would go to the church for Compline.

Later on, they changed it. We would have spiritual reading, examination of conscience, Compline and then anticipate Matins the night before. We got up later, as it was just too hard on the school people getting up for their schedule. It was much easier on the monks, so Fr. Abbot Bonaventure started changing that schedule.

During June and May, we would have devotions to Mary so we would have Benediction and the Litany of Mary, and it was just a long, long evening. Then you would come back to your room. Now as novices, we had to go to bed right away. I will never forget when we came back the first night as novices: we were in bed at 8:00. It was still light out and hot, and we were all there in this big dormitory.

What were your jobs as a junior monk?

Fr. Abbot Bonaventure appointed me senior deacon my last year in the fratery. I wasn't the senior in the class, but I was picked over the one who was. I felt bad about that. I had to appoint all the work to the fraters. The senior deacon was kind of like a superior. And then I was ordained. I thought, "Oh, I am out of the fratery."

However, the first part of July, Abbot Bonaventure called me in and said, "I am going to appoint you *socius*." I thought, "I am never going to get out of that." So I was *socius* for three years and assigned the work for all the juniors and the novices. Then I was made second master of ceremonies and, after the first year, I started going to graduate school.

In '64, when it came time to go to graduate school, nothing was said to me. A sign went up and I was told I was going to Butler University in Indianapolis and do parish work at the same time. Fr. Theodore [*Heck*] called me in and picked my three graduate courses. I had nothing to say about it, didn't have any decision on what I was going to be majoring in or what I was going to be teaching.

Has it changed then?

Oh yeah, they discuss all that with you now. I stayed with Fr. McSween at St. Francis de Sales. The first day I went there, he said, "I know, Father, you are here for graduate studies and to study, but I thought you could offer one Mass each day and help out on the weekends and have the rest of the time for studies." He was very kind and always loaned me the parish car to get back and forth to Butler University.

What was your major?

I was majoring in American history then. Our academic dean in the seminary college, Fr. Thomas [*Ostdick*], called me up in Indianapolis at St. Francis de Sales. He said, "Oh, I am coming up to take you out for supper." I, being naïve, thought, "Isn't that wonderful? He wants to come up and take me out for supper."

So he took me out to a real nice steak supper and afterward said, "I am really here to ask you to change your major from American history to political theory." This was right in the middle of my course work. Fr. Ralph [*Lynch*], who was teaching political science, was going out to California and they needed someone to teach political science, so I changed my major.

I went to the dean of the department and he said, "Well, it is going to be harder as you have to really start catching up in those courses." So my minor was American history and my major political theory. I did have Dr. Comfort, who was the head of the political theory and political science department, and he was very kind. I would say this for Butler: all the professors I had there were really great men. They were very thoughtful and kind, and I think they almost felt honored that a priest was in their class. They treated me with the deepest respect. Several of them were Anglican and they were just very respectful.

Dr. Comfort directed my dissertation, which was "A Doctrine of the Two Swords" [*relations between church and state*] as reflected in the writings of four people: St. Augustine, St. Thomas Aquinas, John of Paris, and Dante. He picked them out. He did let me have some input and, once I started, he was very free and open. I wrote the dissertation and Dr. Comfort read it and then I had a second reader. He was a PhD from Yale University and taught international relations. He said that he certainly approved of what I did.

Then I had to defend it. The man outside of the department for religious education took something out of context and would not accept it. I had to change that. I tried to show and tell him you have to see that in light of the whole chapter. Dr. Comfort said, "Fr. Brune will change that."

I was sick because that was the final copy – all that typing and the money I paid for it. When they left, Dr. Comfort said, "Now, Fr.

Brune, you have to stay here. We have to discuss something." I thought, "Oh, no." But he said, "I was real proud of you and it was very good."

I said, "Well, I will have to change that." And he said, "You are not going to change that. That professor doesn't know what he is talking about and he is not going to look it up. Forget it, you are going to keep it the way it is." I could have hugged him, I was so grateful.

Work

What were your major work experiences?

In '62, I started to teach in high school. I taught world history in the beginning and then American history for a while. Then after three years as the *socius*, Fr. Abbot Bonaventure appointed me as assistant dean of discipline in the high school. Then I took over as the manager of the bookstore in the minor seminary under Fr. Martin, who was the business manager. I still stayed on as second master of ceremonies.

The job as manager of the bookstore was not easy, because I was teaching courses in high school, was assistant dean of discipline and trying to run a bookstore. It was just a lot of work. The job at the bookstore was bad because we were competing with the major seminary – the theology students themselves ran that bookstore.

Fr. Martin didn't like this and told me, "Next year, you will take over as the manager of their seminary bookstore." We changed all the locks so that their keys wouldn't fit. The first day, oh, they were furious. I called the workers in and said, "This is the way it is now. I am the manager, I have all the order blanks and nothing is ordered without my signature. It has to come through me and there will be a lot of changes. If you don't like it, tell me and then get out."

Some were deacons and they were used to running everything themselves. However, I had the backing of the three rectors for our schools – Frs. Theodore, Hilary [*Ottensmeyer*] and Herman [*Romoser*].

Then the third year, we moved everything together and raised the prices – no more discounts. Again, the students were just furious with me. Those years were really hard years and I was glad to give that up. Of course, they moved on and the new students came in and they didn't know what it was like in the past.

When I was finishing up with my whole year of graduate studies and writing my dissertation, we voted to close the high school. We phased it out one year at a time. We only had about eight students in the last class, a very small number. Fr. Kevin [*Ryan*] was the principal.

Each student got a full high school education, but a lot of the parents – when we decided to close it – yanked their kids out. Students got diplomas recognized by the State of Indiana and North Central accreditation. The State of Indiana saw us as a first-class high school and they still recognize that. When I finished my master's, I started teaching on the college level in '68.

I taught one semester of political science, which was my major, and never taught that anymore because they wanted me full-time teaching all the American history courses. Fr. Ralph came back and Fr. Damasus [*Langan*] wanted to get out – he taught all the American histories – so after that I taught all the American histories. This included Colonial, Revolutionary period and all the way through.

Then I taught international relations and a course on the presidency of the United States. I had permission from Fr. Thomas [*Ostdick*], and we discussed how we were going to teach that class and what we were going to do. They were bright students. That course was just tremendous and I really enjoyed it. Then for the real bright students, I had a reading course for them. They had to read many, many books on American history and then give papers on it. I really enjoyed that, too. I taught 10 years in the college from '68 to '78.

Then what did you do?

Then in '77, they asked me to be pastor downtown at St. Meinrad Parish. There were so many things that had to be done. Fr. Raban was there for five years and he was sick and things kind of fell apart. The physical plant was in terrible shape, and they didn't have any religious ed program. I got out of teaching then and just became the full-time pastor downtown.

I was three years at St. Meinrad and four years at St. Mary's Parish in Huntingburg, and those were good experiences. Downtown [*St. Meinrad Parish*], Fr. Kevin was with me the whole time. Over at St. Mary's, Fr. Benet [*Amato*] was with me the first two years and then Fr. Sean [*Hoppe*] the second two years. So I always had an associate with me at both parishes. Now, they [*current pastors*] are all by themselves. They don't have any associates.

St. Mary's was very big. I had three Daughters of Charity who taught; they were excellent. We had 550 children in the religious ed program and 1,000 families – 3,000 people, so it was a large church. Downtown, we had about 300 families and 1,000 people. I enjoyed it and it was a good experience.

Then Fr. Abbot Timothy, on Easter Tuesday of my fourth year at St. Mary's, told me, "I am bringing you back to the monastery." I realized it was good because the longer you stay out, the harder it is to readjust to come back to the monastery. I will never forget what he assigned me to.

What was that?

I went to the Development Office and was the manager and took care of all the details, the secretaries and all the rest. Then in the second year, they asked me to become alumni director of the Seminary Alumni Association, which I did. The following year, they asked me to take over the Summer Session as alumni director and the Summer Session.

We had some wonderful reunions. I had that work for eight years. So I had the alumni seminarians for nine years and then eight years the Summer Session. Then I was in charge of the Saint Meinrad Sunday Parish Program, along with being alumni director and meeting with pastors, inviting them to set up a Sunday that we could preach about the seminary and vocations, and inviting people to share in that with their financial gifts. I was all over Indiana, Ohio and Kentucky. So I went to many, many parishes and was good at keeping contact with our alumni pastors. So I was on the road an awful lot and that kept me busy.

How many years did you do that?

I was in the Alumni Office for 10 years and then I went on sabbatical. Fr. Abbot Timothy called me in and said, "I wish you would take a sabbatical." So I said, "Wonderful." And he said, "Why don't you take that refresher course on Benedictine spirituality at Sant' Anselmo, the international house of studies, in Rome?" I said, "Fine, I'll be happy to do so." I wrote Fr. Vincent [*Tobin*], who taught there, to see if I could sign up for the next year. This was right before Christmas, and he faxed me saying they were filled up and they had no room for me.

So I went to Abbot Timothy to tell him I can't get in. He said, "Oh, I am disappointed. What do you want to do?" I said, "Well, I would like to start on Ash Wednesday and work until Holy Week and finish my dissertation for the Master of Divinity." I had been taking a reading course on English monasticism up to the Reformation under Fr. Cyprian [*Davis*] and I had to do a paper on that. I had done all the other coursework required.

He said, "Fine." "Then on Easter Tuesday, I would like to go to Europe and travel throughout Europe visiting monasteries." I thought he would say no to that one. He said, "Fine." I traveled all over Europe. It was just a marvelous sabbatical.

So after the sabbatical, what did you do?

When I came back, Fr. Abbot said, "I am not going to appoint you to any new jobs because I am stepping down next year. I don't want to put you in a job and then the new abbot comes in who might have something else for you to do. So I am going to have you do pastoral work." I took over two parishes in North Little Rock, Arkansas, where the pastor was on sabbatical.

Abbot Lambert was elected. He called me in the morning after his election and said, "I want you to be the oblate director." I said, "Well, Father, I am supposed to take a whole semester at the Hammond, Indiana, parish." He said, "I will take care of that."

And he appointed Fr. Timothy to that position, who had just resigned as abbot. Timothy came up to me and said, "I am taking your work." We were classmates. So I took over as the oblate director and have really enjoyed that. All the jobs I have enjoyed, but I have really enjoyed my work as the oblate director.

Briefly describe what you do as an oblate director.

As the oblate director, you are really directly under Fr. Abbot because he appoints you. Fr. Abbot is the oblate director and I am just the person who fills in for him. So I am sort of the liaison between the oblates, oblate novices, and the monastic community and Fr. Abbot. I guess my main work is to try and form oblates in the spirit of Benedictine spirituality and the unique spirit of Saint Meinrad Archabbey.

I strive to do that, first of all, through the conferences [*lectures*] that I give, the Oblate Newsletter and the novice instructions we send out. I then reply with answers to their questions and do consultation for those who might stop in the office, even though I don't take on spiritual direction. I don't think it is wise for the oblate director to do that. I will refer them to other monks if they want spiritual direction.

Mostly, my job is to arrange meetings of the chapters, retreats, days of recollection and get the newsletter out. I get other mailings out like at Christmas, the *Bona Opera* [*promise of Lenten abstinence and/or good deeds*], renewals [*of oblation every November*] and special events such as study weeks. Just keeping up with the correspondence has grown so much – especially with email – and is a large part of my job.

Updating all the different manuals – handbooks for the Oblate Council, the Finance Committee and the oblate chapter coordinators – is part of the job. I also try to keep a special relationship with oblates and oblate novices who cannot join a chapter, through correspondence or telephone calls. Of course, I try to keep the oblate library up to date with all the newer books and I have refocused the whole oblate library with the help of oblates. I have enjoyed the work tremendously and it has certainly deepened my spiritual life by working with oblates.

Prayer

What is your most favorite part of the Rule *of St. Benedict?*

Well, I really like Chapter 4 on the "Instruments of Good Works," or the tools of good works. One reason I like it so well is it is so practical and covers everything about the spiritual life. Now there are other beautiful parts of the *Rule*, but that chapter has always inspired me. I have given a retreat on it. I have also given conferences on it because it is so down to earth, and I think it points out so well that, for St. Benedict, it is doing the ordinary things of daily life where we find God.

These rules apply to the ordinary things. St. Benedict does not expect the extraordinary of his followers. He wants them to do well what they are supposed to be doing in life. These tools start with the commandments, and throws in even "Thou shall not kill." There have been times when the monks have tried to kill the abbot – even St. Benedict. So he knows that has to be in there.

He also covers the beautiful things of kindness and service, relationship to God, relationship to one another, relationship to the monastery and relationship to those outside. The *Rule* covers the whole facet of living our life as followers of St. Benedict.

What is your key to living Benedictine spirituality?
Well, for me, certainly the Liturgy of the Hours is so important, so inspiring, and I have always taken that very seriously. Even when I was out in parish work or away from the abbey, I never let go of my Liturgy of the Hours. I pray faithfully, no matter where I am, because I see that as so important. I might be very distracted at times and I don't deny right here in the choir too, but by the very fact that we are faithful in praying this each day in itself will keep you close to God.

Let me share a story. One night a diocesan priest who had just been assigned to a parish in Chicago came home late and went by the pastor's bedroom door. The door was open a little bit and there was the pastor in his shorts smoking a cigar, drinking a highball and praying the Liturgy of the Hours. The new priest said he was kind of scandalized by that. But the longer he lived with the man, the more he realized that prayer meant something to the pastor and reflected on his wonderful ministry to the people and his relationship with God.

It is important, no matter how tired I might be or if much is going on where I have to pray, that I pray it. That is one of the keys to living here in the community with the monks. It is accepting them, and them accepting me with all my weaknesses and limitations. Community life is most important for me as a monk.

I have been out in the parish many times and I have had other pastoral assignments, but it was always supportive to me to know that my confreres back at Saint Meinrad are praying for me and they still accept me when I return. I feel right at home with them when I do return, and that is a very strong key to my life as a monk at Saint Meinrad.

What has been your most difficult time or experiences over your lifetime?

I guess the hardest thing for me was when I was assigned to a parish my first time, going from Saint Meinrad and trying to adjust to a parish life. I found that very hard. You see, evenings in the monastery are mostly for the monks, and evenings in the parish are when all the meetings with your contacts, couples, and spiritual direction takes place. I found that very hard to adjust to. And even after seven years of being in a parish, to come back to the monastery and readjust to the schedule was hard.

Sometimes working under non-monastic supervisors, and I don't mean they are not good people, but sometimes they did not understand our schedules as a monk. They just thought we could do more or we should be out more, not realizing we had a little tension between the monastic life and trying to fulfill what they were hoping to achieve. Some of them were very capable people and we were blessed to have them, but because they were so capable they set a very high standard for you at times. At times, that could be hard.

How about your happiest time?

As I said, I enjoyed all my jobs, but I think one of the best and my happiest have been my years as the oblate director. I guess, in a sense, I am helping others to live a Benedictine way of life. In turn, helping them deepens my understanding of the *Rule of St. Benedict* and it helps me to strengthen my love of living the monastic life.

I found that my years as an oblate director have been very helpful in that area. It doesn't mean we don't have stress and frustrations at times. Some oblates could be difficult at times, but for the most part it has been a wonderful experience. I hope I have been helpful to them in living and having a deeper love of Christ according to the *Rule of St. Benedict*.

Changes in the Church over Your Lifetime

As you know, St. Benedict became discouraged by the general disregard for spiritual ideas in his own time, and some observers today are of the opinion that society is once again falling into indifference to the meaning of a virtuous life and lack of spirituality. How has this affected Benedictine spirituality found within the abbey and the Church, if at all?

I mentioned when I first came to the monastery it was a very structured way of life and it is still, in many ways, a very structured way of life. But it is not as tight a structure as it used to be, and I do see a need for that structure and framework within our life. We have a certain rhythm living a Benedictine way of life, and I think we need that in the Church.

It is beautiful sometimes working with the oblates, because it puts structure in their spiritual life and the fact that you have to pray Lauds and Vespers and *lectio divina* [*spiritual reading and contemplation*]. It is important that some pray the Liturgy of the Hours faithfully. There are days you can't do it, and that is understandable.

I think we need a certain spirit of the Benedictine way of life in the Church. Maybe people won't come into the oblate program, as such, but when they see oblates praying the Liturgy of the Hours after Mass, or before Mass, several parishioners have said, "What are you doing?" Even to see that can be a sign or a demonstration of God's love.

Many changes have affected the contemporary Church. How different is the Church today compared to pre-Vatican II?

Well, with the Liturgy of the Hours, after Vatican II, we were permitted to go to English. I was on a special committee to create an English Liturgy of the Hours as an experiment and was the secretary of that group. Fr. Aidan [*Kavanagh*], who is now deceased and taught at Indiana University, was the chairperson of that committee. I think Fr. Simeon [*Daly*] was on it and two or three others. We had to create an English Office that was prayed in the Chapter Room, separate from the rest of the monks who were in the church in the Latin Office. Certain monks were invited to attend with Abbot Bonaventure's approval.

I will never forget being at those meetings and how exciting it was to have the English Office created. It was my job to come up with the responses after the readings. Then these were taken to the main church. The brothers, who were praying their Office in English, then joined us as a whole community that prayed together in English.

Then I will never forget the first concelebration [*two or more priests celebrating the Mass together*] of the Mass in English. At that time, not everybody could concelebrate. Perhaps only 10 would be chosen for a particular morning to concelebrate the Mass. The altar was now facing us in the choir and that was exciting.

I am so grateful personally to Vatican II that we have the Mass in English. I am not saying there is not room for a Latin Mass, but I feel like I want to praise God in the language I understand. Not that I couldn't make sense out of the Latin, but I was always trying to think about the meaning of the Latin to give praise to God.

Another thing I found very beneficial to the Church after Vatican II was the importance of bringing lay people into the Church and having them participate in the Church liturgy. That carried over into the monastery, especially now under Abbot Justin [*DuVall*]. We have community meetings where we are invited to share our thoughts in small groups and then take it to the big group, the community. The abbot listens carefully to what the community members say and makes the final decision. So what has happened in the Church has also come into the monastery.

Compare the morale of the monastery today with that of 30, 40, 50 years ago. To what extent has the decline of vocations had an impact on the Church or on the monastic community?

Well, when I first came to the monastery, we had over 200 monks and now we are down to 80-something. When I came to the juniorate [*monks not yet in final vows*], just in the fratery we had 35 men, so that does somewhat hurt the morale. We have had to adjust to that.

It doesn't mean that we are going out of business right now, but eventually we might have a monastery with only 40 monks. We will have to consider how much can we do and what we have to let go. It is unbelievable what comes out of the community meetings now, which I think is the Spirit working within the community.

So in some ways the morale might even be better even though there were more monks back then?

Oh yes, I think right now we have some well-educated monks and very bright young monks. It is beautiful to see what they can bring to the community. It is beautiful to see that and how blessed we are with the quality of the men we have now.

Perhaps the most important change in the seminary curriculum is the de-emphasis of Latin. Even though the Mass is to be celebrated in English, was eliminating Latin from the academic curriculum a good idea?

Well, I'm always grateful for all the Latin I have had because I can read the *Summa* [*instructional guide for theological students*]. I can read the primary sources of Latin and even the breviary. I am glad we had that experience where we prayed in Latin, but I don't want to go back to it.

It is good to see that some of the monks are taking special Latin under Fr. Vincent, just to have an understanding of these documents that are so important in the Church, so that you can go and look at them and read them. I am glad, too, when I was in the seminary, to have Greek and Hebrew. I think it is good that seminarians have some understanding of Latin with regard to the documents of the Church.

In the post-Vatican II years, what has been gained?

I think a big gain is more participation by the laity now in the liturgy and being part of it. I am very grateful for having English in praying, which led me to understand what we were praying when we pray together. I am a little concerned at present that the Church seems to be backtracking on some things in regards to the Eucharist and the Mass. Not in an extreme way, but I do have a little concern at times.

I hope we will not have just one Office for all the monasteries. The beauty is that the Liturgy of the Hours is different in every monastery you go to, but that liturgy expresses well the spirit of a particular community.

Today, I think there is a much better spirit between the superiors and the monks under them. I have heard stories of Abbot Ignatius and how he was so strict – there was a certain amount of fear of him. Well, when Fr. Abbot Bonaventure came in, that let up a lot and then Abbot Gabriel [*Verkamp*], being out in a parish for so many years, certainly had a different approach in working with the monks.

Under Timothy and Justin, there was a lot more willingness to listen and to allow us to express our concerns and opinions. Lambert tended to be a little more firm in making decisions as the abbot, but again that was his approach, his way of running the office of being the abbot. So I think that is a positive part. I have deep respect for him as the abbot. He was my classmate.

Has there been anything lost since the Council?
There are always going to be problems, and everything has not been perfect since Vatican II. There were some extremes in regard to liturgy and kinds of kooky things happened. I think we have been very fortunate and very blessed at Saint Meinrad. We have always had a moderate and balanced approach in the liturgy and didn't go off on extremes.

Even in the seminary, too, we had our tough times during the Vietnam War and the hippie culture, but we tried to keep it in the middle and bring them back. When students were coming in during this period, they had very little understanding of the Church. Trying to explain to them what it means to be a part of the Church and then get them ready for priesthood was quite a job. I think we have been successful all these years with very fine administrations in the schools.

Another concern I see in the Church today are strong divisions. The conservatives are more oppressive, even to the point they don't seem to want to sit down and talk to others. This is sometimes reflected in the monastery with the young ones. Some of them want to go back to some of the things we had gotten rid of.

We need to be willing to listen, try to understand, be compassionate, but it works two ways. We should not become so caught up in our own way of thinking that the others don't have a chance. I am a little concerned about that, and that is now found strongly in the Church. I see some of that in the monastery, too, between the older and the younger ones.

Over the last 40, 50 years, there has been a decline in religious vocations with the number of retirements and deaths in the religious population. What has been the meaning of these changing patterns to the monastery and the Church at large?

We are down to under 90 monks and we are still carrying out a lot of the apostolic works and are beginning to realize we just won't be able to do that in the future. We will have to make some big choices of what we are going to do. I think Fr. Abbot Justin is beginning to realize if a monk comes to retirement, we just can't send another monk into a parish. We just don't have them anymore and we have to start giving up parish work.

But how can you give it up altogether? Because I think it is a very important work for us. But maybe we need to do it closer to the monastery, where we will try to take care of the spiritual needs in the local area. But even in the local area, we gave up Mariah Hill, we gave up Ferdinand, and so I think that is hard when you have to give up something you have been doing many years and realize we don't have the manpower to do all of that now.

What are your hopes for the future of the monastery?

As pointed out previously, we are a smaller community, and I hope even as a smaller community we will have continuity in serving the Church as we have in the past, especially with the seminary work. My own personal opinion is that it would be a great loss if we lost the seminary.

We originally came to serve the spiritual needs of German-speaking Catholics, at least in the local area. I hope we can keep some of that. I think it brings us down to reality and I think any monk who has been out in a parish, like myself, comes back with a more practical approach to living the monastic way of life because of the experience of working with people outside and a much deeper understanding and compassion for them. I hope for the future we will continue to share our Benedictine values, such as our prayer life, the Liturgy of the Hours and helping to share that with the people.

I am very happy with my years here in the monastery. I am very grateful, very grateful, to my monastic community and their willingness to support me, to accept me, to encourage me and to grow in my spiritual life.

I have a lot of gratitude to the superiors, too. All the abbots I have been under, I am very grateful for their leadership and what they tried to do in helping me personally as a monk and their concern for me as a monk. So I thank God each day.

What do you see as the future of the Church?
Well, I always say this, "The Spirit knows what he or she is doing." I think we could say, "Oh my, what is going to happen?" Well, for 2,000 years, the Church has weathered many serious problems but seems to get through it somehow or another. And it is because Christ said, "I will be with you till the end of the days."

Profile based upon: Fr. Meinrad Brune, OSB, to Prof. Ruth C. Engs, October 13, 2009, Interview Transcriptions, Saint Meinrad Archabbey Archives, St. Meinrad, IN; additional comments from Fr. Meinrad, November 2015.

Chapter 5: Br. Andrew Zimmermann, OSB

Br. Andrew has had decades of service in Central and South America. He served in Peru and Guatemala and currently works with the Spanish-speaking community at the Guadalupe Center of the Diocese of Evansville. He is a shining example of the "old school lay brothers" whose primary mission is the work of the community.

Born December 23, 1934, in Richmond, VA, Br. Andrew was given the name of William. He went to St. Benedict's grade school and Thomas Jefferson High School in Richmond. For his last year of high school, he attended St. Placid Hall, a school for prospective brothers at Saint Meinrad, where he graduated (1954). He was trained as a tailor. Br. Andrew made his profession March 11, 1956, and his solemn profession in 1959.

Until he was appointed to San Benito Priory, Huaraz, Peru (1964-83), he worked as a tailor. In Peru, he went through the massive earthquake of 1970. From 1983-89, back at Saint Meinrad, he worked as the vestarian [one who takes care of clerical vestments] *and in the duplicating and mail rooms. A few years later, he was appointed to a parish in Lima, Peru (1988-92), to work with youth.*

Br. Andrew became an administrator and youth worker in Guatemala at Priorato San José from 1996 until 2004. When he returned to Indiana, he was appointed to the Guadalupe Center, a mission to the Spanish-speaking

community, helping with transportation and legal issues, which he
continues to do.

Prof. Ruth C. Engs interviewed Br. Andrew Zimmermann, OSB,
June 30, 2009; additional information added September 2015.

Childhood and Early Years as a Monk

Tell me about your childhood, family life, and early schooling.

I was born in Richmond, Virginia, I presume in a hospital,
December 23, 1934. I was a Christmas gift, the only boy in the
family. I have three older sisters; one sister is in Bristol, Virginia – a
Benedictine sister. One is married and one is an old maid. My father
was a mechanic and he worked part of the time for the state. Then
he switched over to Reynolds Metal, where he was working until he
died in an automobile accident in 1956, I believe. My mother died in
1951, so I am an orphan. I don't remember much about the first
house we lived in on Sheppard Street because I must have been
quite small.

By the time I started school, we were living in a house on
Hanover Avenue and I didn't have to walk a long way to school. I
went out the back door and crossed the street to the Benedictine
sisters, who taught there. Also, all I had to do is go out the front
door and across the street to church run by the Benedictine priests.
They called it the priory. I never knew a rectory was anything but a
priory; the priory was from Belmont Abbey in North Carolina. I
can't remember if I went to kindergarten. I might have gone, but I
don't remember if they had kindergarten in those days or not.

What was the name of your school? Was it a Catholic school?

It was St. Benedict's, of course! The teachers were all nuns. In
seventh grade, I think, I got a lay teacher, first one – ooh horrible –
but it ended up okay; I was a little rebel and didn't like it.

How about high school?

When I got through grade school, I was going to go to Belmont Abbey to be a brother. Now, how did I know to be a brother, I don't know. I guess I got that vocation from my mother, because I didn't remember when I didn't think I wouldn't be a brother. I was going to be a priest, but I guess during the fourth grade I decided, "Hey, I can't even learn the Latin of an altar boy" and gave up thinking of being a priest.

Did you work as a youngster?

During the school days, I must have been 8 or 9 years old, I started working. I took my little wagon and walked five blocks – kids nowadays can't walk a half a block – up to Safeway and A&P [*grocery stores*] with my little wagon on Saturday and carried ladies' groceries home to their houses. Food was still on rations, so I presume it was before the war was over [*WWII ended in 1945 and rationing ended in 1946*].

How much did you get paid for hauling groceries?

I don't know, 5 or 10 cents a bundle. One time I took two bags of groceries – I can still see them sitting there on the porch. The lady told me, this is my address. Well, there was an Ellwood and an Idlewood Street. I don't remember which one I went to, but I went to the wrong one. A couple hours later, she came back and said, "Where's my groceries?"

Well, I go back to where I left them and they were still sitting on the front porch waiting for me to pick them up and take them back in the right direction. Then, I started working for a lady helping to clean her house. She took in servicemen on weekends and I got paid 10 cents an hour there. My sister Aggie came and helped sometimes.

I carried afternoon newspapers for two years and morning newspapers for two years. In the summer of my sophomore year, I started working in a grocery store. I told Daddy I wanted to work at something and he said, "Go ahead, you find a job." So I went out and I don't know if he said anything or not, but it was the grocery store he bought all his food from and I got hired right away. So I worked there during the summer.

What did you do at the grocery store?
Mostly bagging and stocking. Then one night a week, I stayed and mopped the floors. Another night we stocked shelves until midnight. During that summer, some weeks I put in like 80 hours a week, but since that was against the law, I got two envelopes—one for 40 hours with money taken out and one with 40 hours with no money taken out. Then, I worked on Friday nights. That was the only time the grocery was open until 9 o'clock. All the rest of the time, they would close at 6 and were closed on Sunday. There were no Sunday grocery stores back then.

What kind of health care did you have when you were young?
Health? Never had a health problem.

Did a doctor come to your house if someone was sick or what?
Oh yeah, when we got sick or something, the doctor came to the home. The doctor worked in his office, which was only, I think, two blocks from my home. The only thing I ever had was my tonsils taken out when I was a kid, but I think that was because my sister needed hers taken out and the doctor said, "Let's take the two out at the same time." Well, I don't think they do that anymore.

Before you came here, what kind of hobbies did you have and did you smoke or drink?
Well, did I smoke? Let's see, one Sunday, don't know how old I was, but I likely wasn't too old, I sat on the front steps with a cigarette in my mouth smoking away. The boy down the street who

was in the Navy gave it to me. My daddy came out and told the man, "You're cleaning up after him."

That afternoon I went to a movie with an aunt and her two kids and I got sick. Coming home on the bus, I got sick. Nowadays, I know it wasn't from the cigarette because it wouldn't have been that long after the fact. I don't think I ever smoked a whole pack of cigarettes in all my life.

Did you drink as a young man?

No, I don't think I drank until I came here, except at Christmas, when I would drink eggnog. Actually, my parents told us if you are going to smoke or drink – because Daddy didn't do anything to me for smoking – do it here. So, he just saw me and that was it. I don't think my two older sisters – they were goody-goodies – drank. My oldest sister, Aggie, didn't drink that much in high school. When I was working at the grocery store, I did buy her beer once or twice because she was underage. I was younger still, but I could get it because I was working in the grocery store.

Did you do anything with your church when you were young?

I was in the school choir one time until Christmas time. After that, they didn't need any more warm bodies. They kicked me out, and I think that is why I still don't want to sing as I wasn't a good enough choir boy.

How did you find out about the brothers?

I presume from the good little sisters, because I had a stack of 100 to 200 different religious brochures by the time I came to Saint Meinrad. They must have been giving them to me all the time, because I never wrote for them. I didn't go to Belmont after I got out of grade school. I went over and saw Fr. Rembert Codd, OSB, who was a Benedictine at the priory, and he told me, "No, go to high school at least one year." So I went to Thomas Jefferson High School, a public high school, instead of going across the street to the Catholic high school.

I know Daddy must have talked to Fr. Rembert because other classmates of mine came to Thomas Jefferson, but they went right back to the Benedictines real quick. Since I wasn't college material and Benedictine High School was more or less a college preparatory school, and also since my daddy did moonlighting keeping up the schools and church around there, I guess he didn't want to ask for financial help for me to go to school with the uniform and the expense of going to a private school. But I am sure he talked to Fr. Rembert, because nothing was ever said about me changing back from the public school to the Catholic school.

In my junior year, I was working in the summer and I asked to take off a week to come here to see Saint Meinrad. When I came here, they gave me a brochure on St. Placid Hall [*high school for potential brothers*] and I ended up coming here for my fourth year of high school to St. Placid Hall. The classes I took here in my senior year were tailoring, an English class and religion classes, and that would have been enough credits to graduate from high school.

So you graduated from St. Placid?

Well, I guess as much. We didn't have a graduation ceremony but I did use those credits to take some college courses later. So, it got validated somewhere along the line.

What did you do after St. Placid Hall?

I came to the monastery.

What was the reaction of your family and friends when you decided to become a brother?

There wasn't any reaction really. I think it was expected and I don't think I even asked permission from my parents. I just told them I was coming because my parents trained us, more or less, to be independent – to think for ourselves.

Why did you decide to come to Saint Meinrad and not Belmont or some other monastery?

I talked to Fr. Rembert at the Benedictine church. He didn't want me to go to Belmont because they were all old priests and brothers at that time. I never saw him again until I went over to ask him for a recommendation to come to Saint Meinrad. It was just little brochures that I had picked up or the sisters had given me that made me decide where I was going.

Why did you decide to become a monk?

Fr. Claude [*Ehringer*], who was the novice master here when I visited, asked why I wanted to come to Saint Meinrad. I said, "I don't know, I just want to come." He said, "You don't want to come to serve God?" I said, "I guess so." I never thought over the thing; it was like a fish taking to water. I'm not a good Benedictine. I am of the old school lay brothers. I came, more or less, to work and I enjoyed the little simple liturgical life we had as brothers. I hated going to the Abbey Church for Vespers and Latin and things of that sort. I hated going to choir practice.

Br. Andrew, as a young monk

What was your formation like when you were a young monk?

The first two weeks I was here, I did the candidate and the novice's work. After that, I was put in the tailor shop under Br. Innocent [*Benkert*]. I became an untouchable. Br. Innocent was on vacation my first two weeks I was here. He came home and I was in the tailor shop working. I never had to leave for another job. After a while, I didn't even check the sign [*for assignments*] to see where I was assigned. I knew I was going to the tailor shop.

So, I never did [*clean*] bathrooms. The juniors [*temporarily professed monks*] used to have to do bathrooms. As novices, we had one conference [*lecture*] in the morning or the afternoon – an hour and a half conference with Fr. Claude – and they were good for sleeping. Don't ask me anything about the spiritual reading books he gave me, because I kept telling him they make me go to sleep.

What was your typical day as a junior monk?

At that time, we got up at 3:40 in the morning and then we went to the brothers' oratory and we had Office [*early morning prayer*] and Mass. Then if we were lucky and didn't have to serve a second priest with his Mass, we got to go back to bed for an hour or so until we had Prime [*morning prayer*]. I think Prime was 6-6:20 or something like that, and then we had breakfast. We went to work, I think, at 7:30.

What did you eat for breakfast?

In those days, we had "sewer lids" once a week with "motor oil" on top of them – that was pancakes with syrup. Coffee was always mixed with everything under the sun in it. It might have cocoa leftover from the previous day; they just kept adding stuff to it.

You said that after breakfast you went to work, so what did you do in the tailor shop?

Sew, what do you think?

I mean, did you make garments from scratch? Or did you repair things?

Oh, I worked mostly with Br. Innocent and was trained to be the cassock maker. I did monsignor cassocks with all the red frou-frous and all that stuff on it. We had also in the shop Bill Steinmetz, who was an old man, and he did all the patching.

These habits were mostly made of patches. Sometimes the habit was milled [*thickened*]. Basically, I was making cassocks for the priests. At that time, we had Br. Phillip, who was making habits. Let's see, Fr. Pius [*Klein*] was in at one time and Br. Gabriel [*Thibert*], and they did all the habits.

How many years did you do that?

Until I went to Peru in '64.

Compared to your earlier days, when you were a junior monk, what changes do you see in formation to be a monk?

Well, now it is more lax. In those days, we went to work, we got off work, we had reading to do, and then we had common recreation until Compline [*Night Prayer*]. Nowadays, we don't always even have common recreation. I mean, there is recreation but no one shows up. The only time they show up is if something is going on, such as a party. We also had strict separation in those days – there were three communities here.

There were the brothers, the fathers and the fraters [*those studying for the priesthood*], and we did not associate with each other. We each had our own recreation room and our own agenda. Now the fraters went with the fathers to church and did everything with them. The brothers were, more or less, work orientation. We did have two groups of brothers, the German brothers and the English-speaking brothers, but we did recreate together.

Can you tell me anything about the German brothers? Did you interact with them?

We seemed to get along pretty good, but we didn't recreate that much together with each other. We would have tournaments and they would specialize in chess or something they played. I worked with Br. Innocent; he was a German. Then there was Br. Franz; he was over the shoe shop. Fidelis [*Benkert*], I think, was the one up in the bakery and we had Br. Conrad in the power house.

We had Br. Mark [*Michel*], who was the oldest person in those days until Fr. Theodore [*Heck*][5] came along – he was 90 something. When we had a vacation at Camp Benedict on the Blue River, the German brothers had one week and the English brothers had three weeks. We weren't separated but there was a 20- or 30-year gap in age between the two groups.

Tell me about the change from three groups to everybody as one community, which is found now?

I wasn't here.

That was when you were in Peru?

Yeah, I missed all that fun and games.

Well, before we go on to your experiences in Peru, do you have an amusing story from your early years here as a junior?

I found humility real quick when Fr. Abbot asked for volunteers to go to Peru. It struck a note and I said I would go. I

---

[5] Fr. Theodore Heck's biographical profile (1901-2009) is in: Engs, Ruth Clifford, editor, *Conversations in the Abbey: Senior Monks of Saint Meinrad Reflect on their Lives* (2008).

wrote my sisters, because my folks were already dead, and said, "I volunteered to go to Peru but don't worry, I will never go. I am too important. I am in the tailor shop and nobody can take my place." Well, I went. I found out I wasn't so important. This put me down. It helped me with my humility a little bit.

Work

Peru

Tell me about that whole process of going to Peru and the work there. How did you get there? Did you go directly to Peru? Did you already know the language?

Fr. Michael [*Keene*] and I went down together. We wanted to go by boat but Abbot Bonaventure said, "No, you can't count on boats getting there on time." Well, afterwards we found that the price of boats was twice the price of plane tickets. I think he was looking at the price tag more than anything else. So, we flew down there. When I came into the Lima airport, I found it was a desert country, dirty just by the nature of being a desert, and no green.

Coming into Lima from the airport, I saw all these buildings with iron doors on them. I found out later that this was normal when the stores closed. They pulled down these iron shutters to protect them. But, I think that if the abbot had been there with a round-trip ticket, I'd gotten on the next plane and gone home. When we got into the wealthy part of the city, they had nice green lawns and things. Then we went out to Cieneguilla, a valley about an hour drive from Lima. It was kind of nice out here away from the big city.

How long were you at the school?

In theory four months, in practice three months. I think we went from November until March, but we had a Christmas break for two weeks. While we were at the language school, I didn't learn much. Once in a while, I would sit down with the gardener and we would talk, and I most likely learned more trying to talk to him than the teachers. At Christmas, we went up to Huaraz [*the priory*]. At that time Kenneth [*Wimsatt, Fr.*], Benedict [*Meyer, Fr.*] and Germain [*Swisshelm, Fr.*] were there. They went the first year and Michael and I came the second year.

So, how did you get up to Huaraz?

They came down in a Jeep to get us. It was about a 12-hour trip, and half of that or more was on a dirt road. It wasn't that far really, about 200-250 miles north of Lima, but the dirt road took a long time to drive on.

Describe what the community looked like when you got there.

Well, it wasn't much of a community. They lived in an old seminary. It was rectangular and had a court, two floors. We lived on the second floor. There was no running water, except in one bathroom. The students lived in another wing; they also had one bathroom. Your room opened out onto a balcony and you went out and went to the shower. It had cold water and came from the melting snow on the mountains and it was cold!

There was just one shower. I almost took a shower one time but when I went, there was no water and I gave thanks to the Lord and never had that temptation again. There were hot baths about five miles from where we lived, and we would go there about every week and also take the boys and let them swim in the hot pool so they got a bath too, although they would use the cold showers at the school.

How about drinking water?

We just used to filter it, boil it and filter it, but it was nice and cold and good.

What did you eat there? Where did you get your food?

Well, nuns were cooking there and they gave us special food, different from the students. We didn't like having separate food and kept fighting them, but they kept giving us one dish and the students another dish. We sat in the same dining room eating. I think, eventually, we finally convinced them to cook the same meal. Then the students got better food and I think we all did.

Describe a typical meal there.

A typical meal would be rice and beans, maybe a little meat. The poorer people would have potatoes and beans, as potatoes were grown there. But we had meat. Sometimes you wondered if it was meat or shoe leather. The cows were usually very old and tough by the time they killed them.

You would put five pounds of meat into a pressure cooker and you came out with a half a pound, but it came out tender. I enjoyed the meals, basically. Peruvian cooking is very good and I am surprised there is not a bunch of Peruvian gourmet restaurants here, because they are very good at cooking meals, particularly a lot of fish food.

What did you drink? Did you have wine at every meal?

No, I guess we drank water or lemonade.

Did you have wine for evening meal like you do here on Christmas or Easter?

Well, we did later, but I can't remember wines at the meals because we were eating with the students. Later, we had alcohol and we would leave the bottles out for the two weeks of Christmas season and hardly emptied any of them. Most of us really didn't drink that much. When we did have wine in the house, I had to put out two kinds, a very sweet one for the Peruvians and another for us. So we didn't have that much of a problem.

Did people smoke at your house in Peru?

Yeah, and we would buy the cheapest old cigarettes you could get – Incas. I didn't smoke; they stunk. I can tell you a trick we played on Fr. Theodore [*Brune*]; this was Fr. Meinrad's brother, not Fr. Theodore Heck. We were playing bridge one night with one of our Peruvian friends, Ricky and his wife, who was from the United States. Theodore and I were playing bridge with him, and he saw that Ricky had a pack of Camels on the table. We had stuck Incas in the first part of the Camel pack.

Theodore said, "Oh Ricky! Can I have one of your cigarettes?" He took one and said, "Oh, this Camel is so good!" and about halfway through his second one, he happened to see Inca on the cigarette. He said, "Oh, I thought there was something wrong with those cigarettes."

Describe your cell [room] *at the house.*

The first one was a good-size room. All it had was a bed and a washstand. I did have a little kerosene heater that I could use to heat my room up. We also had a Primus kerosene stove to heat water to wash with. I didn't have any fancy cell. It had wood floors and a bar on the wall to hang up clothes. After I was there about a year, we moved up to Los Pinos, a little hotel we bought.

After we moved up into the hotel, it was nicer. A lot of the rooms had private baths. It was a small hotel that, I guess, wasn't making money. It was good for mountain climbers coming down to Peru for a couple months a year. It was on the other side of the city, up on a cliff looking down on the river and a whole view of white snowcapped mountains across the valley that we could see all year long. A nice part of this place is that we never had snow. So we didn't have to worry about it, but we could go to the snow if we wanted.

So, this hotel became your priory?

Yeah. For a while, the kids at the school came down to the priory and would have meals in their section of the dining room. We put up two prefab buildings; one was a dormitory for them and one had four rooms for classrooms. We also had a bathroom built for them. The kids only came down to our place at mealtime.

You said you sometimes went up to the mountains with snow. What kind of recreation did you do there?

Camped out. I used to like to go camping, but didn't like to go on the snow for mountain climbing, as it was too much work. To get on the snow and just touch it, that was good enough for me. In the daytime, you could walk around in your shirt sleeves. At nighttime, our canteens would freeze over. Fr. Joel and I went a few times and then sometimes I would take students up for the weekend. We would drive up and just put out our tents and camp out.

We would go up to Llanganuco [*in Huascaran National Park*], a lake at about 15,000 feet up. The snowline doesn't start until a little over 15,000. I went into the lake to go swimming and I was only in it for about two minutes. When I got out, my back was burning me like sunburn from the cold, but the kids got in the water and would stay and stay and stay. They didn't seem to think it was cold. Around the lake in the daytime, it was nice; at nighttime, it got cold.

How far was this lake from the priory?

Let's see, to drive there was a three- to four-hour drive. When I went with Fr. Joel, we would hike usually for about two or three days. The longest hike I did took 10 days for tourists, but we did it in six days but we walked from 8 in the morning to 5. I took this hike with Mike Rouke, who was a volunteer who had come down from the college [*Saint Meinrad College*], because he wasn't sure if he wanted to go on or not. Well, he found his wife down there. They got married and he planned on coming down each year with tour groups, because he liked mountain climbing.

He and I did the Lake Llanganuco - Santa Cruz walk, in which you go up one canyon, cross over the mountain, come down another canyon and come out. It was about a 10-day tour – two days getting there and two days getting out – because by the time you get up there, you did not get far the first day. One morning we woke up with a foot and a half snow all around us. We waited for the snow to melt, but it wouldn't melt, so finally by 10 o'clock we tracked off in the snow – and lost the path. We went up the mountain and came down. We didn't go up very high and it wasn't that far up, but that was more than enough mountain climbing for me.

What was your work in Peru?

I taught English once at the school, but I didn't like it. I taught gym class for several years, but I was gone so much. So I hired a young man to be my assistant who had finished high school but didn't want to go to college right away. So, when I wasn't around, he was there.

I also had administrator duties. Fr. Bede [*Jamison*] was the administrator, but died in the 1970 earthquake and Fr. Joel took over. The seminary had farmlands and other property, so I ran them. I was also the treasurer for the community.

Raban [*Bivins, Br.*] was in charge of the kitchen and did the buying for the kitchens, but I would go to Lima and buy stuff wholesale. I would go to Lima at least once or twice a month. Usually, I would just go and come right back, which was a three- or four-day trip – one day down and one day back.

In Lima, you can do one thing in the morning and one thing in the afternoon. And it wasn't that easy getting around, even though I had a car. Some places were closed in the afternoons. Because of some legal work, I had to see the lawyer about things that belonged to the seminary and not the monastery.

For example, we were always in a fight to get the renters to pay their rent for haciendas or farmlands. The seminary basically lived off farming, including sugar. But it takes two years to get the first cutting from a sugar crop. One farm was about 100 and the other about 50 acres. We had some lawsuits to get our money from the renters.

Tell me about the earthquake.

It was May 30, 1970. I was taking my nap like a good Peruvian and, about 3 in the afternoon, I got shook in my bed. I went outside and Fr. Theodore, who lived on the second floor, came running out in his shorts. He was taking a nap and said, "Andrew, I am in my shorts, should I come down?" I said, "I don't care." But he didn't waste any time coming down.

We went to the middle of the patio. The only thing that actually fell down was the dining room, which was almost all glass overlooking the cliff. I guess it didn't have much wall. The kitchen was damaged and our little Peruvian cook was in the kitchen frying potatoes. My room was cracked. We had built what we called the back house. It was four bedrooms of adobe, and they were damaged. The nuns' part fell down. But on the whole, we were not too badly damaged. We had to tear down some things afterwards, but we were able to get the furniture.

Who was affected in the community by the earthquake?

Fr. Bede and Fr. Pius had gone downtown to Santa Elena School. They were having a little show, because Fr. Bede and the superior at the school had a feast day, I think, one day apart and the school was having a celebration for the two of them. Fr. Bede and Fr. Pius were in this school.

Br. Raban had gone down to the town but, instead of taking the direct way into town that he ordinarily took, he was taking the roundabout way. Well, it was a wise decision, as the quake came during that time. If he had taken the direct way, it was filled with rubbish. As it was, he was in a pickup truck and nothing happened to the truck.

Fr. Pius said he got into a room and a beam fell on top of him, but hit the piano and that saved him. He doesn't know how he got the bars off the window, because the window had bars on it, but after the quake maybe they were all loose. When Bede died, he was protecting a little girl, I believe, as they found her alive under him. In the town, the streets were very narrow, a little wider than one width of a car. After the quake, all the streets you walked around were on second-floor level because all the buildings had collapsed. When the two-story buildings came down, there was no place for people to escape to so that is why so many people died. They had no place to go.

Was anybody injured up at the monastery?

No. Fr. Bede died and the superior of the nuns who cooked for us died, as they were all down at the school. This was the same group of Franciscan nuns who ran the school. It was also a bad day for the superiors of the Franciscan nuns who had a high school in town. Their Mother General was up from Lima with the treasurer, and all the nuns had gone on a trip that day, except for two who stayed home because one was sick and one stayed home to be with the sick nun.

The big shots went through Cañon de Pato, which is a narrow canyon that has around 20 tunnels. It goes down to a hydroelectric plant. Because the plant was under control, they know they went into that area, but they never came out and never found the car. So it must have fallen off into the river and gotten covered over in a big landslide down in the river.

Tell me some more things about your work in Peru.

I lived up in the dormitory with the students for a while. When we no longer had students, I still stayed up in the dormitory but young men came up. They used to play football and, somehow or another, they got in with me. Two of the boys had home problems; they were repeating the third year in high school three times.

Basically, they didn't go to classes. One's father was a shoemaker and he was having problems. His father wanted him to go to school or start working in the shoe shop. He stayed over a lot with me and stayed away from his family. In the end, it worked out. The other boy lived with his mother and stepsister, which was a big problem, and on top of that he was a thief. One time when I was in Lima, he went into the guest house and stole one of the toilets.

A toilet?

Yeah, and the water was running out all over the guest house. He had brought a little kid to watch out, but the little kid didn't like the amount of money he was to get, so he asked one of our workers, "How much is a toilet worth?" So the two kids were told they couldn't come up there for a year. Well, after a month or so, he begged to come back.

So I talked to Fr. Joel, the superior at that time, and the kid was allowed to come back. I almost felt like his father. When I left to come up here, what happened to him, I don't know. When I went down again, I saw him. Some of the people said he went back to drinking. He stopped drinking when he was with me, and I think he was drinking again. But at least I saw a change at one time.

Who were some of the people from Saint Meinrad who were there?

We had a whole mob of them. Let's see, Fr. Bede died down there in an earthquake; Frs. Kenneth, Michael, Theodore Brune and David are now dead. Fr. Giles and Br. Hillary left and are also dead. Who else? Fr. Benedict, Fr. Germain, Fr. Joel [*who went to the*

Trappists in Chile], Br. Xavier went to Christ in the Desert [*monastery*]; he also is dead now. Br. Raban, Br. Dominic [*Warnecke*], Frs. Noël [*Mueller*] and Pius [*Klein*].

However, it was basically a gringo community, and the few Peruvians we had come never stayed. We would try to speak Spanish when they were around, but we might switch to English when they were not around. When they would come in, we would switch to Spanish. After a number of our people had left, we started to get vocations. When we closed the place, we had three or four men in temporary vows. One was ready for solemn vows. Luckily, he didn't take them because when he left, he was married within a month.

One of the boys we sent to the Benedictines in Los Toldos in Argentina; he made solemn vows there. I presume he got ordained. When I was in the parish, I saw him. But Abbot Timothy [*Sweeney*] wanted to close it and so it got closed. I thought it was funny we kept the parish with three priests in it, instead of closing the parish and bringing them up to the priory. But then maybe other people wanted to go home, I don't know.

So, when you left, when you closed it down, there was still a parish?
Yes, because I went back to the parish later. Fr. Christopher [*Shappard*], Fr. Theodore and Fr. Michael were in the parish. After a year and a half, I went back down to help close up, since I had been the administrator and had power of attorney and everything from the schools and all. I knew the legal works to go through. So I went down for about a month to close up the place.

How long were you there and what did you do when you came back here?
I went down in '64 and, after 19 years, I came back up here in 1983. I went crazy. They gave me a beautiful job title in the Business Office. I was purchase agent, but nobody wanted to buy anything

through me. Br. Luke[6] said, "Well, we could send letters out to all the companies and say if they didn't have a purchase order number, we wouldn't pay the bills." They were trying something, but it didn't work and I was going crazy.

So then what happened?

They sent me to see a psychologist, and then he sent me over to see somebody in Jasper for a second opinion. The guy with the second opinion told him what I knew all along: "He just wants something to do."

So in this job you were bored?

Yes, I had a beautiful title. I think I saw the psychologist for about a whole year. But the guy in Jasper knew right away what was wrong so, after the second year, the abbot said, "Why don't you go back to school?" I had come up from Peru once to do a summer business course to learn a little accounting. So I went over to Vincennes College in Jasper to continue that course.

After the first year of classes, Br. Luke wanted me to come back to the Business Office. But I was not going to go to work and go to school, too – it was too much. Abbot Timothy called me in one day and said, "You are going back to the Business Office." He didn't even ask me if I wanted to continue school. Most likely, if he had asked me, I would have said, "Yes," but I was just as happy not to. I am not much on school.

So what did you now do in the Business Office and did you have other work assignments?

I did different things. While I was in the Business Office at that time, I had other jobs like running the duplicating room, running the

---

[6] No longer with the community.

mail room, writing checks for things and running the vestry, so I
was in and out.

What did you do in these jobs?
I would open the vestry for about a half hour a day for people
so they could get clothing, and every two weeks for one afternoon. I
would go out and buy stuff for the monastery, eat out and have a
good time.

When the students were there, I didn't do much of anything in
the mail room or duplicating room. I just had to check on things,
because the students ran them. During the summer, then I would
have to sort the mail and get it around to people.

When I came back here, I wanted to return to Peru.

This is after you closed the monastery down?
Yes, and after six years, around '98-99, Fr. Michael asked me to
come down and work with the youth in the parish. So I said, "I
don't like Lima. I don't think I would like parish work. It would be
the last place I would go, but that must be where God wants me."
And so I went down and I really enjoyed working with the youth
and the catechist program.

I had this lady, Emma, who was my right hand, my left hand
and foot. I get ideas, but I need somebody else to carry them
through. One time, after we had a small group of First
Communions, I said, "Emma, where are all your students?" She
said, "Oh, they go to church on Sundays." And I said, "Oh?"

So about a month later, Emma said, "Andrew, I am going to
different Masses and you are right. They are not there." And I said,
"Emma, let's change over to the new program of Catechist Familia."
So, she and I took a course in Catechist Familia. It basically works
with groups – the family, the parents. Parents would meet in small
groups of about six couples. One of the couples is the monitor and
they would talk about practical things.

The parents would take the theme to their kids on a kid level and then the kids would come to church. At church, older youth would be there and they would play games and check their homework. So we did not teach them; the parents had to teach them. We just saw that they did their homework and played games with them to make sure they were learning.

I didn't know at that time, but it was basic liberation theology. I would like to see it work up here. I think it would make the parents more conscious. The first year we had 50 kids and, out of those 50, there were 35 families. During that year, three of the parents straightened their marriages out. However, some of the nuns and the old catechists didn't like this program since we did not need them anymore, even though it was approved by the archbishop.

In 1992, I was ready to get out. As I said, I start programs, but I am not the type of person to keep them going. I left Peru at a good time. The Confirmation groups were functioning. I didn't want anybody teaching the kids catechism who was over 25 years of age, so we started a summer school to prepare catechists. My idea was one main catechist and a group of two or three helpers who would be in formation.

After four years, it was just Michael and I down there. Theodore was down there, but he was having health problems so he had to come home. So Michael was trying to do everything himself. Sunday he would have three or four Masses and would give a talk to one of the groups Sunday nights. He had wedding practices Saturdays and about 30 baptisms a week. Well, that was too much for him. After various other problems at the parish, the abbot wrote to Michael, "Neither you nor Br. Andrew can stay in Peru." So we came home.

Guatemala
What did you do when you came back here the second time?

I had the vestry again. I was going out a lot because I did transportation. Br. Michael was supposed to be the chauffeur, but he would only take one trip a day. When there was more than one trip, I would take them. I wasn't overworked, but I had enough to keep me out of trouble.

Then what happened?

Abbot Lambert [*Reilly*] was elected abbot in 1995. Fr. Theodore Brune asked to go back to Peru and Lambert gave him permission. Then Lambert said to me, "Andrew, don't you ask me; you are too important here." Well, I think it was the same year he was elected; in November, I picked him up at the airport and we went over to New Albany to a little Italian restaurant right off of I-65.

While we were eating there, he said, "Andrew, would you like to go to the priory in Guatemala?" I said, "If that is what you want." And he said, "That's not what I want. I am asking if you want to." Well, it took me a long time to decide. That night I said, "Well, it must be God's will," so I put a note the next day in his box and said, "Yes."

So what did you do there?

Administration. I was in charge of the kitchens, I was in charge of the guest house, I was in charge of the workers. I was in charge of the farm until I got Br. Dominic down there, and he took the farm off my hands since I don't like farming.

I was also in charge of the students when they weren't in class. Being in charge of the students was my principal job, as far as I was concerned. Evidently, at different times, I must have griped to the abbot, as he kept telling me to come home any time I wanted to. I said, "No, I am down here for the kids." The other part was secondary. I was there for nine years and I loved it, working with the kids.

What did you do?

I was just in charge of them and I was trying to get their confidence and trust and I was doing it. For example, Saturday afternoon they could go downtown. One kid came home Saturday and came right to me and said, "Andrew, I am drunk," and I said, "Get in my room; we will talk later." When I went back to my room after supper, he is in my bathroom on the floor asleep, and had vomited all over the floor.

But I didn't find him, he came right to me and that is what I was trying to do – build their confidence and trust. I told them, "If you tell me, you won't get punished and we can talk about it. But if I find out and I have come to you, then there will be punishment."

So you were like a surrogate father to them?

Yes. Right before the end of the school year, two students in the fifth year decided one Saturday not to get up for Mass. One of them came in to see me that night about 9 o'clock and I said, "Pedro, I have been waiting for you and Allen to come in all day and justify why you were not up for Mass this morning." "Oh, we were coming in at 10." I said, "Too late, call Allen and let's talk about this."

Then to the two of them, I said, "Okay, look I have been trying to give you independence. I want you to act with freedom and responsibility. Well, evidently you have the freedom but you are not responsible, as you still act like little boys." I said, "Change dormitories, and go to the dormitory for first grade." They didn't like that.

So they said, "How about we don't take any more weekends home and we will work Saturday afternoon?" I said, "You are asking for something worse than I am giving you, but I'm going to accept that." I never saw kids work so well. One of them later told me that, at first, they would just play around, but then they said, "No, the punishment was just," so they would do a good job. I liked working with the kids and, when I left, I wanted to go back.

The reason why I finally left was because they named a Fr. Christopher rector. He was a native and he never liked the way I worked with the kids. He took the rectorship only if I wouldn't be with the students. So I came home.

Guadalupe Center

What did you do when you came home?

Worked with the Guadalupe Center [*a mission to Spanish-speaking people that is affiliated with the Diocese of Evansville*].

Do you work there every day?

No, it depends on what my schedule is. I take people shopping, to the doctor, kids to school and things like that. Yesterday, I had a very busy schedule. I left here at 6 a.m., which is 7 a.m. Eastern time to go to Huntingburg to pick up a lady and take her to the doctor at 8 o'clock in the morning. Then after that, I went to the Guadalupe Center and there were two Mexican men waiting for me to take them to Indianapolis.

So, driving people around is your main job with the center?

Yes. The two Mexicans came on the train – that means they most likely were on a freight train. They needed to be dropped off in the center in Indianapolis. When we got there, I said, "I can drop you off in front of the Mexican Consulate or I can drop you off where there are Hispanic stores." They said the stores.

So I zigzagged up and turned down Washington Street and, sure enough, before long we started seeing Hispanic stores, so I just dropped them off there. I gave them my card and said, "I am not charging you anything, but I expect you to send a donation to the center or to me when you start working." Sometimes they do; most of the time they don't.

Describe the function of the center that you are working in.

They try to do all sorts of programs. They usually have ESL classes—English as a Second Language. They have bilingual classes where they match one to one – one Spanish-speaking to one English-speaking person – and they have some kind of health program. They have three people who are, more or less, fulltime in the center. One of the nuns works with immigration forms and things of that sort.

Are their clients migrant workers or illegals?

Some legal, some illegal. Most of the ones I work with, I bet, are illegal, but I don't know for sure. I don't usually ask. I know some of them. I am mainly a driver and do things like that. I also take the troublemakers, kids that are having troubles or can't learn. I would never have learned Spanish, except I was forced into it. I didn't learn it from studying it.

Are you fluent in Spanish?

As far as talking, I have no problem. I can talk Spanish almost as well as English. Now don't ask me to read or write it. I can understand reading and writing, but I usually do it on my computer and have it translated on the computer and then, more or less, correct the translation.

Some people tell me my letters aren't that bad. I am not an English language person. One time in Peru, I was with Benedict and we were walking down the street. We passed somebody and I said, "Buenos Dias." Benedict said, "Andrew, that was very good," and I said, "Yeah, but how do you say 'Good afternoon'?"

I don't know whether I was that bad, but I did have a hard time in the Spanish class. And when I got the diploma, I tore it up. It was a lie – actually it only said I finished the Spanish course satisfactory. I learned to speak it during my last nine years in Guatemala because I lived it. I very seldom spoke English in Guatemala during those nine years. It was just Fr. John [*not from Saint Meinrad*] and I there, and we were not that good of friends. I bet I didn't speak over 10 or 15 minutes of English a day.

Do you just travel to the Guadalupe Center when you are needed?
Yeah, because they have three people who are, more or less, fulltime in the center. One of the nuns works with immigration, too – with the immigration forms and things of that sort. I enjoy working with the Hispanics. I am quite content with this work.

Prayer

Since Benedictine spirituality is a balance of work and prayer, let's discuss prayer. What is your favorite part of the Rule*?*
I have no favorite part. I saw that question and I said, "I don't know what my favorite part of the *Rule* is." I guess my favorite part is no rule. This part is going to be quick.

That's fine. What is your key to living Benedictine spirituality?
I don't believe I live Benedictine spirituality. I told my sister that once, and I told somebody else, and they both got after me and said, "You are." I guess I am of the old mentality of the lay brethren, like I said earlier – the liturgical life, I don't miss it.
I go when I am home, but if I am not home, I don't miss it. I often think we try to put on a big show here instead of really having a devotional service, although most lay people come in to see the big show. I would like to keep things simple. I think that is why I liked being in South America all the time in small communities. Anything we had was a simple service.

What has been your most difficult time in your life?
Like I said earlier, the most difficult part was when I came home and left the troubled kids back in Peru.

How about your happiest or most enjoyable time in your life?

Well, the most enjoyable for me was working with the youth. I enjoyed working with them a lot. When I was in the parish, one year I wanted to start a summer school and told one young man, I was going to tell the groups I was working with that we are going to have this summer program.

He told me, "Don't you dare. Ask them." Well, I learned you ask them and they would do anything. If you tell them, they would do nothing. So I enjoyed working with the youth and seeing them in action in Guatemala. I was gaining the trust of the kids and I think that was one of the best things I did.

I had one student come back one weekend from going home and he was all down and out and sad and he said, "I told my mother I wanted to kill myself and she said, 'You are crazy, go outside and play football.'" So he sat down and talked to me. I don't believe he wanted to kill himself, but we talked and at the end of the school year he came to me and said, "Andrew, thanks for listening to me when my mother wouldn't listen to me." It was things like this that I found joyful.

Joyful in religious life – I don't know. I did learn to put my trust in the Lord and, since that time, things have gone good. I have been in seventh heaven since then, just letting Him carry the ball and say, "Yes," whether I wanted to or not. I was very slow at learning to let go and trust in the Lord. It took me about 30 years, but now that I have learned, I am very happy.

From your experience, as a monk, what would you want to pass on to younger confreres? Some words of wisdom?

You have to lose your own self-will. The young people sometimes say they want to come here because they like the music, buildings or grounds. I just wonder if they are going to stay. I just came. I had no reason to come, no reason to stay. It just felt normal to me. But to say you are coming because you like the music or the grounds, I think that is all wrong. Their reasons for coming here must be deeper.

I often wonder if we are asking them enough nowadays. I think we make life too easy for them. I know when I was young I think we liked to do things hard. We were willing to give up things. I remember reading not too long ago that young monks look like saints and run around in their habits and look so holy, but the older monks look like devils and they are saints and really holy. We go through stages. I guess as you go through life you just see things from a different way.

My chapel is my easy chair in my room. I sit back, relax and just enjoy myself, not necessarily doing anything. I used to go to church and pray a lot, but now I do my prayer in my room – that is my chapel. So I guess we evolve. Maybe we need the first fervor to carry us through to get to the second stage. I don't know.

Changes in the Church

There have been a lot of changes in the contemporary Church, particularly with Pope John XXIII and the Vatican II Council. What has this meant to the monastery and the Church?

Well, definitely changes, drastic changes. I can't say whether for the better or the worse.

What are some changes you have observed in the monastery and the Church?

I guess we have more freedom but, of course, that is good if you use it right. But I'm wondering when we are young – are we ready to have all that freedom? Then I just don't understand why the juniors take a trip down to Gethsemane [*Trappist monastery in Kentucky*] a couple of times a year. Is that forming them for our community? I can't figure it out.

So you see this as a change then?

Yeah, and I don't know if it is for the good or not. I think they should have to stay home and live this life to see whether or not they want to stay here. As far as changes in the Church itself, like switching to English, I wouldn't want to go back for anything. I don't think that anything John did was wrong. I think the Church was too closed.

However, I wish Pope John would have pushed for more things and opened it up more. I am not even against women getting ordained, but I think priests should be allowed to be married first. I suspect that would be the first stage and I have no problem with it. What did women do in the town where Jesus lived back then? Their only occupation was a family or a prostitute, but that doesn't exist here anymore.

Jesus was working with a strictly male society, but society is not that way anymore – but try to tell those people in Rome. I don't agree with a lot of stuff in the Church. That is why it is good I am not a priest. I would be excommunicated within minutes!

What else did you see from Vatican II?

I think people now take charge of the parishes much more than they used to. Before, the priest was the boss. I think the people have a lot to offer and, when I was working in Peru in the parish, we couldn't have worked without the people. They did everything.

Have you seen that change here?

I don't know about up here. So much of the work was voluntary work down there. Up here everybody wants to get paid. We could never have run the parish without help, and the help was all voluntary down there. I remember talking to one of the young priests when he was at St. Benedict's [*a parish in Evansville*]. He was at a youth group and asked the group about something they wanted to do for the community. The first thing they wanted to know was how much they were going to get paid. There is no sense of service or volunteering.

One time, with Br. Placid [*McIver*], we visited a lot of the Mormon shrines from New York to Nauvoo in Illinois. We stopped at different places and at Nauvoo they almost have a city. They said one person is paid and the rest are volunteers. I like the Mormons' spirit in the sense that they volunteer. I found out that when they go on missions, the youth pay their own expenses for two years. We don't have Catholics wanting to do that.

So you would like to see more volunteers among Catholics?

Oh, I would. I would love to see churches send youth to [*Third World countries*] so they could get experience with what the rest of the world was like.

Have declining vocations had an impact on the Church and on the monastic community?

The Church, I think, has turned a lot over to lay people out of necessity. I know these little parishes around here used to have two and three priests. They're getting along with only one priest now. Maybe it is better that we most likely are becoming more like a Protestant-style church. I suspect the Protestant churches always had the involvement of lay people. In a lot of the churches, the lay people hire and fire the pastor. Maybe we should start doing that in the Catholic Church. The priests would have to wake up, but I don't know.

Even though the Mass is now celebrated in English, was eliminating Latin from the academic curriculum a good idea?

The only thing I could think that it would be good for would be a common language. But since we have such instant translations, I don't think it even plays an important role there, anymore.

Striking changes have been made in the liturgy and in parish organization since the days of the Council. Do you see this as positive or negative?

Well, I think it is for the better, although it seems like now the Pope [*Benedict XVI*] is trying to close the door and going backwards again. In my opinion, the more open and the more freedom the Church has, the better. It is like Obama [*Barack, U.S. president*] saying, "Let's keep things open and not hide things." I think that is good for the Church. We are not saints; we are humans.

That leads right into the next question. What has been lost or been gained in the last 40 or 50 years in the Church?

Well, what has been lost for the Church is they can't get by with whatever they want to. The lay people are starting to yell. I guess we are starting to think for ourselves, and I think some of the priests were in back of those things. One of the things, I think, would be birth control. I know nuns down in Peru said, "I would give birth control pills to ladies any day, because half the time they don't have a choice." The way I look at it, what would Jesus do? In his day, you didn't need birth control – they didn't live long.

We keep dead people alive nowadays. There is a little Hispanic kid who should be dead. They knew he was going to be born defective and he is now living off machines. He is 2 or 3 years old and can't eat and they have to feed him through a tube. He should not have lived. We keep people living that should be dead. So I don't know. I think these things have to be refigured – are they doing it?

I am not even sure about divorces. They are so common and it seems like people are happier in their second marriages. There is a man who comes to church frequently and he can't go to communion because he is divorced and remarried. What does that say to the family? Maybe it would be better for the children if the family is united. That is a Church problem.

We are living in such a different society. When Jesus caught the woman in adultery, the town was going to stone her to death. He forgave her and told her not to sin anymore. My Jesus is not the same Jesus the Church is seeing sometimes. I think he is understandable and loving and can understand human problems. I am not a priest and I am not a theologian. I have my personal opinions, and they are not approved by the Church. Nor is it likely to happen.

What are your hopes for the future for the Archabbey and the Church? And where do you think the Church and monastery are heading?
I can't distinguish the two. The Church is part of the monastery and the monastery is part of the Church. Where are we headed? That is the $64,000 question. Whether we are heading right or not, I don't know. I think the program Saint Meinrad is running, "One Bread, One Cup," for youth, is the right direction. I think the more that we can influence younger people, not necessarily seminarians, is the best way. The Church is the people and whatever you do in that line is good.

Is there anything else you would like to say?
The only thing I can say is that, at present, I am completely happy.

Profile based upon: Br. Andrew Zimmermann, OSB, to Prof. Ruth C. Engs, June 30, 2009, Interview Transcriptions, Saint Meinrad Archabbey Archives, St. Meinrad, IN; additional comments by Br. Andrew, August 26, 2015.

Chapter 6: Fr. Stephen Snoich, OSB

Fr. Stephen, an expert builder, first became a brother and later a priest. He was noted for his construction of guest houses at both Saint Meinrad and Prince of Peace Abbey in California. He served as supervisor of the monastery buildings and manager of the campus laundry in addition to pastoral duties.

After his ordination, he was associate pastor of St. Benedict Church, Evansville, IN; chaplain at Monastery Immaculate Conception, Ferdinand, IN; and pastor of St. Augusta Parish, Lake Village, IN, until a few months before his death.

Born in Shenandoah, PA, on June 24, 1929, Fr. Stephen was given the name John Joseph. He attended school at Roosevelt Elementary and J.W. Cooper High School, where he graduated in 1947. He studied for one year at St. Joseph College in Philadelphia. He then worked in construction, qualified as a journeyman carpenter, and worked in the Philadelphia area for 10 years.

In 1956, Fr. Stephen entered the novitiate at Saint Meinrad and professed his vows as a brother on April 7, 1957. His first major project was overseeing construction of the St. Jude Guest House – the "old" guest house. In 1962, Fr. Stephen was assigned to Saint Meinrad's new foundation, St. Charles Priory, Oceanside, CA (now Prince of Peace Abbey), where he supervised the construction of their guest house. In 1970, he returned to Saint Meinrad.

After returning, he completed his college courses, began studies for the priesthood and was ordained March 12, 1972. He received a Master of Divinity degree from Saint Meinrad Seminary in 1973.

Fr. Stephen was associate pastor at St. Benedict Church, Evansville, (1977-93); chaplain at Monastery Immaculate Conception, Ferdinand, IN (1993-2004); and in 2004 was assigned as pastor of St. Augusta Parish, Lake Village, IN, until early October 2012 when failing health necessitated his return to the monastery infirmary, where he died three months later on January 6, 2013.

Prof. Ruth C. Engs interviewed Fr. Steven Snoich on July 29, 2009.

Childhood and Early Years as a Monk

Tell me a bit about your childhood, your family life and what kind of job your father did.

I was born on the Feast of John the Baptist on June 24, 1929, in Shenandoah, PA. My father wanted his first son to be named Stephen, but my mother insisted on John, as I was born on the feast day of St. John. My parents were both Catholics and I was of Lithuanian ancestry. I was the oldest of three children.

Mother was a seamstress prior to marriage and, after children were born, she retired from working in a dress garment factory – the Spount Garment Factory – to take care of her children. Daddy was a coal miner working in the deep mines of Maple Hill Coal Colliery, a coal mine owned and operated by Philadelphia and Reading Coal and Iron Company.

My town of Shenandoah sits over one of the richest veins of anthracite coal deposits in the country. There were deep mine pits very close to the town limits and numerous tunnels by the miners were dug beneath the town in order to remove the coal. These tunnels eventually collapsed and damaged structures. Several churches, schools and businesses were condemned when I was growing up.

The Depression years of the early '30s found many coal miners out of work and only worked one, possibly two days, in any two-week pay period. It was very difficult, but we survived. My parents did without the luxuries of life. They skimped, scraped and saved every penny so they could send my two sisters and me to college for an education, which they did not have.

How about your schooling?

Growing up, I went to the Roosevelt School, which was the new grade school – elementary school – at the time. I went to high school at the J.W. Cooper High School after it was remodeled to make it structurally safe after the tunnels collapsed. These schools were public schools. The only participation in Catholic school was religious education in those days.

They did not have a release time at school, so we had to go to summer classes in order to receive religious education on the sacraments. So my sisters and I went to summer classes. It was probably about five weeks in the summertime to receive my First Communion and then Confirmation was later.

How old were you then?

I was about 9 years old, and it was rather interesting because the pastor at that time would not allow us to receive our First Communion with the Catholic school children because we went to the non-Catholic school. So the Catholic school children received their First Communion in August, I believe it was August the 15th, and we public school children received our First Communion in September. I don't want to say it was a penance but, nevertheless, it was at a later date.

The pastor came around twice a year to visit the families, for a census-taking in the summertime and a fuel collection in the wintertime. Every time he came to our house, he would ask, or tell, my mother, "I want you to send your children to Lithuanian school." My mother said, "Well, Father, if you would pay their tuition, I would be happy to send them to the school." The father never came through with the tuition, so we continued on in public school.

Another reason we didn't want to go to the Lithuanian school was it was at least 15 blocks away from our home, and there was no way our mother could see us walking through the streets that distance in the wintertime. Public school was just a block away, so that was another reason we went to public school. So I was educated from grade school right through high school in a public school system and graduated in 1947.

Tell me some more about your religious life as a child.

My parents' Catholic faith was a top priority in their lives and the day began with praying a litany of one of the saints. They were members of St. George Lithuanian Church. The church was about 10 blocks away from our home on Emerick Street, and in a coal mining town there are a lot of hills and valleys that you walked through, although the streets were paved.

While we were still infants, one of my parents stayed home with us so the other could attend church. Mother stayed at home with us children while Dad went to early Mass and when Dad came back, Mother went to church. We all walked when we were older. We had no car; we walked to church for the 7 a.m. Mass. Mother and Dad were very good Catholics and made sure we went to church every Sunday, rain or shine, winter or summer.

Were you an altar boy?

No, never an altar boy. When I came to the monastery, we served the priests, but I was never an altar boy.

Did you have a job as a youngster?

During my school and high school years, it was at the beginning and during the Second World War. All the young men in their late teens and early 20s were drafted. Joseph Zanecosky owned and operated a local grocery and butcher shop. He asked me if I would be willing to be a delivery boy. I was about 10 or 11 years old at the time and he said he would like me to deliver orders for him.

So I did, and in addition I stocked the shelves every day and cleaned the store after school. If I recall, my first payment was a bag of fruit, working all week for a bag of fruit. Then eventually he saw that I was doing a good job, so he gave me a dollar a week for delivery and working all day, Friday night and Saturday.

Now this man was the majority owner of a packing plant where they slaughtered hogs, and he had as much meat as he could use. In fact, other butchers from the town during the wartime came to him to get the meat for their own use. So I worked from Friday after school making orders up – our showcase was stacked with orders.

People would order a week ahead of time if they had company coming. This butcher told me, "Now I want you to watch me cut meat because you are going to be a butcher someday," and I was only about 10 years old at that time. It was on-the-job training to become a butcher, and I was able to cut meat to his satisfaction.

Did you do this all through upper elementary school and high school?

Yes, all through high school I was working in the butcher shop. Actually, it was good training for me to be with people. I not only spoke with people, but with the Lithuanian language. They were mostly Lithuanian and Polish customers, so I had to learn both languages.

Tell me something more about your neighborhood.

I grew up in an environment where the neighbors were all Lithuanian and all coal miners. Everyone had a yard in the back of the house. They were row homes and company homes built by the Reading Coal and Iron Company way back in the 1880s. So we lived in an old home that was built about 1880.

The miners built a community brick bake oven in one of the neighbor's back yards. The oven was rather large. It was about eight feet wide, six feet high and anywhere from 10 to 12 feet deep. An opening at the bottom of the oven allowed one of the neighbors to start a fire Friday night or early Saturday morning; Saturday morning was bread baking day. Every family in the neighborhood baked either bread or rolls. People would stack their bread and buns on both sides of this oven for baking.

We kids at an early age – before I worked in the butcher shop – called ourselves the Emerick Street Gang. We 5-, 6-, 7-year-old kids were the first ones to reach that oven Saturday morning. When the first loaf of bread came out, the ladies would put the loaf on a shelf that was built right outside the oven, along with a knife and a bowl of homemade butter.

The homemade bread was still warm and we were the first ones to test the bread. This was our early Saturday morning treat before our free day began. In the afternoon, we attended the local Strand Movie Theater, where a movie was being shown of one of our cowboy heroes and a continuation of the weekly serial. The movie was over early enough to go to confession.

Our mother was stern in telling us to make sure we went to church and go to confession every Saturday. It was very interesting that the mothers made sure us kids got to confession Saturday afternoon and, "Yes, Mom, I will get to confession," and all of us said the same thing. So Saturday was a busy day for us kids.

Did you have other recreation as a child?

It was interesting growing up in that environment. Everyone was Catholic, mind you, and we had a full Saturday of playing games, such as baseball in the summer or just getting away. We walked through the hills – coal banks – to walk up into the mountains. During the fall, football was the game of the day. The cold winter months brought on winter sports, ice skating and skiing.

The Shenandoah Volunteer Firemen flooded our baseball field with water from a fireplug that was located a short distance from our baseball field so we could ice skate and play ice hockey. Our skis were made from barrel staves that were curved up and a strip of leather held our shoes in place on the ski. The bottom of the barrel stave was rubbed with wax for speed. We did a lot of skiing on the coal bank hills surrounding the town.

Back in your hometown, what kind of health care did you have back in the early '30s?

The miners had some type of hospitalization if they got injured, but there was nothing to my knowledge for our family. When we were born, I don't have any idea how that cost was covered. Neither Mother, nor us three children, were ever sick enough to enter a hospital. My daddy was injured several times, but never had to go to a hospital for it.

The coal either scraped you or you got cut by falling lumps of coal. I know many times Mother would patch up areas on his back or legs where he was injured by some tools or machinery or something, but he never had to go to the hospital. So as far as health care, I've no knowledge of what type of system they had in those days.

When you were in high school, did you smoke or drink?

No, never smoked or drank, even though Dad made homemade wine. He never gave it to us kids unless we had a cold;

then it was for medicinal purposes. That is the only time we had it. It was elderberry wine and it had to be heated. No, we never partook of any wine during our early years, but Dad was a winemaker. He also made root beer, and we kids enjoyed root beer along with my mother.

What did you do after high school?

After leaving high school, I went to Philadelphia with the intention of getting a college education. There was a neighbor who went to St. Joe's College [*Saint Joseph*] in Philadelphia, a Jesuit training college. Since he was there and I knew him rather well, I told my parents I would like to go to St. Joe's College.

Now my parents were not wealthy in any way whatsoever, but they lived very scrupulously and were frugal. They saved to educate their three children in something they did not have. My sisters studied nursing and graduated from St. Mary's School of Nursing in Philadelphia with registered nursing degrees.

When I went to St. Joe's College, I had to find a place to stay. During my college days and many years later, I lived with a family who had placed their name with St. Joseph's College seeking students as roomers. My dad and I rode the train to Philadelphia – we had no car – and then rode a bus from here to there to look for a place for me to stay.

We went to two houses and my dad was not satisfied with either one. And we went to the third house and a young mother, a little girl about 4 years old, and an elderly woman came to the door. As soon as I arrived at the door, the little girl hugged me by the leg. The young widow's name was Mrs. Emilie Hagerty and her daughter's name was Judy. Her daddy had just died a year before, so she just took to me right away.

My daddy immediately said, "You are going to stay here." As time moved on, Emilie married Charles Murphy, and they were blessed with three more children. I had a very close relationship with the Murphy family. Emilie's husband Charles, "Murph," and I were close; he was the brother I never had.

Much of my young adult life was guided by the Murphy family and they were an important factor in my persevering in the monastic life. So it was a lifelong relationship that I had with this family that lasted 60 years.

Emilie worked as a bookkeeper for the neighboring Samango Concrete Construction Co. Now I had Saturday and an afternoon free. So I worked for this construction company. I had the opportunity to learn about concrete work – concrete sidewalks, steps, driveways, foundations. I also received my first taste of the carpentry trade and construction work. When school ended, I worked full time with this company.

You see, after the second semester at St. Joseph's College in 1948, I found out how much it cost my parents financially for my first year of school. I couldn't believe how much it was and I had three more years to go and my second sister also wanted to go into nurse's training.

For the three of us, it would have drained every cent my parents had saved. So right then and there, I decided I was not going back to school, but was going to work. So I told my parents and they were both very upset that I decided to stay on with the Samango Construction Company and not go back to college.

Toward the end of the summer, the boss offered me a position as a foreman of a large project for 96 homes. Now you have to realize I was just in my early 20s – just a kid – and I had a lot of laborers working for me. These men were all black Americans and were wonderful men, but they were tough men, and each had a knife attached to his leg.

But they respected me because I worked with them. Even though I was the foreman, I went down into the foundation and worked right alongside them. I showed them how to do the work and I showed them if I could do it, they could do it.

How long did you do this?

Well, maybe a year and a half. I finished this job of 96 homes and then I had an opportunity to join an apprenticeship in the carpentry trade, so I took advantage of that. But the boss at Samango was upset, as he wanted me to stay. I worked as an apprentice for John McShain, the largest contractor in Philadelphia.

I completed my apprenticeship carpentry program and became a journeyman carpenter. In a very short time, I became foreman on the Temple University construction job site in north Philadelphia. I held this foreman position until I entered Saint Meinrad monastery. So I worked with John McShain as an apprentice for four years and two years as a journeyman.

How did you get from construction to Saint Meinrad to become a monk and a priest?

While working in Philadelphia, one day at confession in my parish church, St. Callistus, the priest asked me if a vocation had ever crossed my mind. I said, "I don't want to be a priest. I am dating a girl, I love my carpentry trade very much and there is no way I am going to be a priest!"

He said, "There are vocations other than the priesthood. Marriage is also a beautiful vocation, but you must pray for a vocation." And that kind of put, should I say, a bug in my ear. After this, I prayed asking God to help me decide my future.

Shortly after I gained my journeymanship, and when I was foreman at the Temple University site, the superintendent thought we should take some time off, as it was winter and work was slow. So I visited my uncle in St. Mary's, Kentucky, where he was a layman professor in the minor seminary – St. Mary's [*College*].

He took me to Gethsemane, which is a Trappist monastery. The monks were working on a building project and were thoroughly enjoying themselves. I told my uncle, "They are doing the same work as I am and look how happy they are up there." It was not the dog-eat-dog life I was working.

My uncle knew some of the monks at Saint Meinrad and, sensing that I might be interested in a vocation, he wrote them – this was 1954. Fr. Claude [*Ehringer*], who was the novice master, invited me to visit Saint Meinrad. I drove to Saint Meinrad and it was love at first sight. I stayed about a week and returned to Philadelphia to my carpentry job. After some difficult decision-making, I asked to be admitted into the Benedictine community.

I told the superintendent at my job about my intentions to join the monastery and he was very upset, as they were grooming me for a superintendent's job. However, Mr. McShain, the president of the company who was Catholic, had some idea of religious life and said, "If you don't persevere, your job is always waiting for you," and I thanked him and began as a candidate here September 8, 1955.

How did your family feel about you coming to Saint Meinrad?

My sisters and my mother felt as long as I was happy with what I was doing, it was fine. My uncles were upset with it, because I wasn't carrying on the Snoich name. In fact, one apparently disowned me. I never got any feelings either way from my father.

Fr. Stephen, as a young monk

Describe something about your early years in the monastery.

When I arrived in September 1955, Fr. Claude said, "I will take your toolbox," which I had brought with me. I said, "Take it? That's my life in that toolbox. That's my bread and butter." And he said, "Well, you won't need it anytime soon." That is just the way it was in those days. So I entered with that attitude, I guess, of, "Well, okay."

In April 1956, three of us worldly men entered the novitiate and a year later, on April 7, 1957, the three of us professed our simple vows and received our new religious name – Br. Leo [*Sinkula*], Br. Daniel [*Linskens*] and myself, Br. Stephen.

Brs. Leo and Daniel have since reached their earthly goal. They were truly wonderful examples of what it takes to convert from the worldly ways of life to the monastic way of life. My parents and sister, Anna, were present during my profession of simple vows.

While professing my vows – there was no microphone in those days – I read my new name loud and clear, so my dad could hear me. My mother and sister said Dad's face just glowed as he finally had a son named Stephen. Dad said, "God is good!"

How about recreation as a younger monk?

The different jobs that I did were sort of a priority over extracurricular activities. But I did not avoid recreation. When I was supervising the building of the guest house, I would be playing cards – bridge – with the brothers. And Fr. Marcellus [*Fisher*], who was the first manager in the guest house, would come to our recreation room and say to me, "Here you are recreating and I am worried about the guest house. Here you are laughing and joking."

I said, "Fr. Marcellus, when I am on the job, it is my job to worry about the guest house construction. It is always on my mind. But when I am recreating, I am recreating. When I am praying, I am praying. And when I am working, I am working. It will be finished. Don't worry about it."

Do you have another amusing story from your early years?

When we were first digging the foundation for the guest house here at the abbey in 1957, there was a golf course there. Fr. Michael [*Keene*] got so upset with me, because I was taking his golf course away for the guest house. I told him talk to the abbot. Fr. Michael wouldn't speak to me for months because I excavated his golf course.

Work

As I mentioned, Fr. Claude had taken away my toolbox when I arrived as a candidate. It wasn't long, just a couple of weeks after I had been there, that the carpenter shop had an order for 50 eight-foot-length solid oak dining room tables for a community of sisters. Br. Rembert [*Ringler*], an old German brother, and Br. Lawrence [*Shidler*] and Br. Samuel were in the carpenter shop.

Br. Samuel got sick and they needed a third person to handle these tables, so Fr. Claude immediately said, "I want you to go to the carpenter shop and help the brothers up there make these tables." So there I was in the carpenter's shop – that was my love – so I fell in with the carpenter shop. It had nothing to do with my tools, but it was rather interesting.

The archabbot would ask me from time to time how I was doing and that he understood I was a carpenter construction foreman. About three or four months after I had been there as a candidate, the archabbot called me into his office and said, "There were problems with the water filter system and if we don't do something with it, we are going to have to close the place down."

The archabbot asked me if I could supervise the building of an up-to-date filter plant. I said, "I probably could build the plant if I had a set of blueprints." He opened his desk drawer and pulled out one piece of paper and said, "Here it is." I said, "Where are the rest of the blueprints?" He said, "That's all I have."

This one piece of paper had the floor plan for all the filtering equipment, pumps, chemical vats and the huge tanks that filtered the water. I told the archabbot, "This is only the floor plan. I would have to design the building around this floor plan." He said, "Can you do it?" "Probably" was my response.

Now the novice master insisted that I was not to miss any of the novice instruction or work, such as cleaning the restrooms and floors, like the rest of the candidates and novices. Several times when I had to pour concrete, I had to be on the job at 4 a.m. to wait for the concrete truck to arrive so I could have the pouring of concrete finished in time for novice instruction at 11 a.m.

It was also very important to me that I keep my prayer life a priority, along with daily Mass and receiving the Holy Eucharist prior to my work day. Three local men did much of the work on the building, but they could not read a blueprint. However, they were willing to do just about any job with some supervision.

It was at this time that I was introduced to a dragline, which is a machine used in strip mining that removes topsoil from an area. The monastery had purchased this dragline knowing that building projects were being discussed for the future; however, they did not have a monk who knew how to operate it. Now I had to get the basement dug for the filter plant and the dragline was here, but there was no operator for it.

So Fr. John Thuis, who was more or less in charge of maintenance and of physical plant, but knew nothing about construction or heavy equipment, said, "Well, it is there, and you have to learn how to operate it." So it was for me a self-taught, on-the-job training to operate that dragline. Later, by the time I did the excavation on the guest house, I was pretty good at it.

Work continued during the winter months and the building for the new filter plant was almost finished, even before the end of my novitiate. The archabbot called me into his office and said, "Novice

John, have you seen the sign in front of the church?" I said. "Yes, it says, 'The monks are going build a guest house.'"

He replied, "You think you can build a guest house with the monks helping?" I asked, "How many of the monks are skilled in any of the trades?" The archabbot said, "Not any, but you could teach them." I said, "Well, again, if I had blueprints, I guess I could."

The archabbot went to a table on the other side of his office and unrolled a set of blueprints, which consisted of only five pieces of paper. I said, "Fr. Abbot, this is really not enough to build a guest house. There are no details on it at all; it's just pictures." He said, "Well, that is all they gave me." I told him a much more detailed set of prints is necessary.

The archabbot then called the architect and asked for a more detailed set of prints. The architect told him, "Well, you tell that brother if he considers himself a construction man, he can build the guest house on what blueprints you have, because his men will construct a building on what you have in your possession."

I was still in the novitiate and the archabbot said, "Kneel down, Novice John, and I will give you a special blessing for a successful completion of our new guest house." So I went ahead, but I had to do all the details myself.

When did you start?

We broke ground March 15, 1957, when I was still a novice; I was the superintendent of the construction. As a novice today, do you think novices do that? No, no way would they give a novice that responsibility. But I guess God provided. April 7, 1957, was when I made first vows and got my name Br. Stephen.

Once I surveyed the area for the new guest house, I began excavating the basement. The footings were the basis for the guest house foundation. The archabbot told me that he wanted the fraters – monks who were in the seminary studying for the priesthood – to help. It was the end of the school year and they were free from classes in the summer.

He said, "I want them to work. I want to see them sweat." I said, "Well, Fr. Abbot, they are really not much use to me, as they don't know the difference between a hammer and a hatchet." He said, "Well, you can train them." The archabbot sent me 16 fraters to work on the guest house and they did a fine job in digging the footings, as well as pouring the concrete into the trenches, which were to be the base for the foundation walls.

The archabbot came around the job site very often and remarked many times, "See, I told you they could learn if you would teach them." But I would show the fraters what to do and I would constantly be on the move watching them so that they would not mess up. There were also three laymen from the town who were working for me.

During building of the guest house, many times I would be approached by one of the department heads saying that they needed maintenance done in their department. It would be some emergency thing, so I had to leave the guest house. If the maintenance was bigger than I could handle, I had to take one of the laymen to help me do it.

Now, all the monks working on the guest house talked about their week at camp [*Camp Benedict*], which was the only time the monks had some time away from the monastery. So I asked the archabbot if it was OK for me to plan a week at camp. He said, "Absolutely not. Your responsibility is with your men supervising their work on the guest house."

His answer was somewhat disappointing. So I was thinking ahead. If I planned to pour concrete for the entire west wall of the basement of the guest house, once the wall was poured, the wood panels had to be removed before another wall could be erected.

The fraters had removed wood panels on a previous poured concrete wall, so they knew the procedure very well of removing panels. The monks approached the archabbot and told him they knew exactly what to do and that Br. Stephen should have his week at camp. The archabbot was somewhat reluctant, but agreed. So off I went to camp.

Work progressed at a good pace considering the non-skilled help I had and, three years later, 1960, the time was getting close for our class to profess solemn vows. This should have been April the 7th of 1960. In February or March, I said to the abbot, "Fr. Abbot, our final vows are coming up." He said, "Well, your guest house isn't finished and you can't take an eight-day retreat to prepare yourself for vows."

He said, "Do you have a date for it to be finished?" I said, "I can't give a date yet." So the archabbot said, "I am going to extend your vows." So Br. Leo and Br. Daniel and I – all three of us – extended our vows. In July, I told the archabbot, "We are just about finished and are ready for occupancy at the guest house." So he made an inspection and said, "Okay, you can make your retreat and make your final vows on July the 16th, the feast of Our Lady of Mount Carmel." Our families were the first occupants of the guest house in 1960.

After the guest house was completed and you said your final vows, then what did you do?

On several occasions, I requested permission from the archabbot to enter the seminary and study for the priesthood. He always told me, "Pray and God's will be done." He went on to say, "Br. Stephen, your work is more important to the community than being in the classroom. You can be a priest the rest of your life, but this work has to be done first." Then he would give me a project that someone requested or another set of blueprints.

So for two years after the guest house was finished, I did a lot of maintenance here on the hill, as there was a lot of work to be done. It was at this time that the monk in charge of the stone quarry asked me to remove some topsoil at the quarry, so the men could begin quarrying the sandstone for commercial use.[1] The dragline was moved to the stone quarry and about two acres of topsoil to the depth of 20 to 30 feet began. Abbey Press had a lot of maintenance, so I did maintenance from 1960 to '62.

In the summer of 1962, I went to camp and the abbot came out and said, "I want you to go to California and build a guest house at our daughter house, St. Charles Priory" [*now Prince of Peace Abbey*]. I said, "Well, okay."

I went out there in July, and again there was only one piece of paper to build a guest house, one piece of paper. I had to do much of the designing and detail work for the building. Two young brothers and I were the only ones working on this guest house. I also had to design the atrium for it, and they wanted a tree indoors in the center of that atrium.

They had no idea what that is going to involve, so I told them, "No." They called up the abbot and the abbot said, "Whatever Br. Stephen says, you better do it." So anyhow, we didn't have the tree in the center, but I designed the atrium.

One day when I was working in the foundation of the guest house, a lady came by and we chatted for a while. Some months ago, to my surprise, I received a letter from a lawyer in California and was named in her will. It amounted to several hundred thousand dollars and a gold ring.

The old farmhouse across the road from the guest house here was torn down and the money was used to build a new three-bedroom house over there. This house, called Ravens house, is used by monks for their visiting families and also for their private retreats or vacations. It was blessed last month [*November 1, 2012*].

---

[1] For more information on the stone quarry see: Engs, Ruth C. *Conversations in the Abbey* (2008), 354-358.

One day soon after I was there, a Navy doctor came out to the priory and he saw me dragging my leg and said, "What is it with you, Br. Stephen?" I said, "I don't know, Doc." He found I had no feeling in the leg. So he told Fr. Rudolph [*Siedling*], who was the prior out there, "This is very serious."

So, I was sent to Mercy Hospital in San Diego. I had a myelogram right away, which found I had two ruptured discs. So they operated, fused my back and put me in a body cast to immobilize the back when they found out what kind of work I did. The cast was from my hips all the way to my armpits.

I came back to the job site and walked around with this big body cast. I looked like a sumo wrestler. I went to the job site every day and was trying to supervise people who knew nothing about construction. The superior called the archabbot and told him the situation. I received a call from him telling me that I had to be away from the job for a while. So I spent several weeks with my parents, as well as the Murphy family, who were now in New Jersey. The body cast had to be on for six months.

One day I received a call from the archabbot telling me that no work was being done at the guest house in California and that I should plan to return and do no more than supervise. After six months, the body cast came off, but I had to wear a body brace for a year. Two years later, with minimal help, the guest house was finally finished.

When the archabbot arrived for his final inspection of the new guest house, once again I asked him if I could return to Saint Meinrad and begin studying for the priesthood. This time he approved, with the condition that I study for St. Charles Priory. That hurt me very, very much. Saint Meinrad is my home. My heart was broken when this condition was made to study for St. Charles Priory, because my heart and soul were here on the holy Hill.

However, that was the way it was back then. When a brother wanted to study for the priesthood, they immediately moved him out to another monastery. When I came back here, it was very tough, as I was a traitor to the brothers and they let me know it. I was the first one to come back home to study for the priesthood.

So this practice has now changed?

Oh yes, that has changed; it's drastically changed. Now you are entering as a monk and there is no separation anymore between brothers, fraters and priests. Back then, brothers had their own recreation room, fraters had their own recreation room, and everything was separated in those days. You were not even allowed to communicate with each other unless it had to do with your work or on special feast days.

So then what happened after you were told you could come back here to study?

As soon as the abbot told me of the condition, I prayed and told myself no matter what it took to reach my goal – ordination – I would pray for perseverance. The next four years of studies were difficult, because I was returning to school after being away from the classroom for 18 years. I worked very hard at my studies. Graduation from college came four years later and then it was on to theology at Saint Meinrad.

Did you ever do any other construction work?

Yes, in 1969 when I graduated from college, I was approached by the archabbot about supervising renovation on the Archabbey Church. This was the summer between semesters and I was looking forward to my beginning theology program. The good Lord works in mysterious ways. Fortunately, I was able to remove everything from the church that could be removed and prepare the nave of the church for the pouring of concrete for a new floor. The age-old choir stalls were removed.

The high altar, weighing over two tons, was the last relic to be removed from the sanctuary. It was separated piece by piece and transported to what was later named St. Joseph's Oratory in the crypt. A later phase of renovation was a major change to the interior of the church. This was contracted to a local engineering/construction company, and I had little to say or do in this project.

Describe your years leading up to ordination.
I did not rock the boat for fear they would say, "You have go to another seminary." I wanted to stay here, so I didn't say one word. I was studying for St. Charles Priory all this time. Right before I was being ordained as a deacon and to make solemn vows – which fraters made back then – Fr. Adrian [*Fuerst*], who was the rector of seminary, approached me.

He said. "Br. Stephen, I know you are not happy with St. Charles Priory. This is your home here, so why are you studying for St. Charles?" I said, "In order to go to seminary here, the condition was that I had to study for St. Charles Priory." He looked at me and was shocked.

Less than an hour later, I got word from the archabbot – the successor to the former one – that he wanted to see me right away. Now when Adrian left me, I guess he went right to the abbot and told him the situation. The abbot said, "What is this I hear about you studying for St. Charles Priory?" I said, "The only way I could go into the priesthood and study here was to study for St. Charles Priory." He said, "Well, what do you want?" I said, "What I want is to study for Saint Meinrad Archabbey." He said, "Foolishness." That was his famous word, "foolishness."

So the abbot gets on the telephone and calls Fr. Claude, who was the prior out there at the time, and said, "I have someone here who wants to say something to you." I said to the prior, "I want to study for Saint Meinrad, not St. Charles Priory." He said, "If that is what you want, it is okay with me."

The abbot then said, "Okay, you're a member of Saint Meinrad Archabbey now." I thought to myself, "I suffered for eight years." I was the first brother from Saint Meinrad to study for the priesthood here and to stay here. After that, other brothers studied for the priesthood here, including Fr. Pius [*Klein*] and Fr. Meinrad's [*Brune*][2] brother, Fr. Theodore, who has reached his heavenly goal.

So what happened after that?
I was ordained a deacon and made solemn vows to Saint Meinrad Archabbey, and on March 12, 1972, I was ordained a priest. Upon ordination, I was assigned as a supply priest helping pastors in local parishes on weekends. I was in charge of the monastery laundry plant for five years after ordination. I also had the responsibility as house prefect in charge of maintenance in the monastery. In 1973, I finished a Master of Divinity degree from Saint Meinrad Seminary [*now Saint Meinrad Seminary and School of Theology*].

Then after about five years, Abbot Timothy [*Sweeney*], in 1977, asked me to go to St. Benedict's Church in Evansville and I said, "Fr. Abbot, I made my vows to Saint Meinrad; I really don't feel like I want to go into parish work." He said, "Father, you also made your vow of obedience and I want you to go." I said, "Well, okay." Obedience is a powerful thing, so I went and I loved it. I loved the parish work!

I spent 17 years as an associate pastor working with Fr. Camillus [*Ellspermann*] as my pastor and they were truly wonderful years. We were a good team. We had a number of other monks helping us out from time to time in the training program. We had a school there and a variety of activities were going on continuously, so it was a very active parish.

---

[2] Fr. Pius' and Fr. Meinrad's bios are also in this book.

But you know I did not have one moment to myself there. The office was in the rectory and, when that happens, you don't have any time to yourself at all. I was busy from the time I got up in the morning for first Mass at 7:00 until I put my head on a pillow at night. Counseling was a continuous thing from after Mass until evening.

In 1980, I had a massive heart attack. I was in the hospital and the doctor said, "Do you know how this heart attack came about?" I said, "Well, you know it shocked me. I was doing physical work all my life, heavy work, and here I have a job behind a desk and I get a heart attack." He said, "That is only part of it; the main thing is the stress you are under." I said, "You must be kidding."

He said, "No, you probably have a lot of counseling." And I said, "I do from morning until night and that can be very stressful." He said, "Your heart is damaged pretty badly, but we can't do anything now as your heart is going to have to revitalize itself and get stronger before anything is decided." So six years later is when they did open heart surgery in 1986.

When I was at St. Ben's, Fr. Camillus was on his second sabbatical so I went to the abbot and I said, "Fr. Camillus is going to ask for a second sabbatical and I have never had one. The abbot said, "We don't give sabbaticals to associates." I said, "You must be kidding." And he said, "No." So what could I do? I accepted it – obedience.

After I had the heart attack and open heart surgery, I came back to the monastery for a while to recuperate. Abbot Timothy called me into the office and said, "Remember when you asked for a sabbatical?" I said, "Yes." He said, "I want you to take the sabbatical now."

So I went back home to be with my parents and the Murphy family for a few weeks, but they had no one to replace me at St. Benedict's so they called me back. So I went back to St. Ben's. The assignment at St. Benedict's lasted until July 1993.

It was during my years at St. Benedict's that I returned to some of my previous hobbies of wood carving, stained glass window artwork, windows sandblasting and egg sculpturing, which continues to this day.

When you left St. Benedict's after so many years, what did you do?
The archabbot, in 1993, assigned me as chaplain to the infirm and retired Benedictine sisters in the Monastery Immaculate Conception in Ferdinand, Indiana. Being chaplain to the sisters was truly a delightful and heartwarming responsibility. I was also appointed chaplain to the coworkers at the monastery.

If somebody would get sick in the hospital, I would go and visit them in the hospital and in their home. If a death occurred, I would visit the family, and I would have the funeral. If they came home from the hospital and got back on the job, I would visit them to see how they were doing.

These assignments lasted until July 2004 when Archabbot Lambert [*Reilly*] assigned me to St. Augusta Church, Lake Village, IN, where I am still pastor at the present. At this small parish, for the first time in my life, I can sit and relax and fall asleep in a chair, which I was never able to do before. They treat me royally up there. They need a priest, of course, but it is a two-way street. I love it!

[*Due to failing health, Fr. Stephen retired and came back to the monastery in October 2012.*]

Prayer

What is your most favorite part of the Rule of St. Benedict?
Obedience is an important part to me. I was a foreman before I came here, and the men who worked for me respected me and when I told them what to do, they would do it. So when someone would tell me what to do, I would obey. This was also true with the monks here. Since I was telling them what to do on construction, I expected

them to do it. Likewise, when someone told me what to do, I was expected to do it and I did it.

What is your key to living Benedictine spirituality?
Seek God in everything you do. I have told this to my people in the parish, time and time again. Everything is for the glory and love of God, everything we do. Not only prayer, but the moment we get up in the morning we are God's creation; we are his instrument. No matter what we do, it is for the glory and love of God. I think the entire *Rule* is important. I can't pick out one particular part over another. It is all important to me.

What were your saddest or most difficult times as a monk?
The saddest time was when I was told I couldn't study for Saint Meinrad for the priesthood.

What have been some of your most happiest or joyful times in your life as a monk?
My final solemn vows to Saint Meinrad Archabbey was one of the happiest times of my life. Ordination would also rate at the top, but deciding to come here was important, too. I think ordination and being accepted back into the community again, as I was happy knowing I was accepted. But I was still too young to realize the importance of being accepted.

Changes in the Church over Your Lifetime

What have been some of the changes in the Church and Archabbey you have you seen since Vatican II?
The people themselves. Some of the monks said that people don't change, but people do change. It is our surroundings that change us and we have to adjust to our changes. We are changing, we are accepting the changes and that is what I did. I accepted the

changes as they came; I didn't fight them. They were needed. I think everything was needed in the Church.

I remember my dear mother had a prayer book that she took to church. One side was Latin and the other side was English, and she found this difficult. I said, "Mom, take it with you to Mass, but accept a little bit at a time. If you try to learn the whole thing, you are going to throw everything out the window." They then adjusted pretty well to it.

When I went into the hospital for pneumonia several months ago, I couldn't get a priest to take the weekend Mass, so I prepared one of my parishioners for a priestless Sunday. My secretary called her and said, "Father is in the hospital. We will not be able to have Mass." The secretary cancelled all the weekday Masses. I told the parishioner, "I prepared for a priestless Sunday," and we talked about how to do it on the phone and I told her she was ready for it. She did it and it was acceptable to the parishioners.

Okay, so this is a change you see in the Church after the Council because a priestless Sunday wouldn't have happened before then?

Definitely, it wasn't even heard of. A priestless Sunday would not have happened, but it was not only me. In some areas where the priest cannot get to a church regularly, the church has a service but minus the Eucharist. The Eucharist is not distributed. The scripture is read for the Sunday, songs are sung, prayers are prayed together and the Our Father is prayed together.

Are there other changes?

I don't see any further complications, for example, married priests. I can't see that and I can't see women reaching that goal. Now we do have married priests who have converted from another faith and have come in with their entire family, as they are married. Other than that, I can't see anything in the future that would change this tradition.

How about change in the monastery?

I have seen a tremendous change since I came and other monks have seen the same things, but we have to accept the changes; we have to. When I came here, they told me to bring a small suitcase with working clothes. Two changes of working clothes and now they come with a U-Haul. They come with their computers, they come with their TVs and radios, and that is a change and we have to accept it.

The monks now have their private bathroom. Well, that is good. Men coming from the world have their privacy now. When I came, it was different. I am not against it; I am in favor of it. I am in favor of having a bathroom in my cell upstairs; yeah, I am glad.

Even though the Church has been de-emphasizing Latin, should it be eliminated from the academic curriculum?

Uncle Al, who influenced me to come to Saint Meinrad, was a Latin scholar and taught Latin in the minor seminary. I would visit him from time to time when I was in seminary. The first thing he would ask is, "How is your Latin?" One time I told him, "Well, it is a dead language, Uncle Al." Oh, I thought he was going to fall over. I said, "Latin is going out; it is not required anymore," and he said he couldn't believe it. He couldn't believe it because he was a professor of Latin and he got mad at me.

Anyhow, why is it not required as it used to be? I had some Latin in college and at that time the professor would give us a research topic. It was either in Hebrew or German and most of the references were in Latin. So if you didn't know any Latin at all, you were sunk. That isn't done anymore.

For academics, Latin is okay. But for the average person in the parish, I don't think it is necessary. Even though it is the root of many languages, people don't think about that today and care less if it is the root or not. So I don't think it is as necessary as it was in the past.

Assuming we cannot go back to pre-councilor days, what has been lost and what has been gained over the last 50 years?

Today young people have more choices than they did years ago in terms of jobs. In my hometown, a coal mining town, you either followed your father into the mines or were a school teacher, a nurse, or married a coal miner and that was it. There were few other job opportunities in a town that was a small coal mining town.

My daddy said, "You will not go into coal mining. You can do anything you want, but you will not go into coal mines – not the deep mines." You could, of course, have a religious vocation. Today, youngsters have so many choices waiting for them when they graduate from high school. Years ago, it wasn't that way, so this has resulted in a decline in religious vocations.

So you see more career choices for youth as a cause for the decline in religious vocations?

Yes, but another reason for a decline in vocations is you had many religious teaching in schools, and they had an influence on students. Youngsters did not get much religious education at home. The sisters and priests sort of influenced them by their presence. I tell my people, "Today it is your activities, your presence, whatever you do, that your children are going to take up." I have seen that. In my case, I think my parents had a lot of influence on me for eventually going into a religious vocation.

Have there been changes in parishes and among the laity?

Until both of my parents died, their mornings began with the Litany of the Saints and the rosary every day. When I visited them in the summertime for vacation, I saw the *Litany of the Saints* and the *Daily Reader* in the living room. I said, "Mom, what saint are you praying today?" She would tell me it was the litany of St. Ann, or the Blessed Mother, or the litany of the Holy Spirit, or whatever.

Both my mother and dad would pray, even though Dad was not an overly religious person, but they were good holy people.

So you see this as a change as people are not praying daily as much anymore?

People are not doing this anymore. I have told my parishioners, "Families that pray together will stick together." I witnessed this when growing up. When my grandmother lay in bed dying, her two sisters, mother and me prayed the rosary in Lithuanian around her and we were close. My cousins prayed the rosary every night growing up as youngsters.

When I visited them in Louisville, I prayed with them. Now, I guess they don't do this anymore. When they had grown up and left their home and I visited their parents, their parents would say, "Pray for my cousins as they are looking for a divorce."

Youngsters years ago weathered the storm more than they do today. Now they want to throw the towel in right away. I try to prepare young couples for marriage and they come in for pre-marriage counseling. Then six months later, the couple comes to me with problems and they want to have a blessing. I say to them, "How is your prayer life? I don't know you. I haven't seen you in church at all."

Well, they say, "Mother and Dad go to church." But I haven't seen them in church. They make 101 excuses. So I don't know. I tell the parents, "You are the example." And I know the parents come to church, as I have seen them, but I haven't seen the couple. What can I say? I am not the only one who sees this today.

Due to the many changes over your lifetime, what are your hopes for the future of the monastery?

Well, I think the monastery is failing in not having monks learn more trades other than academics. It seems that all the men coming in now are academically inclined and want to go to school and to pursue higher education, but I think they should be told, "You should learn something mechanical."

We don't have one monk in the plumbing department, no monk in the electrical department, none in the maintenance department, none in the tinsmith [*sheet metal*] department, and none in the mechanic department. Years ago, we had monks in all of them. Today we don't have one monk in the trades and I think that is our failure.

So a hope for the Archabbey would be that monks need to come with trades or learn trades?

Yes, at one time, we had priests in charge of the farm. I don't know if it is because of my background in the trades, but I feel that is our failure. But, of course, I have no control over this. I don't have any say in what they are doing. That is the superiors' decision, but I feel that is going to be a downfall.

Years ago, we had a school – oblate school. They went to the oblate school with a minimal amount of academics, with the last year learning a trade with a possibility of coming into the monastery with a trade background. Today, there is no reason why they can't, in addition to academics, learn a trade.

The last question: what are your hopes for the future of the Church?

Well, the Church has survived many changes in the past. It is going to survive whatever awaits us now.

Profile based upon: Fr. Stephen Snoich, OSB, to Prof. Ruth C. Engs, July 29, 2009. Interview Transcriptions, Saint Meinrad Archabbey Archives, St. Meinrad, IN.

Also: Snoich, Stephen, "Coalminer's Son." Essay presented to: Sisters of St. Joseph, Chicago, IL, circa 2006.

Email: Fr. Stephen Snoich to Prof. Ruth C. Engs. "Respond to your request on renovation." August 13, 2009.

Snoich to Engs, "Raven House," Private communication, December 11, 2012.

Chapter 7: Fr. Timothy Sweeney, OSB

Fr. Timothy Sweeney has had a variety of leadership positions in the community. He served as a philosophy teacher, novice and junior master, and prior (second in leadership), and then was elected archabbot. After he resigned this position, he served as administrator and pastor in several parishes in Indiana. At present, he is the community's archivist and administrator of two small parishes.

Born July 24, 1935, in Indianapolis, Fr. Timothy was given the name of Robert. He attended St. Philip Neri Elementary School in Indianapolis. Fr. Timothy entered Saint Meinrad Minor Seminary in 1949 and graduated from both the minor (1956) and major (1961) seminaries. He received the licentiate in sacred theology (1963) from the Pontifical International Institute of St. Anselm and lived in Rome from 1961-63. In 1968 he received a PhL in philosophy from the Institut Catholique, Paris, France.

Fr. Timothy made his first profession August 15, 1956, his solemn profession August 15, 1959, and was ordained May 7, 1961. His first appointment was as teacher of philosophy at Saint Meinrad College. He served as subprior (1972-75), master of novices and juniors (1972-75), prior (1975-78), and archabbot (1978-1995).

Upon his resignation as archabbot, he renounced pontifical signs. He then became administrator of St. Bridget Parish, Liberty, IN; Our Lady of Perpetual Help Parish, Hammond, IN; and pastor of the Parish of the Immaculate, Owensboro, KY; and St. Paul's Parish, Tell City, IN.

In August 2009, he was appointed a faculty member at Saint Meinrad Seminary and School of Theology, and in 2013 as the archivist for the community and the Swiss-American Congregation and as administrator of two small parishes. He currently serves in these positions.

Dr. Ruth C. Engs interviewed Fr. Timothy Sweeney on September 2, 2009; additional material was added October 2015.

Childhood and Early Years as a Monk

Tell me something about your early childhood and family.

I was born in Indianapolis in 1935. My parents, James and Helen, were both of Irish Catholic origin. I had one brother, who was three years older than me, who is now deceased. I grew up in St. Philip Neri Parish on what is now the near east side of Indianapolis. It just celebrated its 100th anniversary.

What was your father's occupation?

My dad started out as a manager of the retail meat market for Kingan and Company in Indianapolis. It was a big wholesale/retail meat packer, slaughterer, and shipped meat out. Dad was the manager of the retail market on Washington Street. It no longer exists now. When they closed the retail market and just had wholesale, he became a supervisor of the trucks that carried the meat out to various areas all the way to Pennsylvania.

My mother did not work; she was a housewife until I was about sixth or seventh grade. Then she took a job working in an insurance company – Aetna, I believe. Because her older sister Marie worked there, I think Mom wanted something to do, so she also started working there. We were active members of St. Philip's Parish. My parents were practicing Catholics, not overly religious, but they were practicing Catholics. I was an altar boy.

How about your early schooling?

I went to school at St. Philip's eight years, a parochial school, and I did fairly well in grade school. Then I came to Saint Meinrad in 1949 to high school at age 14. They used to have a high school then called the minor seminary.

My brother Jim was three years older than me and went to the Saint Meinrad major seminary and was studying for the Archdiocese of Indianapolis. My parents were very happy that their older son was considering being a priest. We would come down and visit with him. In those days, there were some regulations about visiting. About seventh or eighth grade, I started thinking about the possibility of becoming a priest, too. Well, my parents were not too excited about that. It was enough for one of their sons, but not both, as they only had two. Dad said, "Well, if that is what you want to do, give it a shot." Mom was a little more negative about the idea.

Why was that?

Grandchildren! I only found that out when she was dying of cancer and I was visiting her. My mother died of cancer in the late '50s. I was already a monk and the abbot gave me permission – most exceptional in those days – to go home once a month and visit her. Once when we were talking, I asked about her hesitancy for me becoming a priest or monk and it was only then that she said, "Well, I wanted some grandchildren." I said, "Oh, I never thought of that." When you are young, you never even think of things like that.

Did you have hobbies and activities?

I played sports, basketball, football and baseball. Even when I was in the seminary, during the summer we would go home, of course, and I belonged to a PAL [*Police Athletic League*] club. I think it was an American Legion baseball team. We played the championship game at Victory Field – the old Victory Field. I don't know if it is still there. That was a big deal and I had completely forgotten about it.

What kind of health care did you have as a child growing up?
Oh, I can't recall we had any health care.

When you were sick, did the doctor come to you or did you go to the doctor's office?
Old Doc Sheenen, who had just returned from WWII in Italy, came to the house one day because I got spiked in my lower right leg playing baseball and blood poisoning set in. I remember Doc came to the house and gave me penicillin and told me, "If it weren't for the war, you wouldn't have this." Evidently, penicillin was discovered roughly about that time [*it was first used in WWII*]. He said, "Otherwise, we would have to treat this with sulfa drugs and it could go on for a long time," but it cleared up pretty quickly with the penicillin.

When you were a young man, did you smoke?
During the summers, we started smoking. The rule here was that you had to be a first-year collegiate to smoke, and then you could only smoke cigars or a pipe. It was only when you got to the major seminary, which would have been comparable to your junior year of college, that you could smoke cigarettes. During the summer, we cheated but not much. I can remember Mom caught me one time and said, "Wait until you are 18." My dad smoked, but I waited until I was 18. That would have put me almost in first year of college.

When did you stop?
When we entered the monastery, we could not smoke. So when I became a novice, you had to stop smoking. When you were ordained a priest – or for the brothers, when they made final vows –

then you had to go and ask the abbot if you could smoke, which I did, and he said, "Okay." So I smoked from 1961, in some form or another, until December 31, 1999.

Why this date?
Abbot Lambert [*Reilly*] said, as of 2000, we had to stop smoking, so I did.

Why did you decide to become a monk?
Well, I came to Saint Meinrad as a student for the Archdiocese of Indianapolis, much like my brother. About my junior or senior year in high school, I was exposed to some rather outstanding monks, all of whom are dead now.

Fr. Adrian [*Fuerst*] was my confessor, and it wasn't as if he was soliciting people to enter the monastery, but we had long talks and discussions. Fr. Kevin Ryan was not my confessor, but Kevin taught physics and nearly flunked me in high school physics, but I always admired him. The

Fr. Timothy, as a young monk

choir, community prayer and also the whole idea of preparing men for the priesthood were intriguing.

Now the funny thing is that – OK, now you want to join the monastery – but nobody got too excited about that here among the monks. Finally, they said, "Well, you have to go see Archbishop

Schulte," who was at that time the archbishop in Indianapolis. But you never went to see the archbishop, for heaven's sakes!

I can remember setting my appointment and going to see him. I remember him saying, "Now, do you like to get up early in the morning?" I said, "Not particularly." He said, "Well, you are going to have to do that if you become a monk. Do you like to sing?" I said, "Well, you know, it's all right."

He answered, "You are going to have to do a lot of singing. Do you want to teach?" I said, "Yeah, I guess." "Well, you will probably end up teaching. All right, son," he said, "you go ahead and go join the monastery. It is all right with me. But let me tell you, if you decide that is not the life for you, don't come back to the Archdiocese."

I think when I look back on it, his answer didn't surprise me at the time. First of all, there were a plethora of [*people with*] vocations. But, secondly, the idea of switching was kind of an indication of instability of character, if you couldn't make up your mind what you wanted to do. When we look back on it today, we think that is odd that they considered it a character flaw.

When did you become a novice?

I entered as a novice with Fr. Meinrad [*Brune*] around 1955. There were 10 novices when we entered. Only Meinrad and I are left and that is not unusual. When I was novice master, I did a little study under Fr. Henry Brenner, who had been novice master for 30 years.

I took the number of novices who entered and compared it to the number of novices who made first vows, which was about 50%. Now that was back in the '30s and '40s. Then I took the number who made first vows versus the number who made final profession, 50% again. So if you had 10 who entered, roughly speaking, two would be there at the end.

That is very interesting information.

It is, but it was not scientifically done. I just took names over a period of about 30 years when he was novice master.

Going back to your years in the novitiate as a young monk, describe something of the tone and nature of the discipline in which you were formed.

Well, basically, at that time, and it is very similar to today, you simply follow the normal *horarium*, the daily schedule, as a novice. You had novice instructions with the novice master, who took the *Rule of St. Benedict* and kind of explicated it.

You then did basically "house work," as we called it, and I always looked upon that later as the kind of work that doesn't necessarily occupy your mind. You just go cleaning the bathrooms and ordinary housework, where your mind really was sort of free. That is basically what we did. We were young fraters – this is what they called us – because we were studying for the priesthood.

Also, when I look back now, and from what I hear from others, the most famous story of our formation is this: Archbishop O'Meara of Indianapolis wanted a meeting of the priests council in the '80s. He said, "Well, let's set a date for August whatever." They said, "No, no, Archbishop, you can't have it at that time, because that is the Saint Meinrad Alumni Reunion."

He told them he was flabbergasted that they wanted to go to an alumni reunion at the seminary. He said when he went through the seminary in the '30s and '40s, it was tough. They put the guys under lots of pressure to see how they would hold up. Saint Meinrad was much more familial, not patriarchal, except for one or two fathers who stand out and are still in the verbal history of the Abbey.

By and large, the men who taught and ran the seminary were much more familial, and I think they got that from the Benedictine life. So our formation and the tone of our formation were, by and large, never harsh. It was much more of a family; it wasn't Marine Corps training.

How about a humorous story from your early years?

We all had to play some sports. Now, that was okay by me, as I was somewhat of an athlete, but some of the monks were not particularly active. Where this monastery is now situated was a big open area. We use to play tag football around here and, in those days – now we are talking about '55 to '57 – we had to wear an old habit when we played football.

I remember tagging somebody, but he couldn't reach me, and so he grabbed and grabbed my scapular and tore it right in half. Fr. Bernadine [*Shine*][1] was the novice/junior master. He said, "Well, you have to say *culpa* for that in Latin, *schiso vestimento*, I tore a garment, and I think from now on you should take your habit off when you play football," which we did.

I think when we played softball we continued to wear our habit. When any of them played tennis, they didn't wear their habits, especially in the summer. There was no air conditioning; it was humid, Indiana humidity.

Describe a typical day when you were young.

In those days, you got up at a quarter to four, you had Matins and Lauds, and then you served at the private Masses of the fathers, and there were plenty of them. There were two rows of private Masses. You always wanted to get in serving the first row. Then you went to breakfast and then you came back to choir, had Prime, in those days, and then you had a break.

[*The public prayers, also called Divine Office or Liturgy of the Hours, are now combined at Saint Meinrad. The canonical offices of praying the psalms in this former time period consisted of eight daily public prayer*

---

[1] Transferred to Prince of Peace Abbey in California.

events. Private Masses have been replaced by the priests concelebrating the regular daily Mass.]

The conventual Mass was at 7:30, but you had Terce before Mass, which is one of the short hours, and then you had Sext afterward. You then went to school. In those days, the instruction was basically classes, very few papers. To my recollections, we had no seminars; it was all class work in class with a textbook, except later when a couple of fathers came back from the *Biblicum* [*Pontifical Bible Institute*] in Rome, where they acquired a new way of teaching sacred scriptures; but that was a little bit later.

Then at noon time, we had None and then we went to dinner. The main meal was at noon, or there about, in the middle of the day. And then in the afternoon, if it was a regular school day, you went back to school until it was time for Vespers. It is foggy now, but then you had supper and then Compline about eight o'clock. That was the end of the day, and night silence began. Now in the summertime, instead of going to classes, you did some kind of work.

What kind of work was this?
They assigned me to the library, the old library, and I was up on the third floor. Old periodicals were there. My job was to find out what was up there and to record it, etc. Basically, that was the only thing there that was interesting.

I would go home to visit my mother who was dying and she always confused the terms "abbey" and "abbot." So she would say, "What do you do?" I would say I am working in the library. This is summertime and she would say, "No, you tell the Abbey that you should be outside." I said, "What do you mean?" She said, "Your grandfather died of consumption, TB."

I never knew that. I said, "You never told me that. I have been filling out these health forms and I just didn't know."

"Well," she said, "in our day, we never talked about that because only the poor got consumption." I thought that was interesting. She was born in the United States, but her father, my grandfather, I never knew what he died of.

They had four children. My grandmother, who I never knew either on my mother's side, ran a boarding house on the south side of Indianapolis, but she couldn't take care of all four children. So, the oldest one, Marie, she kept. My mother, Bart and Agnes, she took back to Ireland. She might have kept Bart because he was so young.

Mom went back to Ireland and lived there, until she was about 10 or 11, with relatives and friends of Grandma. Then, when she was 10 or 11, Grandma had enough money and brought her back to the States. I've got the manifest when she came into Ellis Island. There it was: Helen Cahill, age 10 or 11, had $10 on her and this was 1912 or '13.

She was to be met at the dock by a Griffin from someplace in New Jersey. I suspect it was a cousin or something. Now there she is, 10 or 11 with $10. I am sure he put her on a train and sent her to Indianapolis. A little girl like that, I couldn't believe it.

Is there any particular incident that helped you in your formation in becoming a monk or a priest?

Not really. It was simply a gradual acceptance that this is what I wanted to do, and I kind of depended upon the community and the novice/junior master to say, "Yeah, you have the wherewithal to do that. You look pretty good to us from our point of view." But that is what I wanted to do, anyway.

I was interested in my studies for the priesthood. I was infirmarian for the fraters, which meant I had to give shots, which today we would never do. I remember we practiced on a grapefruit and, of course, in those days flu and colds spread quickly. I remember giving penicillin shots.

The most famous story I heard was Fr. Edmund [*Morthorst*], who was infirmarian for the whole complex. One of the old German brothers died. Edmund filled out the death certificate – you could never do that today – and cause of death. Edmund wrote in "natural causes" and mailed it back in.

Somebody in Rockport [*the county seat*] didn't think that was good enough, so he sent it back and said it had to be a little more specific. So Edmund – if you knew Edmund, you would understand this – filled out another one and he put "heart stopped," and they accepted it.

Did you have health care or a doctor here?

Yes, the Gootee brothers, for 20 some years, Tom and Francis. Tom would come over at least once a week and anybody who needed to see the doctor, Tom would take care of. You had students who were infirmarians, like Fr. Edmund and later Fr. Camillus [*Ellspermann*], who were capable of seeing if a problem had to go to the doctor or, when they got the Jasper hospital, went there to be with them. Health care was pretty slim when I look back. When Br. Daniel [*Linskens*] came back [*from schooling*], health care stepped up three or four stages.

Work

When you were a young monk, what assignments were you hoping for? What work were you assigned to do?

When we were fraters preparing for priesthood, as the time approached for ordination, I was asked, "What three areas would you like to teach?" I was certainly hoping to teach. I remember I put down First Theology – most of us just came out of theology. Second, I put down history, and third, I put down philosophy.

Well, before I was ordained, I was told that I would be going into philosophy, as we needed someone in philosophy. That was all right with me. I thought I could handle that and I was told I was to be sent to Sant' Anselmo in Rome after my third year in the fall of

1961. This was the time of the opening of Vatican Council II. I went to finish theology, as it was a two-year course. So I did the fourth year and the fifth year of theology there and received the Licentiate in Sacred Theology after the examination in '63.

Since you were there during the Vatican Council era, do you have any stories from that?
Well, we were young and very much of what we heard would today be classified as gossip.

Okay, what is interesting gossip you heard when you were there?
Oh, we heard, for example – and it turned out to be true – that some clerics had taken tape recorders into the classrooms at the *Biblicum* and recorded what the professors were saying. There was, at that time, an antipathy between the theologians, mostly the Belgium, French and Germans, and what today we would call the Roman curia.

Being young and hearing names like Congar, de Lubac and Karl Rahner, that is what we thought the future was to be and so we were most interested in what was going on, especially the first session of the Council.

The Roman curia had prepared texts and the bishops said, "No, we will make our own and do our own thing here," and that changed the atmosphere. By the second session of the Council, I had already left Rome. The Council moved in the direction that history has shown it has moved.

That first session was – this is what we were hearing – very much contested. There was a lot of friction between the 3,000 bishops gathered there and the curial officials. The curial officials at that time just didn't know what Pope John was doing by calling the Council. Whereas those Belgium, French and German bishops, in general, really wanted to latch on to Pope John's ideas. And I think ultimately it turned out well.

What are some other things you remember when you were in Rome at that time?

I think the biggest thing about being in Rome is you came in contact with the whole Church, in a sense, a wider Church. German monks, Burmese monks, Austrian monks were there. French and Italians, Swiss and English were there.

We had some Maronite monks from Lebanon. They were primarily from Western Europe, because the Iron Curtain was still there. So we didn't have any Polish monks, to my recollection. I still have a very good friend who is a monk in a French monastery in Brittany, Fr. Filbert.

In Rome, all the classes were in Latin, but you sure had to learn a little Italian to get around. I remember being hooked up with an Italian cleric who came to Sant' Anselmo, the Benedictine college for theology. During our 15-minute break in the middle of the morning between classes, one day we would do English – he wanted to learn some English – and the next day we would do Italian. So at least I picked up enough Italian to travel, to eat, you know, the common sort of things.

Then I became a good friend of Filbert. He spoke pretty good English, but his accent wasn't very good. My French was from Saint Meinrad, where we could basically read French but we had a hard time with pronunciation. It was the old-fashion way of learning grammar, vocabulary, etc. But when it came to pronunciation, our listening and hearing was another cup of tea.

So I gave Filbert a book in English. I remember he gave me *Les lettres de mon moulin* [*Letters from my Windmill*], which is a classic little book that French teenagers would have in school. I would read that aloud and he would correct my pronunciation. And I gave Filbert *Grapes of Wrath* by John Steinbeck. He would read that aloud, even the cuss words, and I would correct him on how to pronounce the cuss words.

We were able to attend papal ceremonies at St. Peter's. I was in the *schola cantorum* [*a choral group*] at Sant' Anselmo. I remember at one of the sessions of the Council – they always began with Mass – they had our schola sing the Gregorian chant for the Mass. So it gave me an opportunity to gape around and see all the stands where the bishops were. But at the end of Mass, the master of ceremony, in a rather loud voice, would say, "*Extra omnes*, everybody else get out." Those were two good years and I passed the exams.

Then what did you do?

Towards the second year I was in Rome, I was supposed to see where a good place would be to study philosophy. Well, I checked the Leuven in Belgium, I checked the Soulchaux in France – a Dominican place, which was famous at that time for studies of St. Thomas from the original texts. I looked at a place in Salzburg, Austria. And I ultimately ended up suggesting that I go to the Institut Catholique, Catholic Institute in Paris, and Fr. Abbot Bonaventure said, "Okay, go."

So in '63, I went to Paris. I stayed at a place called Pax Christi, because a Benedictine from Conception Abbey had stayed there and suggested the place. It is an international peace organization. Pax Christi means Peace of Christ. There is a group here in the United States that is a little bit different. I think they sponsored Monsignor Lalande, who was kind of the head of the French sector of Pax Christi.

Part of his work, or their work, was to sponsor this apartment for international priests who would be studying in Paris so that you would have a mixture of nationalities. We ate together, we had a little chapel where we would offer the Eucharist, but each of us went our separate ways for whatever we were there to study. I lived there for five years.

There were about six priests living in this apartment. They had fixed it so each of us had a room with a desk and some bookshelf space. When I first arrived, there were three French Canadians who also spoke English and that helped me get readjusted. During the summer of '63, I studied French at Tours, France, for two months. Then in the fall of '63, I began courses at the Institut Catholique.

The Pax Christi is in the sixth administrative district of Paris, Saint Germaine de Pres. The famous Les Deux Magot café was right across the street from us and Jean-Paul Sartre lived in that area. At the local parish, there were three priests. I agreed to take the early morning Mass, as I was used to getting up early.

By this time, the Mass was in the vernacular; therefore, it was in French. I couldn't preach in French at that time – I probably still can't – but I could handle the Mass and readings and things like that and go to school. I walked from there, because the Institut Catholique was six blocks away.

I obtained a licentiate in philosophy from the Institut Catholique and started on a doctorate dissertation. It had taken two years to get the licentiate and then I had three years to do the doctorate, but I never got the dissertation done. I am ABD [*all but dissertation*].

So why did you leave before you finished your dissertation?
Fr. Abbot Gabriel [*Verkamp*] said, "Come home and you can finish your thesis back here." I came home in 1968 and immediately began to teach philosophy. I was given the summer of '69 and the summer of '70 to try and finish the thesis. It was on Henry Bergson, on the lack of negativity, which is a metaphysical subject. I was given two summers, more or less free, although I did do some work.

When I came back, I taught about 13 hours a week. I was also assigned to be *socius*, assistant to the novice/junior master. So from '68 to '72, I was *socius*. I also taught philosophy to freshmen and sophomores in our college.

Then from '72 to '75, while continuing to do some teaching, I was also in charge of the novices and the juniors as novice/junior master. At one point, we had about 30. We had three years – '70, '71, '72 – during which I believe we had 10 novices every year. Now, keep in mind, not all are going to stay and they didn't.

How many stayed from that group?
Roughly, give or take, about two out of each group. The group that stands out in my mind had Fr. Harry [*Hagan*] and Br. Benjamin [*Brown*], who are the only two left at the monastery from that time period. In '75, while continuing to teach, I was named prior by Abbot Gabriel. In '78, I was elected abbot and ceased teaching. I was abbot from '78 to '95 – 17 years.

Can you give some recollections of being abbot, some positive and some negative?
The positive thing of being abbot was that it was during a period when we did a lot. It was not intended. I thought building construction was over, but as subprior, between the years '70 and '72, I went to see our Fr. Anselm [*Schaaf*], who was way up in years, in the infirmary in the old monastery, and he said to me, "How are things?" I said, "Well, you know, Father, I think we are getting into a position where we might be able to seriously discuss building a new monastery."

And he said, "Oh, no, no. In 1911, Abbot Athanasius [*Schmitt*] appointed me to a committee to study building a new monastery." Fr. Anselm didn't believe this was going to happen but, actually, that is what happened. Before I was elected, we got serious discussing strategic planning for this possibility. As soon as I was elected in June '78, I started to visit people and the most famous visit I made was to Mr. Lou Jenn – we have a plaque around the corner on Lou.

Well, he was the one who discovered the Jenn-Air ranges. Our Fr. Louis Range had been in contact with him and said, "Now I will bring the new abbot to meet you." We met with Lou and talked about 30 minutes. We didn't have blueprints or anything like that, but mentioned that we were along the road toward building a new monastery and library.

Lou was very receptive. On the way out, Lou said to me – I still remember this, "Well, Father," he said, "I think I can give you a little help. How about marking me down for a million dollars?" I said to myself, "God help us!" I acted like "OK, thank you very much," but I was dumbfounded. I never ran into somebody who could just give you a million dollars, but that was Lou.

What was different from being an abbot when you were an abbot or later, compared to when you first came here?

When I first came here, the abbots were more strict. For example, if you had an appointment with Abbot Ignatius at 8:30, you stood outside the abbot's door until the bell chimed the half hour and then you knocked on the door, not before and not after. It was that Germanic sort of punctuality, which was all right. Abbot Bonaventure [*Knaebel*] was a little more relaxed, although he grew up under Ignatius.

Next was Abbot Gabriel [*Verkamp*]. He had spent many years in the parish. I was his prior for three years and I was told he really had a temper at one point in his life, but only twice did I notice him kind of lose his cool.

But Abbot Gabriel was much different, even though he had grown up in that strict atmosphere. I think the years he spent in the parish kind of mellowed him, and he was much more understanding and certainly much more delegating. You take care of that and he would only step in if you really fouled it up.

I learned a lot from Abbot Gabriel and, of course, things have changed. There is much, much more consultation with the community now. In the old days, you still had the chapter, where any big decision had to be approved by the chapter. But what gradually occurred, especially as we moved toward building the new monastery, we had a lot more community meetings of the monks and open discussions about this and that.

I noticed every time we had a community meeting prior to a chapter meeting where we had open discussion, the monks already knew what you were talking about and their vote was their vote. They were not voting blind. They knew what they wanted. This process held for both building this monastery and the library.

Now, the next project we undertook was the renovation of what today we call Anselm Hall. It was almost as if we had experience in these kinds of things, so that project moved along a lot quicker and a lot more expeditiously. Then the next project we had was the Abbey Church.

When I came home in the summer of '68, I helped tear out the interior of the Abbey Church as one of the "workmen." The whole idea at that time was just to have a very simple setup here for about five years, until we decided what we wanted to do. Well, we were now 25 years later and so we started two things. We started fundraising first, and I made a big point we would not renovate the Abbey Church until we've got the money to do it, no going into debt to do it.

The Development Office enabled us in '77, '78, to seriously consider this renovation, as we now had people who were interested in Saint Meinrad who were giving and would enter into that capital campaign. Our big question with the capital campaign was: could our Development Office do it itself or did we need outside assistance?

We debated this and, fortunately, we came down on the point of outside assistance. Bunea Beaver of a development firm would take care of the logistics of the campaign. If we had to depend upon our people in our Development Office to handle all of the logistics, such as keeping track of all pledges, payments and all that, even though we had computers, that would have swamped them and they would not have been able to do that.

Then John MacCauley, who had helped professionalize the Development Office in the '60s, retired. We then hired one of the people who had been working there, a former student, Dan Conway. Dan was called director of development. After two years, Dan moved on to someplace else.

Then I started a national search for a development director and, when we reviewed all the possibilities and interviewed three or four, I said, "We've got the man right here. Dan Schipp." So we moved Dan up to being director of development. By that time, the title had changed to vice president of development. The basic reason for this change was because when these guys went to conventions, a director of development was not the head man. He was called the VP for development. So we changed the title.

So your greatest accomplishments were constructing buildings and renovations?

I suppose so, yeah.

What are some of the things that you would have liked to see happen, but didn't for one reason or another?

Oh, I can't really pinpoint anything. I did start, toward the end of my tenure, a process of decent strategic planning. As abbot, I invited in – his name slips my mind now – a priest who had done a lot of work with religious communities on renewal-type things. I remember he came for a weekend a couple of times.

My idea was to rejuvenate the community. And if we had been able to carry through with it then, the next abbot would have stepped into, I think, probably a little more invigorated community of monks.

What year did you retire as abbot?

I resigned. Abbot Gabriel did a big thing when he stepped aside as abbot. He would not let us use the word "retire"; he resigned. In 1993, I announced to the community that I would serve for two more years. June of '95 was the official date when I resigned as abbot.

Now it is traditional here for abbots to maintain their title as Fr. Abbot for life and wear the pectoral cross. Why don't you wear the pectoral cross?

It is what we call the *pontificalia*. It means pectoral cross, utilization of the miter and, in procession, the crosier, etc. I had noticed that English congregations of Benedictines have had the custom that their abbots were elected for eight years and then they could renew that for another term.

We never had that custom. Originally, our abbots were elected for life. You might get a coadjutor [*someone appointed to assist*]. Abbot Bonaventure was coadjutor with the right of succession for Abbot Ignatius. This generally happens with bishops.

I remember talking with an English Benedictine monk – now, this was long before I was abbot – and we were commenting on the difference in the terms of the abbots between our systems. The English were elected for eight years. Ours were elected for life. "Well," he said, "one of the problems with our system is: what do you do with the bodies? You elect a man for eight years and then you elect somebody else, and you have lots of former abbots around here."

That was one thing that stuck in my mind. The other thing was that the abbot's role is that of directing, organizing, and inspiring and invigorating the monastery and the monks; but it is also a symbolic role. A symbol of unity and, in my opinion, there should only be one abbot. Now, I know the old timers would not go with that, but I think there should just be one abbot. When you look at the community, you should see only one abbot, but that is my personal opinion.

Did you just decide to eliminate all the trappings of an abbot or did you have to get permission?

Technically, you had to get permission and I did. In 1967 or '68, we changed our constitution indicating that abbots were elected without term, and then a footnote said that they could resign. So when I came up for resignation, I did consult the community and we had a chapter vote. Then I wrote a letter to the abbot president of our congregation. [*Saint Meinrad belongs to the Swiss-American Congregation of Benedictine monasteries.*]

I happened to be on his council at the time, so I presented the letter and said, "Do you want me to step out while the council discussed and approve it?" "No," he said, "you can stay here." And they approved that I could resign from the office of abbot. Then I said, "I also am going to set aside the *pontificalia*." I remember Abbot Patrick, who was the president then, said, "Yeah, well my experience with a resigned abbot is they just do whatever they want to do." So that is the background basically to that action.

Some of the living resigned abbots appear to have slots waiting for them in the cemetery, so will you still be buried in Abbots Row?

I don't know. Probably. That is up to whoever is the abbot at the time I die. As one abbot said, "I could bury you in a ditch."

What kind of work did you do after you resigned?

I spent 14 years in parishes. I was nine and a half years as pastor. When I resigned, I was asked to go to Liberty, Indiana, which is up on the Indiana-Ohio state line. Liberty, Indiana is part of the Archdiocese of Indianapolis. A pastor suddenly died and I was asked to go up and fill in from roughly August and including Christmas 1995. Lovely little place, 150 families, lovely people.

Then I was asked to go to Hammond, Indiana, Our Lady of Perpetual Help, where the abbot had agreed to supply a priest while the pastor, an alumnus, had a sabbatical. So I stayed up there from January till around May, maybe June, of '96.

Then we had kind of an unwritten agreement with the bishop of Owensboro that if he provided a priest to work in the seminary, we would provide one of our priests for parish work. So I went to the Diocese of Owensboro in Kentucky and the bishop made me pastor of the Parish of the Immaculate and I stayed there for nine and a half years. Then Fr. Abbot asked me to come over to Tell City to St. Paul's in 2006.

I stayed there for three and a half years as pastor, and then Fr. Abbot in 2009 said to come home, which I did. I taught one class of logic again after 31 years. I also have spiritual directees. In 2013, I was appointed archivist for the community and the Swiss-American Congregation, OSB.

Do you have any hobbies or interests?

Reading basically, college football. Unfortunately, IU doesn't rank.

Prayer

The next group of questions has to deal with prayer and spiritual life. What would you like to convey to younger confreres, or even to the laity, in terms of prayer and spiritual life?

Well, I think you have to always approach this question from the point of view of who you are talking to. For example, back in '68 or '69, I was invited to go up to Indianapolis to give an evening of recollection to policewomen. I never met a policewoman, but I thought, "Well if they are coming to an evening of recollection, I assume that they are basically practicing Catholics."

So I decided to give a talk about the Second Vatican Council and the importance of the laity. When I got up there, there were about eight policewomen and I found out two of them weren't even

Catholic, so that made six. However, three of those six were involved in what we called "bad marriages," so that left three practicing Catholics.

I thought, "I can't talk about Vatican II. I am going to talk about God and Jesus and fundamental sort of things." You have to know who you're talking to, what their background is, where are they at, and try to adjust what you have to offer according to their background.

What is your favorite part of the Rule?

Chapter 7. Chapter 7 in the *Rule* deals with humility. The famous 12 steps of humility, in my opinion, are both the core of the *Rule* and the core of Benedictine monasticism. Now it has to be understood appropriately and it has to be understood, first and foremost, in what the author meant.

For example, the sixth step of humility is very difficult for us to accept and understand [*The monk is to accept himself as a "worthless workman."*]. But if you see what is behind this step, you can understand its meaning. It is in the section from the sacred scriptures in Luke [*17:7-10*], where Jesus is speaking the parable about the servant who comes in from the field and prepares his master's supper.

About that situation, Jesus says the master is not going to say to the servant, "Oh, you sit down and let me serve you." No, the servant serves the master and works in the field. I think that is what is behind that sixth degree of humility.

Obedience and silence from Chapter 5 and 6 are also there in the steps of humility. So that chapter, and the chapter toward the end of the Rule, 69 or 70, which as abbot I always found most helpful, is on what a monk is to do when he is asked to do the hard or impossible task.

St. Benedict lays out three basic steps. You listen, you find an appropriate time and explain to the abbot why you don't think you can do that, and then give the abbot an opportunity to reflect upon that. Then whatever he says, that is what you do, trusting in God's assistance. I found that chapter as abbot most helpful.

What is your key to living Benedictine spirituality?

Well, when you are in the monastery, to follow the "regular observances," as the ancient monks in the desert used to say. The famous example is when the young monk goes to the Abba, an older monk, and has a problem. The Abba says to him, "Stay in your cell; it will teach you everything." Namely, live the regular life. When you are out in parish, you can't do that. But if you have lived the regular life, you will then carry that over into your work in the parish.

What has been your most difficult and what has been your happiest time?

The most difficult was always dealing with people. That is always the most difficult and I think many people would agree with that. You have in the monastery a variety of personalities and it is up to the abbot to try to adjust himself to that variety. The best experience I think is seeing people grow and develop. I have seen men really grow and mature, not only psychologically, but also spiritually.

Changes in the Church

As you know, St. Benedict became very discouraged with the general disregard for spiritual ideals in his time. Today some observers suggest as a society we are falling back into that again. How have these societal changes affected Benedictine spirituality within the abbey or in the Church?

Well, I will make a distinction: Americans versus others. The American culture has about it that sort of rugged individualism and, in terms of both the monastery and the Church in America, you run up against that. That, in turn, can lead to a certain lax-ism and a sort of devil-may-care attitude about things that are serious. The business or whatever you are involved in, whether it be the monastery or the Church, it is not considered serious.

The second thing you run up against is certitude. It's the feeling of I want to have absolute black-and-white certitude about this, that or the other thing. You get certitude by faith, but not the sort of certitude that many people are looking for. That causes conflict we experience in the Church today, not so much in the monastery, but I think we probably experience it more in the seminary school. Certitude: well, is it this way or isn't it? It is not black and white; there are gray areas.

There are many changes that affected the contemporary Church. Some Catholics feel that Pope John XXIII was overly optimistic and that ever since Vatican II the Church has been paying a heavy price, where others applaud his gestures. What is your opinion on that?

Well, I think immediately during and immediately after the Council, until roughly speaking 1972, we did experience a lot of bizarre things, without a doubt. There was a lot of **dumb stuff being** done in the name of the Council.

Can you give some examples of that?

I think there were some priests who were celebrating the liturgy in a rather bizarre fashion, and I think here in the seminary there were some who were maintaining that the rule of celibacy for priests was going to be lifted. Well, there was just no way that this was going to happen, not in our lifetime anyway, even though it is an ecclesiastical law and can be changed, but it won't be.

So if you are in the seminary, don't expect that five years after you are ordained, they are going to let you, and it won't be retroactive even if it is. Kind of crazy stuff. We had to really hit that hard, so that the guys really had to face the question.

I think that by 1972, in the Church in the United States and certainly in our seminary school, things calmed down and we began to see more clearly what was promoted in Vatican Council II and implemented them in the appropriate way or manner. I think Pope John was moved by the Holy Spirit to do what he did and that, overall, it was good and is good.

How is the Church different today than 50 years ago?

Certainly the liturgy is different; it is in the vernacular. I think 50 years ago you didn't question. It was laid out for you. Now, and it is probably due to Vatican Council II, although we blame Vatican Council II for a lot, there is much more, not in a bad sense, questioning that leads to a better understanding.

If you don't question your understanding and doubts, you will never deepen your understanding. It is kind of like what Aristotle used to say, "You have to tie a knot that is tied before you untie it." I think in these years after Vatican II, a lot of knots have appeared and by seeking to untie them, we deepen our understanding of the matter.

Compare the morale of the monastery today to 50 years ago and to what extent has the decline in vocations had an impact on the monastic community and the Church?

I think 50 or 60 years ago morale was pretty high, but I was young. I didn't know everything that was going on because, by and large, things were pretty well set. Here is the way it is done and you didn't say why. Today I think the morale of the community is basically good. But 60 years ago, we didn't really plumb the depths of what we were really doing. And certainly over the past 60 years, in terms of the monastery, we have learned that our monastic life has depth to it.

For example, when I was a novice, we didn't know anything about the Desert Fathers. It is only within the last 30, 40 years that we begin to see the background of the Desert Fathers, John Cassian and St. Basil the Great, etc. When I was in Rome in '61, I began to see there was a lot more involved in monastic life and in its writings. The writing of monastic life had good stuff.

That was when I was already a priest. There was a big discussion at that time between the black Benedictines and the Trappists. Well, not the whole group, but Thomas Merton and a monk at St. John's Abbey in Collegeville were corresponding back and forth. That kind of thing was going on and a high degree of interest in it was being expressed.

How about lack of vocations?

Yes, that is a whole question of critical mass. If you don't have monks, you can't do various kinds of work. We closed the high school, because we thought they should be in their homes going to high school for maturity reasons. American kids don't mature as quickly as European kids.

When we got to the question of dropping the college, I think part of it was the lack of a critical mass of monks to teach. Certainly, the whole question that I experienced in closing our priory in Peru, South America, was a question of critical mass; we just didn't have the monks to do it anymore.

So, that question of critical mass in terms of lack of vocations is God's way of dealing with us. In the Church, it is even more obvious in combining parishes and bringing in foreign priests. People in the pews see the lack of vocations.

Even though the Mass is celebrated in the vernacular, should Latin be eliminated from the curriculum?

No, and I think they have reinstated it now. I think they have to take at least a year of Latin. We were taught Latin. I had six years of Latin, but we were taught the old method of teaching a language. You would think that after six years of a language, you would be pretty proficient in it, but many of us weren't. I did my courses in Rome in Latin and did an oral examination in Latin.

Americans were noted as not being real swift in Latin – most, but not all, some were good. At any rate, I do think that seminarians don't need to take six years of Latin. One or two years would be good. We put a year now into the seminary curriculum, if for no other reason than being able to understand some of the terms used. Also, having knowledge of Latin enables you to improve your vocabulary. So that is okay by me. I think it is good.

Striking changes have been made in liturgy and parish organizations. What do you see as positive and negative changes that have occurred in your parish experiences?

Certainly without a doubt, the parish councils were a great improvement. Secondly, which is now mandated by canon law, is the finance committee. Third thing, in my experience, was hiring a lay person to be a business administrator to take care of all that. That really clears the decks. I had one in Owensboro and there was one in St. Paul's, Tell City, full time. That person handled all of the physical plant questions, certainly all the finances, getting the salary checks out, making sure the Sunday collections were appropriately marked, etc.

That relieved the pastor of a lot of things, when in the old days he had to do them. I can remember back when I was a kid in St. Philip's, Monsignor Busald, who was our pastor, handled a lot of that. Well, you don't have to do that today, and the people who are hired generally have some kind of background in that area. Most priests don't have a background in physical plant problems nor finances, for that matter.

I would like to see certainly even greater degree of participation of the people in the parishes. One lack, that I personally have experienced, is where you do not have Catholic education, the Church and the parish are going to suffer in terms of the kids as they grow up. When I was in Owensboro, we had a consolidated Catholic middle school and the children got a very good education, but they also had one hour of religion five times a week.

When I came over to St. Paul's, there was no Catholic school. They had about an hour of class once a week. In my opinion, the young adults in Owensboro will have a better understanding of their faith than the ones in Tell City.

In terms of pre-Council days, what has been lost and what has been gained?

Because of the times, there was an abrupt change. For example, in the Council of Trent back in the 16th century, whatever they decided and established took maybe 200 years to become established throughout the whole Church. With Vatican II – bang! – there it was. And certainly the one thing that changed, that hit people the hardest, was the change in the liturgy, communion in the hand and all the liturgical changes. We always have to keep in mind that a lot of changes from Vatican II Council came – bang! – almost too quick for humans to absorb.

I think we did lose some things – a little bit of Latin never hurt anybody. We lost tranquility and certainty in our faith because, to many people, it looked like things were all up in the air. I think we lost that peace and tranquility that our faith does provide us with, to some degree, for some years.

Like I said, roughly around 1972, things sort of calmed down a little bit from '67, '68 to '72, when things were up in the air. I think we lost good music. Some of the music when I came home in '68 was terrible, in my opinion, both in the monastery and in the parishes. It is just going to take time to filter out some of the stuff that is not very good.

There has been a decrease in vocations and, although here in the Archabbey there has been a small upturn in the last few years, an increase in the number of retirements. What have these changing patterns meant to the monastery and the Church at large?

As I mentioned before, there is the question of critical mass and the apostolates that we are capable of handling, but it is not all negative. You have to keep in mind that you can't be running around doing everything. Fr. Abbot has withdrawn some men from parishes and brought them back to the abbey. I think we have been very generous in the past of assisting the local bishops with parishes, and we have had some parishes that we've always taken care of. Fr. Abbot has pulled in some of the men from parishes that were not our historic responsibility, in a sense. So I think by no means that is not all bad.

On the other hand, the Church is suffering from a lack of vocations, but there is always an upturn or upside to that, too. Certainly, parish councils have become much more engaged in the parish, but it differs from parish to parish. Some parishes with a parish council just want to "let Father do it." Other parish councils are very much engaged in helping run the parish. So there are some good points to it also.

Is the Church different today than what it was in the mid-20th century?

It is different in degree, not in kind. I mean the Church is different, and at the same time it is the same. The liturgy is in English, there is much more participation in the Eucharist, in the liturgy in general and in running the parish, and that is different from the past certainly.

Where do you see the Church and the abbey in the future? What are your hopes for the Church and abbey? Is there going to be a Church and monastery here 50 years from now?

God willing! When we built this monastery, we told the architect it has got to last a hundred years, the building, the fabric. In that light, when we decided to have, as the old monks would say, their own facilities, their own bathroom, shower, that was a big question. The monks were split on that 50/50.

But I told the architect, "Okay, we have decided that each cell will have its own bathroom and shower in it." Well, they came back with the estimate on the showers. My gosh, I can't remember exactly, but it seemed like an individual shower was costing an exorbitant amount of money, and I said something to him. He said, "Well, you said you wanted it to last a hundred years. These are the kind of showers they use in coal mines for coal miners and they will last a long time, Father."

I said, "Yeah, but for the coal miners, you've got three, four guys taking a shower because of the workload." I said, "The monks take showers once a day, maybe twice in a day." But the notion that we will be around in a hundred years certainly was present. I think that is true, God willing, we will be around for a hundred years.

What are your hopes for the Church?

The Pope has implied several times that the Church will be much smaller and there will be a remnant type of the Old Testament notion of the remnant of Israel. Certainly, the Church will be around, I have no doubt about that. What size, what quality, I am not sure.

Profile based upon: Fr. Timothy Sweeney, OSB, to Prof. Ruth C. Engs, September 2, 2009, Interview Transcriptions, Saint Meinrad Archabbey Archives, St. Meinrad, IN; additional information from Fr. Timothy, October 2015.

Chapter 8: Br. Giles M., OSB+

Br. Giles has spent many years of service in the important physical needs of the community. These included being a baker, electrician, and head of sanitation and pest control. He also served as pastoral assistant at several parishes and was a volunteer fireman for many years.

Br. Giles was the oldest of 10 children. He was born July 3, 1938, in Moline, IL, and given the name Robert. He attended Sacred Heart Grade School in Moline and Alleman High School in Rock Island, IL (1952-53). He came to Saint Meinrad's St. Placid Hall in 1953 and graduated in 1956. During the 1970s, Br. Giles attended Saint Meinrad College part time and was certified in pest control technology from Purdue University in 1978.

He made his first profession April 16, 1958, and his solemn profession April 16, 1961. Br. Giles worked in the bakery between 1958 and 1968 and again later, until his retirement in the late 2000s. He also worked in the electrical shop (1968-77) and became director of sanitation (1975-91) for Saint Meinrad Archabbey and its schools.

His other duties included being pastoral assistant at two nearby parishes, St. John Chrysostom Church, New Boston, and St. Martin's Church, Siberia. He served on the board of directors of the Indiana Pest Control Association for eight years, was a volunteer fireman for about 30 years and served 11 years as chaplain for the Indiana Volunteer Fireman's Association. He is now retired.

Dr. Ruth Engs interviewed Br. Giles M. on July 30, 2009. Some additional information was added in October 2015.

+*Editor's Note:* Only the first name and last initial for Br. Giles are used due to the AA tradition of maintaining anonymity in public, such as the press, media, books or other publications.

Childhood and Early Years as a Monk

Tell me about your childhood, family life and early schooling.
Well, I was the oldest of 10 children. I have seven sisters and two brothers. After me, there were five girls. I weighed 3 pounds when I was born and I was almost born in Indiana. My parents were on their way to visit relatives at Lakeview, Indiana, right below South Bend. My mother started having problems and told Dad to turn around and go back to Moline, because she wanted to have me with her family doctor. We got back and I was born July 3 at 11:55. If I would have waited five more minutes, I would have been born on the Fourth of July.

My aunt, my mother's sister, came down to take care of things and saw my mother holding me. She said, "Loraine, stop playing with the doll," and Momma said, "No, this is Robert, not a doll." Anyway, I was three pounds when I was born. The doctor put me in a shoebox with an oxygen thing and that kept me alive. He baptized me because they didn't think I would make it. But I fooled them and here I am. I am the oldest of 10.

What did your father do? What was his job?
My dad was lucky and never had to go to the service because he worked for the Rock Island arsenal in Moline. They worked sometimes 20 hours [*a day*] just at the end of WWII. The arsenal was on an island in the Mississippi River. My dad was a machinist who made tanks and ammunition there. I could hear them testing the

tanks as a little kid; things went bang and went into the Mississippi River.

I had an uncle who was in the Navy and my other uncle who was in the Army. Uncle Chuck, my godfather, made a career of the Army. He was a master sergeant and retired after 20 years. I lived where John Deere – the world's biggest agriculture company – was located.

Their office was on stilts because the Mississippi River flooded. So they built it on stilts and, when it flooded, they had a ramp you went up. I didn't realize it was one of the seven architectural wonders of the world and I lived five blocks away from there. I worked one year at John Deere when I went to high school. I didn't realize that was such a big thing.

What kind of religious life did you have at home?

Oh, good religion. Mom and Dad listened to Archbishop [*Fulton*] Sheen on the radio and when it came on television every Sunday. We were one of the first to have a TV in the Quad Cities. My godfather was an electrician. He didn't ever marry and bought us a TV.

It was black and white and in a big console. It had a little dinky square screen with rounded corners. I had to go upstairs and turn the antenna towards Chicago, because the Quad Cities didn't have a TV station yet. They would yell up the steps and I had to turn it right or left or whatever they told. One of the first TV shows was "Kukla, Fran and Ollie."

Were you ever an altar boy?

I served Mass for an old Monsignor Loven. I found out later Monsignor Loven had been to Saint Meinrad and I had to serve him when I was home every morning because I was at Saint Meinrad. I also knew Latin. I didn't realize at the time why he was so delicate about putting a pillow under his knee because he had dropsy [*edema*]. I was so embarrassed because every time I missed the pillow under his knee, he would yell at me, "Put the pillow underneath my knee!" and I felt like a little ant, you know. Sacred Heart Church was the biggest Catholic church in Peoria Diocese.

When you were a little boy at home, what kind of health care did you have?

A dentist. We had a good dentist, but the dentist didn't like me because I wouldn't let him work in my mouth.

Did you go to the doctor or did the doctors come to the house?

No, they didn't usually make house calls in those days. Most of the time you went to the doctor's office. Dr. Dunnaville had two sons who became doctors and one son became a priest of the Peoria Diocese. He had a big family, too, and he was a good friend of the family.

Did you drink before you came to the monastery as a young man?

Home brew. My mother was a home brew drinker and made home brew beer. I was the expert at home brewing at Saint Meinrad's. I would taste this one and, "Oh, yours is better than his." So yeah, I was the home brew expert.

How about your schooling?

I went to Sacred Heart School first. I goofed off when I was in school the first couple of years and I didn't apply myself. A sister there got a hold of me and said, "Hey, you got to straighten out," so I started studying. We had to take a trade and I took tin work in the shop and took printing. I knew the California Job Case [*typesetting box*] inside and out. I printed our school newspaper back home.

In grade school?

Junior [*or middle*] school, we call it today. Then I went to Alleman High School one year. A newly ordained priest, Fr. [*Joseph*] Mackowiak, told me about Saint Meinrad and I was interested in printing because I had printed our school newspaper. He said, "Well, you could go to Saint Meinrad. They have the Abbey Press and you could print there." So, I went to high school here at St. Placid Hall my last three years.

How old were you when you came here?

I was 14 years old and came as a sophomore in high school in 1953. Fr. Pius Klein and Br. Andrew Zimmermann were also here. Pius was a freshman, I was a sophomore and Andrew was a senior. Andrew was typing Fr. Virgil's thesis on the priest who was falsely accused of rape and who later became a monk here – Roman Weinzaepfel. Andrew, Pius and I were good friends and we still are. I missed them when they went to South America.

I was here for the centennial in 1954. Fr. Richard [*Hindel*] was our superior and we had to set the tables where Newman Dining Room is now and everything had to be straight on the table. Abbot Ignatius [*Esser*] was retiring as abbot. He would go up to the dining room and measure and tell us to put the glass perfect, because Ignatius was a perfectionist and wanted everything just so. I remember setting the tables.

You said you served at the Latin Mass. Where did you take Latin?

I had two years and then Fr. Pius Fleming, who had polio, taught me third-year Latin, so I am pretty good with Latin. I still can say it and was one of the last to serve Fr. Joseph Mort. Fr. Fintan Baltz would say only Latin Masses and I served their last Mass before they died.

When you first decided to come here, were you interested in becoming a monk or just going to school?

I was interested in just being a monk. I didn't realize it, but my mom and dad were Benedictine oblates through the Benedictine Sisters of Nauvoo, IL. I was going to be a Dominican, but I had to wait until after high school and then Fr. Mackowiak told me about St. Placid Hall high school and the Press. Well, little did we know at the time that I didn't have a choice of what work I was going to do.

When I entered the monastery, they asked, "Do you like indoor work or outdoor work?" Well, if you asked for indoor work, you got outdoor work and vice versa. I actually asked for indoor work and I got the outdoor work. But I worked in the kitchen once a week and we had to make cinnamon toast. Br. Benno Garrity[1] had a big line of people to make the thing and he wanted me in the kitchen grilling.

Br. Giles, as a young monk

At St. Placid Hall, I had the honor, as a senior, of working in the kitchen under Br. Benno – I think he will be a saint someday – and Br. Wolfgang [*Mieslinger*], the old German. He was the quiet type and very mannered. The reason he was mannered is because he was the crown prince's gardener in Germany. When ladies came here, he bowed and shook their hands

---

[1] Transferred to Prince of Peace Abbey, Oceanside, CA.

and was very gentle.

The other old Germans – oh God, you would think they were going to kill each other. They would get in an argument and hit the table and throw each other against a wall, and poor Br. Rembert [*Ringler*] and Wolfgang were sitting there listening to all that. But then right afterwards, when you'd think they were killing each other, they would go down to the wine cellar and have a slug.

Have there been changes in the Abbey since you were a novice?

Oh, a lot of changes. First, the brothers had their own oratory and were separate from the others. Then they switched over to the English vernacular for everybody and we went with the choir [*sitting in church with the priests*]. A lot of the old bucks didn't like that idea, as we were used to our little oratory. So that was the big change.

The main thing is, nowadays, instead of putting you somewhere which is the opposite of what you want to do, they try, if you have talents, to utilize those talents. I think that is a good thing and a very good change. Today, I would have gone to the Press and done the California Job Case.

Are there any other changes?

Well, you know we are all one now instead of separate. That took a lot of doings. The brothers used a cape like a cuculla, instead of the big cuculla [*large pleated gown with wide sleeves worn over the tunic*]. Then they made everybody change to the cuculla, which I think is great. We are all one community and seniority doesn't matter whether you are a brother or priest. The day you enter is your day of seniority. The brothers can teach nowadays, like Br. John Mark [*Falkenhain*]. Br. Gabriel [*Herbig*] was one of the first to teach in the school or college. He had a heck of a time because they didn't want him, but he had his degrees.

Do you have any amusing stories from your early years in the community?

Oh yeah, Fr. Meinrad's brother, Theodore Brune, used to imitate Abbot Ignatius. Well, one day in the kitchen, I had broken part of a lazy Susan. We had a rule. If a junior monk would ever offend a senior monk, he should ask for his blessing and forgiveness before the sun went down.

So, anyway, I went up to Br. Theodore [*later he was ordained a priest*], who was working in the kitchen then, and said, "I am sorry, I broke your lazy Susan. I ask for forgiveness." So, Theodore started imitating Abbot Ignatius, and here comes Abbot Ignatius into the kitchen and I couldn't yell, "Here comes the abbot." So Abbot Ignatius tapped Br. Theodore on the shoulder and said, "Brother, I see we have competition here."

Fr. Claude [*Ehringer*] was novice master and he had squeaky shoes, so we always knew when Claude came down to our rooms. We had curtains in the doorways. Br. Daniel [*Linskens*] had made a wooden toolbox for me and I had all kinds of tools in it. Everybody borrowed my tools for things, in particular Br. Benno.

Well, one time Fr. Claude's shoes didn't squeak. So I thought it was Br. Benno coming into my room. So, I said, "I'll get him," and I went, "Kootchy koo!" Now, Benno was a big boy and Claude was skinny. Oh, my God, I didn't know what to say. Fr. Claude had just told us, "Whenever a superior enters a room, you are supposed to say, 'Praise be Jesus Christ.'" So I yelled out, "Praise be Jesus Christ."

Br. Ken was next door to me and he went and told everybody. I went into Fr. Pius Flemings' room that day to bring his tray to him and he went, "Kootchy koo!" So I didn't know what to say. In those days, everybody knew that I had to say *culpa* [*acknowledgement of having done wrong*]. I didn't know what to say. So I said *culpa* for scaring a superior and Abbot Bonaventure [*Knaebel*] went, "Ha – ha – ha."

Work

What kind of work did you do over your career?

I first worked for a year in the kitchen and then I worked in the bakery. In those days, you cooked breakfast; then you had a break; and then you cooked lunch and then the evening meal you cooked and then a break. I use to go walking with Br. Wolfgang and he'd say, "Ah, in Germany this is nothing. Ah, in Germany we did this and Ah …" One time he climbed the water tower that was much bigger than it is now. He got on top near the antenna and said, "Ah, if I can do it, you can do it, you know."

Did you know the German brothers well?

I have many good memories of the Germans, Kilian [*Schlittmeier*], Herman [*Zwerger*], Conrad [*Mueller*]. The old Germans – either they liked you or they didn't like you. You could kiss their butt, but if they didn't like you, that didn't make any difference. At the first impression, they made up their minds. That was the old Germans' way of doing things and, luckily, they liked me. Yeah, I knew the old German brothers, yes.

Wolfgang made Angel Bread and Nonsense. Nonsense was a glorified cornbread banged up in a big deep steel Army surplus pan. Br. Benno was training me to be in the kitchen with him and Br. David was training Br. Maurus [*Zoeller*] to be in the bakery. I was in the kitchen one year. Br. Maurus was sent to work at the guest house.

Br. David got me to come to the bakery. I never heard Benno cuss in my life. He was a saint, but he called Br. David [*Petry*] a horse thief because he took me out to the bakery. David was the head and I had never baked in my life. I had never even cooked, because I had sisters.

I did man's work hauling the clinkers out of the furnace and all that good junk, so when I came to Meinrad it was all new. With Br.

David and Br. Benno, we invented all kinds of stuff – a bacon skinner – and we'd make ketchup and pushed it down into barrels in an ice box. Benno was an inventor and I was his right-hand man.

What did you do when you were working in the kitchen?
In the kitchen, I did about everything – cut meat and everything. I got to tell you a story about Br. Wolfgang. The Wolfgang always made Benno start something and then sneak out. He loved guests and he would run off. "Wolfgone," they called him, "Wolfgone boss." And he would go and visit with the guests. I taught Br. Benno how to make bread and he started his bread making out there in California [*at Prince of Peace Abbey*], but I am the one who taught him.

Tell me about your bakery experience.
I baked any kind of cakes, bread and practically anything. One summer I went to the culinary institute [*The Culinary Institute of America*] in New Haven, CT. After I left, it moved to Hyde Park. You had to have five years of experience to attend. Because we didn't have summer school here in those days, I cooked and baked in the French Lick Sheraton Hotel. I worked there a couple of summers. At the culinary school, I was told I was all set, as I had baked at the French Lick Sheraton.

Well, I got to the school and Joe Amendola was my instructor – one of the best pastry chefs, an Italian. We had five in our class – a nice small class. He always said, "If I can do it, you can do it." I have his book yet that he signed for me. We had an instructor named Arthur, but I can't remember his other name. Arthur was a master sergeant in the Army and he treated his people like that. He was entirely different, so I was so thankful to have gone with Joe Amendola. When we graduated, Rose and Eunice Kennedy came. They came into the kitchen and she asked me, "How do you make a baklava?"

The other guys were all laughing at me, because you first had to make the puff pastry. I had to tell them all about how to make the puff. You said a "Hail Mary," as it was very important there was no yeast in that dough. All the layers fattened and stuffed together made it rise. So I explained how to make a baklava and they liked me. In the newspaper, they had a picture on the front page of *New Haven Gazette* of the first religious brother to graduate from the culinary school. Here I was with Rose and Eunice Kennedy. Oh Lord, it was an experience.

How many years did you work as a baker?
I was a baker for about 10 years until Crotty came around 1968. This is Crotty Brothers, the food service. They didn't want the religious working for them and that was a good thing. The head cook took our recipes and threw them away. Cornbread, oh yeah, unfortunate; pear bread – we used to make pear bread and all that stuff – and she threw it all away.

What did you do when the Crotty Brothers food service came in?
Electrician, and I did that for about eight years. I had a hobby of electronics. My godfather was an electrician and I learned a lot from him. I followed Br. Augustine [*Schmidt*] in the electric shop. When he went to California, I took over. Then I went back to the bakery again. I stayed there until I retired a couple of years ago [*around 2006*].

When I was there the second time, I designed the bakery we've got now. I went up to Chicago and got a Champion mixer and the Middleby Marshall oven. It was a used one and we got a good deal from that. So I literally designed the bakery, and we made breads and things like we do today.

At least we didn't have to haul them around anymore, except up the elevator. In those days, we carried the goods in the back of a pickup truck. Not a covered one, just an ordinary pickup truck. You would be going around those curves and down the drive, which was steep, and praying that you wouldn't lose any pies or cakes.

In Benedictine communities, as you know, brothers are generally in charge of the physical aspects of the community, buildings and environment. Was there other work that you did?

Yeah, beginning in '75, I was director of sanitation. I went to Purdue and took the correspondent course. Fr. Damian [*Schmelz*] corrected my papers before I sent them off. Then every year I went to Purdue right after New Year's for a full week to keep our certification up. In those days, they required us to do this three out of five years. I was given the Director of Sanitation title here, so I could go in the kitchen to clean up roaches and so forth. I sprayed and baited.

I was in the Indiana Pest Control Association for a number of years. They called it the liars club. For a meeting, I made a beef sausage – because Jews could eat beef – and took this and bread up to Purdue. A board member was Harry Katz. He was a Jew and his son was a conservative rabbi and Harry was very conservative. One time Maury Oser, grandson of the founder of Orkin, who was in charge of the midwestern account, said, "You can't eat that meat; it is not blessed." So Maury said, "Brother, bless this meat." So I blessed it and he says, "Now, Harry, it's kosher." So I got to know them.

I was on the board for 12 years and one year I was elected president. That was the worst year, because they took chlordane off the market that year. The chemical they should have taken off was Aldrin, which is very bad – they don't even make it anymore. That year I got more phone calls and stuff trying to explain to people to use that and not the Aldrin. Times have changed, but I was going up to Purdue for 25 years to keep my certification up.

Did you do other work?

Well, I wanted to join the fire department, but Br. David wouldn't let me. I was a house warden in the old monastery and you had to make sure everybody was out of their rooms in case of fire when they had to get outside. Then when I became in charge of the bakery – I had two lay people working under me – I told them, "Okay boys, I am going to join the fire department. You can stay here and take the bread out and stuff." I joined the fire department in '68.

Describe what you did as a firefighter.

Well, I was mainly traffic control. [*Until 2009*] for any big wreck, I went out and directed traffic. I am just retiring and I am not going to do that anymore. I am 71 [*in 2009*] and my knees got replaced and now my ankle; I got to wear a brace. I also served as chaplain for 11 years at the Indiana Volunteer Fireman's Association.

Did you do any more chaplain work?

Well, Fr. Kurt [*Stasiak*] asked me to become a pastoral associate, because he knew I had an interest in working in the parish. I worked with Fr. Theodore [*Heck*] – there is a saintly man – in New Boston. He didn't miss a trick, let me tell you. He knew stuff even though he didn't act on it. Theodore was retiring and Fr. Cyril [*Vrablic*] was supposed to take over, but he had a heart attack.

So I went to Siberia and lived out there. I was taking care of New Boston and Siberia. One year it drove me crazy trying to keep the schedule up and get everything ready. Fr. Kilian Kerwin was pastor. He had Fulda, Siberia and St. Meinrad. That was a lot of work for him. He liked the kids and working with young men and it was great. That is what he is doing now up in Indianapolis as a counselor to kids.

I taught religion for a year. One kid thanked me later. I said, "You should learn typing," and he replied, "That is girls' stuff." I said there will be a day you will need your typing experience. So years later, when they celebrated the centennial of Siberia, I went there. This guy came up to me and said, "You were right." Guess what he was? A computer repairman. Fr. Kilian had me bring Communion to the old timers and I loved it. I didn't just bring them Communion, as I learned a lot more about the old people and what they did, and it was humorous.

So in your career you spent pretty much your whole life here at the monastery and later going out into the community?

Oh yeah, and I volunteered. I started learning Spanish because I was going to go to South America when we had our foundation in Peru. They had the big earthquake [*in 1970*] and everything changed, and so I was happy that I didn't go. I have had a lot of experience in my time. "Join the monastery and see the world," so they say. I have been to Europe once. Br. Ivo [*Staples*] and I went in '92. It was his jubilee and he told Fr. Abbot he wouldn't go unless Br. Giles went with him. So we were in Europe.

We went to Belgium. I stayed at Maredsous Abbey. Then I went up where Grandpa was born near St. Andrew's Abbey [*in the Flemish region of Belgium*] and stayed there. They were founded from Maredsous. There was a division [*in the community*]. So all the Dutch went up to St. Andrew and the French stayed in Maredsous, and you can see the differences. The mustaches of the monks up there are different. This old monk had a moustache like my Uncle Poland did. Some oblates of St. Andrew came up for a retreat and they all ate with the monks.

What kind of recreation or hobbies did you have?

I have been in two plays, actually. One was a kitchen cut-up, "Nonsense Now Being Served," and I imitated Theodore Brune. He had this pickled peach business and would go up to people – guests that he knew or when he went with Abbot Ignatius on a trip to different monasteries. Anyway, he would go up to people and say, "Do you want a pickled peach?"

So in this play, I imitated Theodore, and he didn't realize that I was imitating him. Then the other play I was in was "The Caine Mutiny [*Court-Martial*]" and I played the psychiatrist Dr. Forrest Lundeen. What happened was Br. David was supposed to do the part, but he found out he had cancer and didn't want to do it.

I always wanted to do trains.

Oh, tell me about your trains.
Well, I got permission from Abbot Timothy [*Sweeney*] in '77 when I went to the Guest House. We bought a train set up there and it was called a South Shore Limited. I still have it, plus a few others. It was a 27-gauge passenger train made by Lionel. Later I got an HO-scale train and I now have it down on the bottom of the hill in a little house. But they want to tear it down. I have so much train stuff there – where would you put it? I got permission and the Dubois County Museum would love to have them, so we are going to move them over there. So I can't complain.

How about vacations?
In those days, we didn't have vacations so we went to camp. We used to have a camp out at Wyandotte [*land located east of Saint Meinrad*]. Fr. Kurt always liked my Swiss steak and chili. The government said they were going to use it [*the camp*] for a park. They still haven't done anything and it is just sitting there. It is a shame. We could have stayed out there in the camp. So it's the way it is. History is history.

241

Prayer

From your experience as a monk, what would you wish to convey to your younger confreres or even the laity?

Just be honest and you learn prayer is accepting God's will and you are praying for that all the time. You've got to be aware of God speaking to you. You need quiet time, which is hard for me because I am a yakker. I learned that at AA.

What is your favorite part of the Rule?

My favorite part is when St. Benedict tells us there is a certain time for prayer, a certain time for work and a certain time for recreation. That is my favorite part of the *Rule,* when he explains that.

What is your key to living a Benedictine spirituality?

Well, the old saying is we are all different. It takes all kinds to make the world and it takes all kinds to make a monastery. We can get along accepting each other, as we don't try to change somebody. You can't; I found that out. I can only change myself.

What was your most difficult time or experience in your life?

I am known as the crazy brother, because I did all these stupid things when I was a drunk. At the time, I was feeling no pain. I ripped one of the big screen doors off the office in my drinking days when we lived down in the basement down near where the Development Office is now. I went to Guest House for treatment in 1977 and I have been sober ever since!

Abbot Timothy [*Sweeney*] was prior [*second in leadership*] at the time and he took me up there. And I am glad I listened to him, because I wouldn't be here today if it wasn't for him. I inherited alcoholism on both sides. My mother would never tell me about why we left my grandpa's. The reason we left Grandpa was my grandpa and his brother, Uncle Puller, every night would come home drunk because they would go to the taverns.

My grandpa worked in a mustard factory and Uncle Puller, an old bachelor, worked as a groundskeeper at the Rock Island arsenal. I was double-whammied on her side of the family and my dad's side; they all had alcoholism in the family and so it was inevitable.

When I went to Guest House for Catholic clergy and religious, it was the best thing that ever happened to me. In '77, Abbot Timothy [*who was then the prior*] called me into his office and said, "You know we think you got a little problem." So he gave me two choices: the Guest House in Lake Orion, Michigan, or Lady of Peace, which is a nut house in Louisville. I said, "I'm no nut," even though I did stupid things.

I had a miraculous experience after Timothy had called me in. I got this "love note" from him saying to see him at a certain time. Well, I prayed to Mary and said, "I will do this if you do that," and I said, "I will do whatever they say." Something came over me – a calm. A spiritual awakening came over me and I wish I could get it back sometimes, but they say you got it when you needed it.

Anyway, I went down to the prior's office and Timothy said, "Well, Fr. Abbot is waiting to see you. We think you should go to a treatment center." And I said, "Well, I will go," just like that. He was shocked. I didn't realize that I had a spiritual awakening until I later heard somebody else's story.

Abbot Timothy had been at a meeting for superiors down in Florida, and that is how he heard about Guest House. He was the first one to send us there, and Guest House saved my life. This old Scripps mansion in [*Lake*] Orion, where we sobered up, is now a national monument.

We went up last year to celebrate 50 years of Guest House. The house is in a beautiful setting. They are keeping it just as it was when I was there and it's going to be a museum. They built a brand-new place just for the sisters in recovery on the campus and a new men's Guest House and also one in Rochester, Minnesota.

My counselor, Lee Phillips, was a great man. He was the head counselor and he said to me. "You are going to Brighton [*Center*] with Connie," a priest who had heart problems, so he could hear "fifth steps" at this treatment center. I said to Lee, "Brothers don't hear confessions and stuff." He said, "You are going." So I went there.

Connie had to go swimming every day, so we went swimming all the time together. I love swimming. Connie had a heart attack during Mass. I had to finish up Mass. He was feeling sick the night before, so he told me to hear fifth steps of these executives from GM, who were at this center.

Anyway, we had to stay there a whole lot longer after Connie had the heart attack and I had to stay with him. Boy, did I get a sermon about holy obedience and, "You never know what God wants you to do" from another resident who was an Episcopalian. He always called our hosts "wafers."

So at this Brighton treatment center, you were actually there helping as a chaplain's assistant?

Helping, yes, but it was part of my treatment. I was just there to be with Connie, because I was told I had to take care of him. I learned then you just do things – the Lord has ways of telling you to do things. So anyway, I stayed about two weeks at Brighton until Connie was well enough so he could go back to Guest House. He had angioplasty done to him. We kept in contact and he eventually had a triple bypass.

What was the most joyous or best time in your life?

I have been sober ever since I left Guest House. It was a blessing that I went there. I called the Guest House my second vision. Before I went to Guest House, I was suffering and didn't know what was wrong with me. The joyful is after I came back here. I started living again and people accepted me. This lady on the board of the Pest Control Association, who we bought our stuff from, said at a board meeting, "He's not drinking and he's still happy."

I've got to tell you a story about old Fr. Peter [*Behrman*]. Now old Fr. Peter was a good ol' pastor and he wanted a beer at one of our things. In those days, we had keg beer here. So I asked, "Fr. Peter, do you want me to get you a beer?"

"Oh yes, Brother, I would really appreciate that." So I went over and got a beer for him. You could have heard a pin drop because I was taking this beer across the room. And everyone said, "Well, he is not supposed to…" "Here, Fr. Peter, here is your beer." He said, "Thank you, Brother." I loved it!

I am glad I came to Saint Meinrad even though a lot of things happened in my life, but you can see God's will, and I've been sober since '77 and I can't regret that at all. Everybody says, "Oh, the best thing that happened was my second vision." If it wasn't, I wouldn't be here. God is good to me and Saint Meinrad has been very good to me and the community, and I try to return that favor to the community.

Changes in the Church

There have been changes that have affected the contemporary Church. What were the positive and negatives changes since Vatican II?

I think they have mostly been positive; I don't think negative. We should have been doing a lot of this before, such as all of us in one choir [*stall*]. I love the choir today. You walk down out of it and we all go to Mass at the same level – the brothers one side, the priests the other, and we all get along beautiful.

I also think guests should be close to the monks. The only thing I didn't like from before the Council was that the priest had his butt to us all the time whenever he was facing the altar. Facing us now is a positive change they should have always had. Also, now people can do some of the readings, so let's use their talents.

Fr. Raban [*Hathorn*] designed the [*parish*] church here in St. Meinrad. He didn't realize what was going to happen 100% when he started it before the Council began. He had the church designed as a cross with the altar in the middle. Well, they didn't want it and they took him out as pastor and put Fr. Peter [*Behrman*] in.

That is when they built the church, which was horrible, I think, but that's okay. Fr. Raban's classmate built Holy Rosary Church in Evansville and he made it bigger, because it was a bigger parish. That was the first church that had the altar in the center. That was Fr. Raban's. Every time we went to Evansville for a doctor's appointment, Raban had tears in his eyes because that was his church design. He was way ahead of his time liturgically.

Look at the monastery today and when you first came. How about the morale, particularly in terms of the decrease in vocations?

Well, when I came, you had separation. You had the brothery and the fratery, which were the junior priests – they were two different groups. We had the senior brothers and the junior brothers. We were the junior brothers. Br. Lawrence [*Shidler*] and Benedict [*Barthel*] were the first two to graduate in the same class at St. Placid Hall and there was a big difference between the two.

I love all the old ones. I can still remember Br. Rembert [*Ringler*] when he was in charge of the carpenter shop and he tried to whistle and he couldn't. They were great. In those days, the priests had nothing to do with the brothers and they looked down on the brothers. You were lower status and you knew you were just a lay brother. So when Abbot Lambert was abbot, to push his button to get him going on that, I would say, "Fr. Abbot, we are just lay brothers," and he would say, "Oh no, you ain't ..."

How about today?

Oh man, today we are all brothers, and it doesn't matter if you are a priest or a monk. I think the majority of the priests are down to earth and getting along. Fr. Denis [*Robinson*] came to recreation during the coffee break this morning and carried on with Br. Andrew [*Zimmermann*]. So, I like it much better this way and I think the majority of the monks do, because they have a common group now and that helps. I think the community is living the way St. Benedict wrote. We are monks. We are all monks, ordained or not ordained, period!

So I am really happy the way the community is right now, and the spirit overall is very good. We mingle with the juniors, because they have to know us and we have to know them. In the old days, you relied on the novice master or junior master giving a report about them, as we had no contact with them. That was horrible, and now we have contact with them constantly. So you know, I think that is great. We got a good one now. Guerric [*Fr. DeBona*] is novice master and he is good so far.

Has the decrease in vocations had an impact in the monastery from when you were first here?

We used to have the minor seminary and the college. We got a lot of vocations with those.

Even though Latin has been de-emphasized and the Masses are celebrated in English, should Latin be in the academic curriculum for people who are going to be priests?

Well, either that or Spanish. There are so many Hispanics who need priests, and Latin wouldn't hurt. See, I had three years of Latin, so I can still serve Mass in Latin if I had to.

What do you see as the future of the Abbey?

The Abbey is going to be here and the school. We only have the [*Seminary and*] School of Theology, and philosophy [*degree*] now for the ones who don't already have philosophy. I think the school will be here, and I think it is a good thing. I am not against the schools. I get along with a lot of the students and it is nice to know some of the students. I think it is great and I think we should continue with the seminary and continue with our gift shop. That is under the Abbey now and I think that is good.

Now, I didn't like [*Abbot*] Lambert's idea, because of a shortage of priests, of taking over all of Perry County and sending out priests to help the bishop. A lot of them we didn't see for years. Now they are starting to come home and I think that is a good thing because they actually are monks first, then priesthood. I think we will still be here with our school. We need our schools and need to keep them full, like we have now, and having priests going out when they can to the parishes.

What are your hopes for the future for the Church?

For the Church? There are a lot of divisions in the Church, unfortunately. Some people are trying just to have Latin again and so forth. I think the Pope should just say, "Alright, if you want to do your thing, start your own church." I really do, because they are a thorn in the side for us, unfortunately.

I know that the Church and the Abbey will survive. We are going to be a part of it – teaching young men to be priests, which is what our main goal was when the monks first came over [*from Switzerland*]. It was local education of local clergy, not parish work. We are doing that and we will continue. That is why we were founded. The monastery also has trades. I have been a cook and took courses. I took Fr. Kurt's "Death and the Dying" [*course*]. That really helped me being a chaplain. I took his first course when he taught it and it was great.

Would you recommend to young men that they join the monastery?

Oh yes, at least try. Now, all of them aren't going to stay, but at least they gave it a try.

What do you like about being a monk?

How do you say it? The monks get along together and associate together. I like different kinds of people, but we still have one goal – the prayer and the work and following the rules of St. Benedict.

Profile based upon: Br. Giles M. to Prof. Ruth C. Engs, July 30, 2009. Interview Transcriptions, Saint Meinrad Archabbey Archives, St. Meinrad, IN.

Chapter 9: Fr. Gregory Chamberlin, OSB

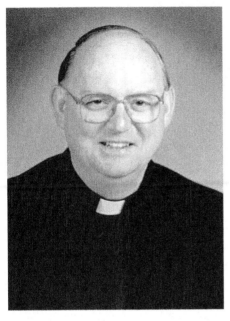

Fr. Gregory spent many years as a French teacher and administrator at Saint Meinrad College, had various assignments in the Development Office, and for 23 years served as pastor of St. Benedict Parish – later St. Benedict Cathedral – in Evansville, IN.

He was born October 12, 1938, in Indianapolis, IN, and was given the name David Andrew. Fr. Gregory completed elementary school at St. Francis de Sales and St. Andrew schools in Indianapolis. He entered Saint Meinrad High School Seminary in 1952 and graduated in 1956.

In 1961, he graduated from Saint Meinrad College with a BA in French and received a Master of Divinity in 1965 from the School of Theology. Fr. Gregory did additional graduate studies at Indiana University, Bloomington (1965); Laval University, Quebec, Canada (1967); and Middlebury College, Middlebury, VT, where he earned an MA in French (1973).

Entering the novitiate in 1958, Fr. Gregory professed simple vows on August 15, 1959, solemn vows August 15, 1962, and was ordained to the priesthood May 2, 1965. He taught French (1966-91) at Saint Meinrad College, became assistant dean of students (1966-71) and later dean of students (1985-88). Fr. Gregory served as acting president-rector of the college (1977-78) and vice rector (1978-81).

He was appointed alumni director from 1983 through 1985. In 1987, Fr. Gregory began a series of substitute relief assignments as administrator or associate pastor. In 1991, he was appointed pastor at St. Benedict Parish, Evansville, and remained in this position until five months before his death in June 10, 2014, after a long battle with pancreatic cancer.

Prof. Ruth C. Engs interviewed Fr. Gregory Chamberlin on July 1, 2009.

Childhood and Early Years as a Monk

Tell me about your childhood and family life.

I was born in Indianapolis on October 12th, 1938, into a lower-middle income family. We weren't dirt poor, by any means, but we didn't have a lot of extra things. My dad was a factory worker who worked for the RCA Corporation for years and years. He was also a fireman for a while and was in the Marines.

My mother helped supplement the family income by working for the Greater American Tea Company, where she delivered tea products to homes like the old milkmen used to do. She was also a teller in a bank and a grocery clerk. I am the second of four children; one brother is older than me and one is younger. My sister was the youngest and she died three years ago. It was pretty much a normal childhood.

How about your religious life as a child?

We didn't have a lot of private prayer together as a family, but we always had prayers before meals and always went to Mass on Sunday. The first four years of school we all went to St. Francis de Sales Catholic School and then they built St. Andrew's Parish right next door to us. So naturally I went to that school and church. I became a server and, because I was so close to the church, whenever anyone didn't show up, I was the guy they got to serve. So that may have had some influence on my vocation, I don't know.

Tell me about your schooling as a child.

At St. Francis De Sales, we had the Sisters of St. Francis from Oldenburg as teachers. I even remember each one of the sister's names. I was scared for my life by Sr. Mary Leigh in first grade because she cuffed me on the back of the head for coloring outside the lines. I remember that very, very well.

I was a good student. I wasn't the best in the class, but I got along very, very well in school. When we went to St. Andrew's, we had the Sisters of Providence from Terre Haute and got to know them. My mother cooked for them and took care of their meals in the convent at the parish, so we got to know the sisters pretty well that way.

Did anyone influence your religious vocation?

My parish priest was Fr. Mathew Harold who had three ways of doing things – the right way, the wrong way and Fr. Harold's way. We did it Fr. Harold's way, no matter what. He was quite the leader in the sense of giving a good example of stick-to-itiveness and fidelity to the teachings of the Church and so on. So he certainly had a great influence on my thinking about being a priest, as well as several other priests who were his associate pastors. I got to know them all because, as mentioned, I lived right next door and was constantly doing something at the parish. So I enjoyed my grade school years; they were wonderful.

What did you do for recreation and did you take vacations?

I played baseball a lot. I was good at baseball and football, but I was terrible at basketball. As I mentioned, we didn't have a lot of money but mother always insisted that in the summertime we take a driving vacation somewhere, because she contended that memories were more important than bank accounts. So one summer we drove out to Yellowstone Park and Wyoming and then to Florida and little places around the city of Indianapolis. It was a fun childhood; I really enjoyed it. We drove in an old 1942 Chevrolet which ran on paper clips and bailing wire, but it got us around.

What kind of health care did you have as a child?

We were always so healthy, so we didn't have a whole lot of health care. I don't remember, but I am sure we had measles, chicken pox and that sort of thing. We had a family doctor that would come to the house. In those days, doctors would come to the house. His name was Ulysses B. Hine and on his storefront office he had "Dr. U. B. Hine," and we always thought that was so funny.

Did you smoke or drink in high school?

Well, I came here to Saint Meinrad Minor Seminary for high school in 1952. There were 119 boys in my freshman class. It was a big seminary in those days. Unfortunately, only 14 of us went all the way through seminary to be ordained. While in the high school seminary, we were not allowed to smoke. During the summers I went home, of course, and I did smoke then. I didn't drink particularly, but I did smoke. In fact, we used to kid that it was a sign of a vocation to smoke. If you didn't smoke, you probably were not called to be a priest because almost every priest smoked in those days.

How long did you smoke?

I quit when I entered the monastery because we were not allowed to smoke until after ordination in the monastery. Then I smoked again until 1985, which was a good many years of my adult life. In fact, I can remember when I put out my last cigarette. It was in the parking lot of the Holiday Inn in Jasper, Indiana. I went there for one of those clinics to stop smoking and that was the last time I smoked. It was February 19, 1985, at 11:00 in the morning.

Did you drink when you were in the monastery when young?

Not in minor seminary. In those days, we had our own winery here, so the monks always had a glass of wine at the main meal. I did drink wine, yes.

Why did you decide to become a monk and what brought you here?

This is really interesting. I wanted to study for the priesthood for the Archdiocese of Indianapolis, but I was not accepted as a student for the Archdiocese of Indianapolis because my mother had been divorced. Later on, my parents' marriage was convalidated [*sanctioned by the Church*]. The archbishop simply said, "That was the rule of the diocese. The son of a divorced family was not permitted to study for the priesthood for that diocese." It nearly broke my heart, of course. I was only in eighth grade at the time and really had my heart set on becoming a priest.

Fr. Gregory, as a young monk

One of the other priests in my parish went to Bishop [*John George*] Bennett in Lafayette and asked if he would accept me and he said he would. Also there was a Benedictine monk, Fr. Bartholomew[1] from Saint Meinrad, stationed in Indianapolis that summer. So one of the priests took me over to meet him and Fr.

---

[1] Transferred to Prince of Peace Abbey, Oceanside, CA.

Bartholomew arranged for me to come and study at Saint Meinrad seminary as a Benedictine candidate.

However, we had to do an entrance exam to be accepted into the school. Fr. Theodore [*Heck*] came to Cathedral High School in downtown Indianapolis to meet with all of the boys from Indianapolis who were entering Saint Meinrad to give us this exam. I remember looking at him and saying, "Gosh, is he old."

He was probably 52 at the time and he died here at the age of 108. So "old" is a very relative kind of thing. I remember that I was always impressed with how old this guy was. When I came here, I had him in algebra as a teacher and, frankly, he was not a very good one, but he was a very good man. He tried to teach me algebra. I have to emphasize "tried" because I couldn't get that stuff for anything, but he was a good man.

So when I came in 1952 for the first year of high school at the minor seminary, I came to study for Saint Meinrad, but I didn't have any idea what a monk was. By the time I had gone through the minor seminary – when it was time to decide whether to join the monastery or not – I had decided I did want to try it. So it was kind of a roundabout way, but I got here, and here I am 50 years later. I will be making 50 years of vows this year [*2009*] as a jubilarian of profession.

What did family and friends think about your decision of a monastic vocation?

They were all very, very supportive. In the '50s, the Church was a lot different than it is today and families were a lot different. Families went to Mass together much, much more and the same was true in my family. We always had prayers before meals and always went to Mass on Sunday. So I was very much supported by both of my parents and my brothers and my sister – the whole family, as a matter of fact. They were very happy that I had decided to do that, and it was a wonderful thing to have that kind of support.

How did you see the Church in your early years? What expectations did you have from it and have they been met?

Well, first of all, I think the position of the Church was much clearer in those days. There was the authority of the bishop, the authority of the pastor, and the authority of the teachings of the Church through the *Baltimore Catechism*. There was a clear notion of what the Church was and I liked that. I had enough faith, even in the eighth grade, to know that the Church would be the way to heaven and I really wanted to get there. So I never had any wonderings about the Church or the value of the Church, and I wanted to be a part of it. I wanted to be able to help other people see the values of the Church.

I never have been disappointed in my expectations of the Church. There have been lots of foolishness that has gone on in the Church and a lot of bad things, but I always like to say, "Peter is still at the helm." The Pope is there and will be, as far as I am concerned, according to the revelation of the Lord, until the end of time.

So I have never had any doubts or worries about whether the Church is going to last. It certainly has gone through some great turmoil, but it has since the year 1 when Peter denied the Lord. Peter and Paul got into arguments on what the Church should be, so there has always been that kind of controversy in the Church. But this has always led to growth and development.

Have your expectations been met?

Yes, I certainly have not been disappointed. Fortunately, I have never, ever, ever felt that I made the wrong decision about being a priest and working in the Church. Thank God for that. A lot of my friends began to doubt and ended up leaving, but I have never been disappointed and never seriously doubted at all. That is the grace of God and I recognize Him for that.

Reflect on your years as a novice, as a young monk or junior. Describe something of the nature and tone of the discipline under which your vocation was formed.

Well, things were pretty – I started to say rigid. What is the word I am looking for? Structured, very structured, but in those times that was expected so it wasn't hard to say, "Well, if I am going to be a junior monk, I have to do this and this and this," and it never bothered me that it was pretty strict.

When I entered the noviceship, I was bright-eyed and bushy-tailed and I thought, "Man, this is great." About three months into the noviceship, I thought, "What in the world am I doing here? I want to be a priest, I want to be out with the people and here I am." So I really almost left at Christmastime of my novice year.

I will always be grateful to Fr. Damasus [*Langan*], who was the novice master at the time. He was very supportive and said, "Well if you have to go, you have to go. One thing I want you to do is come back and see me in three days and I want you to answer this question for me. Have you really tried the life?"

I got angry and I said, "Of course, I tried the life. I have a reputation for doing what I am supposed to." I really got mad at him and then I went back to my cell and I cried. Then I realized I really hadn't been immersing myself in the whole Benedictine thing, the whole community thing. I was living on the fringe of things, doing everything I was supposed to do, but not really allowing the experience to form me.

So after that, it was very smooth sailing until it came to solemn vows, where that was for life. I still had to reconsider. I did want to be a priest, and in the monastery I wouldn't have a whole lot of opportunity to serve as a priest. So I really had to weigh that, but I finally weighed it out and to me it became the best of both worlds.

I had the security and support of community life and yet the opportunity to serve as priest. I had no idea at the time that I would be pastor of St. Benedict Cathedral for 18 years. Nor at the time, I had no idea I would spend 25 years forming other people for the priesthood, so for me it became the best of both lives and of both worlds.

So Fr. Damasus was important in helping you in your formation?

Yes, Fr. Damasus really, really turned me around so that I could solidify my vocation. In addition, I observed a good number of monks in the monastic life. I saw their sense of community and sense of peace in doing that. So I said to myself, "Now here is Father So-and-So. I wonder what he is like." I would kind of ruminate and watch what he did. Those kinds of things also had an influence on me.

What was a typical day and how are things different today?

In a way, this is kind of difficult for me to answer – structure-wise – because I have been living in the parish for 18 years and I don't know the day-to-day things the juniors [*monks before solemn vows*] do now. In our day, it was very structured. You got up, you went to Morning Prayer, you had breakfast, and then you went to whatever assignment you had, such as cleaning the house or whatever – that changed week by week.

Then during the school year, you had your classes, came back for the noon Office, and in the evening you had evening prayer. So you knew what was going to happen the next day. Is it Friday? If so, it is going be this again. I found that a good thing, but now it's not quite that structured, although there are still expectations.

For example, the juniors are allowed to have radios in their room and that was strictly forbidden in my days. There are other kinds of changes. Juniors are out a lot more on field trips. We never set foot off the Hill unless we were going to the doctor for an appointment or something like that, except for one week during the summer. We had a kind of a camp – Camp Benedict down on the

Blue River – and we would go to that camp for one week. It was our vacation in those days.

Do you have an amusing story from your earlier years in the community?

Oh yes, I have several. Fr. Dunstan McAndrews was the athletic director of the minor seminary. He was a member of our community and he marched to the beat of a different drummer. One day he had confiscated some comic books from some of the minor seminarians, as these were strictly forbidden. He was on the way to his monastic cell to drop them off and then get to noon Office.

However, by the time he got over to the monastery area, the bell rang for Office and he didn't have time to drop them off. So he stuck the comic books in his cincture [*the belt on a monk's habit under the tunic*] and, as he was doing the profound vow to the altar, all the comic books scattered all over the sanctuary. It was chaos for a while, but it was really funny.

Abbot Ignatius [*Esser*] was still the abbot when I was in the minor seminary and before I entered the monastery. He had sort of a funny voice. One day we all marched in procession from the hill across the valley to bless the new irrigation lakes, which had just been built over there. Abbot Ignatius intoned, "O Dominus," and a cow mooed just as he did that, and that took care of any piety in that blessing. I will never forget that; it was really amusing.

Another story. Fr. Aemelian Elpers was the dean of discipline; nobody crossed Fr. Aemelian. He taught English and had impeccable handwriting. He would call you into the office to be disciplined and would send you a note with absolutely impeccable handwriting that said, "Please come see me." Those were known as valentines.

You didn't want to get a valentine from Fr. Aemelian, but one time I got a valentine. I was shaking in my boots when I went into his office. I thought I was going to get kicked out or something. But he simply said, "Chamberlin, your handwriting is inbombidable." He couldn't get the word "abominable" out. He just wanted to make me aware that my handwriting needed to improve. When I entered the monastery, he was a totally different person. He was one of the most delightful guys I have ever met, but, boy, I didn't think so when I was in the minor seminary.

One of my professors, Fr. Mark Toon, taught philosophy. We had a two-volume book called *Elementa philosophiae* written by Joseph Gredt, a German [*Luxemburg*] Benedictine. We called this book "Gret" and "Regret." In the beginning of the second year, we were opening the Regret book – volume II – and Fr. Mark, who we also had in the second year, opened his lecture by saying, "Well, same swine, different pearls." I thought it was funny, but most of my class was insulted by it. The monastery is a zoo sometimes.

Work

Now think about your work experiences. What assignments were you hoping for and were you assigned to do what you wanted to do?

Well, I was hoping that I would be able to teach a section of French in the minor seminary high school. Unfortunately, shortly after I was ordained, the minor seminary concept changed. I was a little disappointed in that, but I was still permitted to teach. I was asked to get a degree in French and I taught French for 25 years in the college seminary.

I enjoyed every bit of that. I also taught theology on the college level. I didn't enjoy that nearly as much, because I'm simply not a lecturer. It was really a struggle for me to present theology well. That career ended in about four or five years, but I continued teaching French.

I was surprised, but very happy, to be appointed to the administration of the college. I first became the associate dean of students and then, finally, the dean of students and vice rector. I really did enjoy that challenge because, as I said, I have great respect for the priesthood and to be able to be on the ground floor of helping young men decide whether or not that was for them was a great privilege for me. I really enjoyed that work and had no idea I would ever be asked to do that.

In November of 1966, I was asked to temporarily serve as associate dean of students until June, when I thought that I probably was going to be assigned to a parish and that was okay with me. Well, at the end of that semester, the rector for the college, Hilary Ottensmeyer, asked me if I would like to stay on. I was flattered and told him, "Sure, I would be glad to if you think I am doing a good job." He said, "You are doing a great job." So I stayed on for several years doing this.

What were some of the challenges you had in that job?

The biggest challenge was when Fr. Thomas Ostick became the rector and got sick. He had to take a semester off for a valve replacement in his heart. I became the acting president-rector at that time and found it a great challenge. I am just not an organizer; I am not a planner; I am not a visionary kind of a person. I am a great supporter and second guy. That is how I see myself. People said I did okay in that position, but it took a toll on me because I just did not enjoy that kind of thing.

I found it challenging when I was the dean of students to have to confront people, which is what the dean has to do. That part of the job was never pleasant, but I was able to do it because it had to be done. When I had to be the guy to say, "Do this or you are out," that was difficult. But living with the students and sharing their growth was wonderful.

What kind of problems did students have?

Oh, occasionally they would drink. You can understand a beer or two every once in a while, but it was against the rules and occasionally there would be drunkenness. Sometimes, as the '70s opened up and the whole world went to hell in a hand basket, the guys would get into trouble sexually out in the boondocks, and that sort of thing. Those were hard to handle.

One of them got really messed up with drugs while he was here – not on the Hill, but when he was away from it. I remember having to fly with him to his home and talk to his parents about his drug use. That was a very difficult thing. They were very appreciative.

One of the most difficult things I had to handle as dean of students was when two of our guys decided to elope with two girls up in Canada. I had to be the one on the phone with the parents trying to figure out what they were doing. That was very difficult. First of all, it shouldn't have happened but it did. It turned out fine, as they came back healthy and nobody had actually gotten married. But it was very difficult not knowing exactly how to handle it or what the outcome would be.

One guy was very, very intelligent and convinced the other guy – although it was all false – that he was on the lam from people who were going to try and kill him. So he needed somebody to go with him and developed a whole cock-and-bull story about two girls waiting for him in Canada. The gullible guy thought, "Oh, that will be interesting." It was the craziest thing I ever dealt with. The intelligent guy was very talented musically, academically and every other way, and he always gave the impression that he was very honest and sincere when he was actually pulling all kinds of things like that.

So, those were the kinds of things I dealt with. Less serious things were their struggles with the Church such as, "Oh, I don't have to fast for an hour before communion" or "Jesus didn't wear a wristwatch" – all those foolish rebellion kinds of things. It was sometimes difficult to convince them that there was more to what was being said than just that. So, those were the challenges, but it was a delightful time.

I was also so pleased to be working with the caliber of people I was working with such as Fr. Hilary, Fr. Thomas and Fr. Vincent [*Tobin*]. The Archbishop, Fr. Daniel [*Buechlein*], was my classmate. He and I, when we were first ordained, were assistant deans of students together. Then he advanced to president-rector. That sort of thing is his strength. He is an organizer, he is a planner and he is a visionary, and that is why it was a pleasure to be with him and help him do what he could do.

Were you ever assigned to do something you really didn't want to do?
Around 1983, when I had been at the college for many years as an administrator, Fr. Timothy [*Sweeney*] – who was abbot at the time – called me in and asked me to step out of that role and go into development work and become the director of the alumni program. I didn't want to do that – I just did not want to do that – but I was able to say that to Timothy. He responded, "Well, what do you think you are going to be able to do with it, Fr. Gregory?"

I said, "May I be frank, Fr. Abbot?" And he said, "Yes, be as frank as you want to," and I said, "Damn vow of obedience!" But I did the work and I wasn't miserable doing it. I would have preferred to be doing something else. As it turned out, that assignment only lasted a few years. During this time, I did not have to give up my teaching or spiritual direction with the kids. It was a hard thing to do when you didn't want to do it, but I was able to "mount the attack and muddle through to victory," as they say.

In other words, Benedictine perseverance?
Oh yes, and I was never rebellious about it. I was never griping to other people about what I had to do now. I firmly believe if we are going to be Benedictines and have a vow of obedience, it means we obey what the superior asks you to do, hard as it is sometimes.

So I was never negative about it, except in the joking way with the abbot at the beginning, and he knew what I was saying.

Then what did you do?

Around 1989, I was relieved of my position as dean of students when the new rector came in, as he wanted his own staff, which was fine with me. So, for six months they asked me to work in the Diocese of Memphis, where Daniel had become bishop. I worked in a parish down there and then came back here and continued my teaching.

When I got back here, it just so happened that one of the priests, who was pastor at St. Henry, ran into some problems and the abbot asked me to be administrator over there just for six months. Well, you never do something for six months in a monastery, and that work turned into a two-and-a-half year assignment and then I was transferred down to St. Benedict in Evansville.

While I was over at St. Henry as administrator, I was continuing to teach. However, the college was going down in enrollment, and the enrollment for French classes went way, way down. Everybody was turning to Spanish, which made sense and I wasn't offended by that. When I first started teaching, I had two divisions with 25 guys in each division. When I finally finished teaching, I had four students in one division. So it was easy enough for me to back out of this.

When the abbot called me in to see if I would take on the job at St. Benedict, I really had to think it over. I thought, "What a great challenge and it would be wonderful to do that." But again, knowing my administrative abilities, I thought, "I really better clearly think about it." Because I didn't want to cause trouble within a large parish like that.

So the abbot gave me a week to talk it over and think it over. I talked to the pastor down there and saw that it was very well structured and very organized. So I thought, "Well, if the abbot thinks I can do it and they think I can do it, I probably can do it." So, August 28th of '91, I moved out of the monastery to Evansville and became pastor there.

It will be 18 years August 28th this year [2009] and I have never regretted it. I did at first miss the teaching and the involvement with the students. But in a parish like St. Benedict's, there is not much time to sit back and worry about what you used to do, because there is plenty to do there. I am involved with the school there and all the parish kinds of things. I am very, very happy there and I have no regrets that this is where I ended up.

Is there anything else you want to say about your job or career?

I am totally and completely happy with what has happened over the last 50 years. I have had some bumps – up and down – but I have never ever, ever felt dissatisfied in what I have done. Somebody asked me just recently, "Don't you miss the fact you don't have children?" I said, "Not really." Every once in a while, I might think, "What would my son be like? Would he be in jail or would he be prominent in his community?"

In fact, I am very involved with the children in the parish, in the parish school, as well as the high school. So I have had children in my life throughout my priesthood. So that has been very satisfying. I simply have no regrets whatsoever in what I have done in the priesthood and my life. I am very happy.

[*After almost 23 years as pastor of St. Benedict's, Fr. Gregory, due to a serious illness, entered the infirmary at Saint Meinrad in January 2014. He died five months later.*]

Prayer

What would you like to convey to younger confreres, or even the laity, in terms of Benedictine spirituality?

Consistency in prayer is very important, but that doesn't mean you become a mystic. I don't know what I would do without prayer. Now, that doesn't mean for 15 minutes every hour I am on my knees in prayer. It is the realization of the presence of God. My mother instilled that in me when I was in fifth or sixth grade.

One time an ambulance was going down the street and she said, "Let's stop just a minute and say a little prayer for whoever is in trouble." That really struck me; I didn't know that person and didn't have to, as I could ask the Lord's blessing on that person. So to this day, when I hear a siren, I offer a little prayer for whoever is in trouble. Whether it is a criminal being chased by the cops or an ambulance, they are in trouble. So prayer really is that sense of the presence of God. I urge people to be constant in their prayer, even if it seems like you are talking to a brick wall. Talk anyway and recognize the presence of God in everything.

What is your favorite chapter or part of the Rule of St. Benedict?

It is Chapter 4 on the instruments of good works, and there are over 70 of them. To me that chapter reflects Benedict's common sense. He lists all the instruments [*sometimes called tools*] of good works, and they are obtainable and achievable by everybody anywhere. Benedict was a very practical kind of a person. For example, in Chapter 40, he says, "Wine is not at all proper for monks, yet, because monks in our times cannot be persuaded of this, let us agree, at least, that we do not drink to satiety. Let them have a *hemina* [*half a liter*] of wine a day."

Again, that was Benedict's genius where he recognized the weakness in people. He recognized the potential in people and constantly throughout the *Rule* he calls people to fulfill that potential. Also, the whole sense of hospitality permeates the *Rule*. I have taken that personally to heart. I always try to be as accommodating to people as I possibly can because of the importance of, as Benedict says, "recognizing Jesus in whoever comes." So those are my Holy *Rule* favorites. Benedict was a genius.

What is your key to living Benedictine spirituality?

Once again, for me personally, I think it comes down to consistency in prayer and hospitality. I like to think of myself, and am known, as somebody who is very welcoming to people. I find that very satisfying. So it would be consistency in prayer and hospitality.

Over your lifetime, what have been your most happy or joyful times and what have been your most difficult or darkest times?

My most difficult and darkest time was when I had to leave the college as dean of students and do a different kind of work in the Development Office. It took me a while to adjust to that. I just didn't overnight turn off my feelings. So that was a low point.

But again, I put it in the context of, "What am I called to do? I am not called to be the dean of students in the college anymore. I am called to obey what the abbot needs to be done." That realization slowly took over from my formation and the spirituality that I had built up over the years. I was able to cope with it and be effective at what I was doing.

So your Benedictine formation and spirituality is what made you persevere in something that you did not particularly want to do?

Right, exactly.

What was the happiest or most joyful time in your life?

I think the happiest times were the moments when I was involved with seminarians who made a breakthrough about their vocation or hearing confessions in those moments of priestly service when you can help somebody in their reconciliation through this sacrament. Over 25 working years in the seminary, I never really had any regrets. It wasn't always a party, but I always felt satisfied with what I was doing.

Changes in the Church

As you know, Benedict himself became discouraged by the general disregard for spiritual ideas in his time and today some observers are also of the opinion that we are once again falling into indifference and the meaning of a virtuous life and even a lack of spirituality. How has this societal change affected spirituality within the Church or within the Abbey or even within your parish?

That is a very difficult question to answer; it really is. I am trying to get a good word – a kind of casualness about the faith that is not a healthy thing. It is found in, "If I feel like doing this now, then it is a good thing and let's go do it. But if I don't feel like doing it now, then let's not worry about it." Or, it is reflected in a smorgasbord approach to what the Church teaches.

We have lost a whole generation, in a sense, that after Vatican II, the *Baltimore Catechism* – the manual approach of things – went out the window. It probably was good that happened, but what replaced it was how you feel about this or that. Before Vatican II, we didn't take into account emotions, but all of a sudden that's what it was, and it didn't make any difference what the objective truth was. There is still residue of this attitude around.

Is that a reflection of the hippie generation?

Yes, I think so, absolutely. The Church was simply not unaffected by what happened in the '60s – the flower children, the hippies, the dope and the marijuana.

How about within the Abbey?

For the Abbey, again, I find this very difficult to judge as I was not living in the monastery day by day by day. I think we have a very strong religious community here. I don't think anybody is un-Benedictine because they are not doing things exactly the way I think they ought to be doing it or the way I was brought up here. I think we have wonderful leadership in the community and the leadership allows other leadership to emerge. I am thinking in terms that the abbot needs to be the leader. I think it is a very strong community. I don't think we are crumbling in our Benedictinism at all, by any means.

Some people feel that Pope John XXIII was very optimistic and ever since Vatican II the Church has been paying a heavy price for his initiatives, while others applaud his gestures. What does this all mean in terms of the Church or the monastery?

From my personal viewpoint, I think his election was the work of the Holy Spirit. Pope John XXIII was a different kind of a pope from Pius XII, that's for sure. His roly-poly cheerfulness and his attitude of – I think it is in his autobiography – "Lord, I have this burden of the Church on my shoulders, but it's bedtime now. I am going to sleep; you take care of it," was a marvelous, common-sense sort of thing.

Unfortunately, what many people considered repression in the Church was all of a sudden removed and things swung to the other side. That happened in many, many ways. A lot of the practices of the Church were thrown out because, "We didn't need that anymore."

Conveying the solid teachings of the Church to children and young people in those early times after Vatican II was pretty minimal. So now we are faced with them as parents, and even grandparents, and they don't really know what to pass on. So we have to regroup and find ways of expressing the teachings of the Church in modern terms and not how you feel about this or that. Feelings are important, but there is good and there is evil, and it isn't just your choice that makes it that way. So this also was one of the residues of Vatican II.

When I was in first-year theology, we were still using the manual approach to theology. We had a big volume on moral theology and one for dogmatic theology. Then the post-Vatican changes hit Saint Meinrad like an explosion. We had some rather dynamic teachers, who I think may have gone a little bit too far in their enthusiasm to make the Church come alive.

I remember one monk – whose name I will not mention – at the beginning of our fourth year of theology said, "Well, we are going to get you guys through. There is not much we can do to save you, but now the Church is going to start working." He was not very beloved, needless to say. That kind of thing hit the seminaries – not just Saint Meinrad – but the seminary world as a result of Vatican II. There is still fallout from that. When you read the history of the Church, it is not terribly surprising, because whenever there has been a major council such as Vatican II, there has always been an explosion and residue and I firmly believe the Holy Spirit is in charge.

How different is the Church, or even the parish, today compared to pre-Vatican II?

I think that people who are involved in their parishes, who come to Mass and get involved in other things the parish does, are in great shape. They are just marvelous. I just marvel at the generosity of some people in my parish. I don't mean money only – that too – but their being on fire with what the Church is really all about. Unfortunately, there are fewer people than there used to be, but it is a very strong core of people. About 52-56% of Catholics go to Mass on Sundays now. Well, that is sure down from before Vatican II.

What was it before Vatican II?

It was much higher and I would guess about 80-90% of Catholics regularly went to Mass. First of all, there was a sense of obligation – that is not there now. The people who are coming to Mass now are not coming out of a sense of obligation, but out of a sense of power that goes on there. If we can continue to build on that, we are going to be in good shape. Again, I think some of the reforms of Vatican II will make it possible for the Church to grow that way.

Certainly, it is discouraging when you are working with one of the high school kids whose faith is dependent on parents who never go to Mass. I think that kind of thing is true in society in general. Where are the parents now?

In Evansville, just the other day, they were talking about not being able to have as many counselors in the Evansville public school system because of the finances. "What is going to happen to these poor kids?" people are saying. Well, where are the parents? They are the ones who should be handling their children, but they are not. That is reflected also in the Church.

So parents aren't parenting?

In many, many cases, they are not. It is so discouraging. We have a Catholic school – St. Benedict's – and that is what it is, a Catholic school. It is not a private school and I am constantly harping on that. Some of the parents joined the parish because they could get parish rates for their children at the school.

But you never see them in church and you never see them involved in the summer social and that sort of thing. They want their kids to have an excellent education, which they are getting, but they are thinking in terms of private school, not Catholic school.

Those are some of the challenges. I remind them at baptism, where you give a blessing that says, "And may the parents be good teachers by what they say and do." I stress that all the time to people and it goes in this ear and out the other, if they are even there to hear it. That is one of the frustrations of the work, but it is a good challenge.

What kind of changes have you seen in the parish over the years in the way things are run?

Well, the laity is doing a lot more than they used to. For example, we have a whole army of Eucharistic ministers. We have to because one man simply couldn't do it. I have seen attendance at Mass, unfortunately, go down all over the country. It isn't just a problem at St. Benedict's. The fact that Catholics are supposed to go to Mass on Sunday is now more casually accepted. In other words, "If I can't go, well, it's no big deal."

Unfortunately, that sends out the wrong signals to children in the school, because we are teaching them Catholic doctrine about the nature of the Mass. Then when the parents don't bring them to Mass on Sunday, this is a problem. Those kinds of attitudes weren't quite as prevalent 18 years ago, although it was beginning then, due to all the changes from Vatican II.

Are there any other changes that you have seen in your parish, even minor things such as what they wear to church, etc.?

Yes, as a matter of fact, I just wrote my bulletin comment on that last week. Sometimes people are too casual about what they wear in Church. One article I read said, "We have turned our churches into a meeting hall." I don't believe that because there is a lot of discussion and talking after Mass. I think that is healthy.

But when people come to Mass dressed for the beach, this says something to me about the importance they put on where they are. They wouldn't show up at a wedding dressed like that – I don't think – unless it was perhaps on a beach. So that kind of casualness is there.

Another change is that women are much more prevalent in positions of importance and authority in the parish nowadays. My business manager is a woman and she can spin circles around me as far as business. I was never trained in business and, thank God, I don't have to handle all that, except in a supervisory sort of a way.

Compare the morale in the monastery today compared with that of 30, 40, 50 years ago and to what extent has the decline of vocations had an impact on the monastic community and the Church?

I think the morale is pretty good today in the monastery. However, I think the decline in vocations is a bit discouraging and maybe to some – although not to me, frankly – a kind of fearful thing. It is expressed as, "What is going to happen to us? The median age is growing old," and that sort of thing. I think if the Lord wants us to be here, it's going to happen as long as we continue to work to make it happen. But the decline, I think, does gives a sense of uneasiness.

Even if Mass is to be celebrated in English, was eliminating Latin from the academic curriculum a good idea?

First of all, being a lover of languages, having taught French for 25 years, and having gone through the old Latin, I do think it was a mistake for people to just ignore Latin because it isn't part of the liturgy anymore. Latin has enriched the English language, the French language, the Spanish language, and I think we really ought to hold on to those classical things. It enriches our understanding of other people and so on.

I am glad we don't have the Mass in Latin. I am glad we can have it in Latin if a particular group asks for it. We are allowed to do that unless the particular group is finally saying, "Oh good, now we finally have the real Mass again." There are some who want to have a Latin Mass so they can truly worship the "real Mass." That is really frustrating to me.

Striking changes have been made in the Church since Vatican II. Comment on the positive and the negative changes you have seen.

On the positive side, I think the sense of community is much stronger. The sharing of the sign of peace is an indication of that type of thing. It isn't anymore just "me and Jesus," as it tended to be in the old Church. "Oh, you are going to do that to us. That's fine." But there was never the horizontal part of it. The sense of community and unity and we are in this together is one of the greatest contributions of Vatican II.

On the negative side, there was too much emphasis on throwing things out. It was a classic example of throwing the baby out with the bath water, in many cases. I don't know if some things can be retrieved, but I don't think it means that the Church is dead. We have lost some healthy practices in the Church. We haven't lost any teachings of the Lord and we haven't lost basic theology. We have lost the way to teach it in an effective way, and we have lost the methods to reach people who are on the fringe. So how do we do that? That is the struggle right now.

Assuming you agree there is no going back to pre-Council days, what has been lost and what has been gained?

There is a loss of respect for the teaching authority of the Church. This is not necessarily because of Vatican II. It is because of stupidity on the part of some people who have brought this about. We have lost one generation of people. They believe it is okay to go to Christian formation or a Christian fellowship church. It is a mentality of going to church, but not celebrating the Eucharist. We really have to get back to celebrating the Eucharist, not just going to church.

I have had people say, "Well, it doesn't make a difference. I can go to Christian fellowship because it is closer to where I live and I am still praying, aren't I?" Well, yes, but that is not Catholic. So I think this certainly is one of the losses. The reverence for the

Eucharist is not as strong or as evident as it used to be. Catholics don't come in and genuflect much anymore; some do and some don't.

The adults and teenagers who walk down the communion line to receive communion who are chewing gum indicates that something is missing. The amount of gum that has to be cleaned off the bottom of the pews is unbelievable sometimes. The gains: the presence of the Holy Spirit is stronger and the sense of community is stronger.

What has been the effect of the decline in vocations in the parish?
In the Evansville area, one or two priests have been put in charge of three or four parishes. Unfortunately, some people really do not see it, do not accept it and haven't reflected on what it really means. I think part of the reason they haven't reflected on it is because of the attitude of, "Well, if we don't have a priest, we can do something else." What does that say about their understanding of the priesthood, the Mass and the sacraments?

I keep stressing we are a sacramental church and to have a sacramental church you have to have the priesthood. So I think people are not quite convinced there really is a shortage, especially when there is a gathering of priests. There may see 35 or 40 priests at a meeting and they ask, "What is so short about the number of priests?" Well, that doesn't go very far, folks. The lack of priests is a major challenge in the Church right now.

How about the effect of the decline in vocations in the monastery?
That decline has really affected the monastery. We could be doing a lot more things if we had more monks to do it. When I first came here, there were something like 230 monks in the monastery, and now it is a 101 or so. That obviously affects us here. We have to find better ways of interesting young people in being priests and

sisters and brothers. We are doing an awfully good job here at Saint Meinrad with the programs we have going.

In the Diocese of Evansville, there is a reawakening that we really have to do something. They have a pretty good program going there. If kids do not have a strong faith, they are not going to think they are called to service in the Church. If faith isn't there, if they don't really, really believe what the Holy Eucharist is or know what the sacrament of penance is, they are not likely to think about a vocation.

There is an attitude of, "I don't want to be celibate and I don't want to get involved with it." When I approach guys – as I do pretty regularly – I challenge them by asking, "Do you ever think about being a priest?" The reaction often is, "Well, I really want to be a pilot," or "No, I never thought of it," but most won't say, "Yeah, I am going to think about it." However, there are some who do say they will think about it.

At my parish at the end of every weekend Mass, we have what is called the vocation cross. I call a family forward to accept the cross and then, as a family, they say certain prayers for an increase in vocations in the priesthood and religious life. That is keeping the idea alive. Now, what effect this will have, that is the Holy Spirit's job. I am just doing what I can. At least it is well received in the parish.

Is the Church today different than it was in the mid-20th century?
Yes, it is less formal, it is less structured and it is less imposing. I think it is also more human. I remember when I was in the seminary and growing up as a little kid, to see a bishop was like seeing your favorite movie star – nobody ever saw the bishops. Now, it is not quite the same. People don't have any respect for the "funny little hat," as they call it. So I think that certainly is a change.

What are your hopes for the future of the Archabbey?

We have a very strong community here and we have a strong sense of monastic mission, as well as outreach. That has been the genius of Saint Meinrad since its founding in 1854. There has always been a strong monastic core with a missionary outreach that is compatible with what St. Benedict did. I think if we keep working at interesting people and bringing young men here to "come and see," the monastery is going to live on for years and years and years to come.

I don't see it falling apart, by any means, because there is simply too strong a tradition and respect from Catholics and Protestants alike. I am not concerned about the future. Certainly, we have to watch the shekels, we have to find ways to support it financially, but that always comes if we are doing what we are supposed to be doing in God's eyes.

How about the future of the Church?

For the Church in general, we really have to turn the vocation situation around, whether that might mean a change in the celibacy law – but I am not convinced that is going to do it either. There are some people who are advocating a kind of temporary priesthood. You can be a priest for 10 years and then leave the priesthood and do whatever else you want to. I don't see that in the cards, and I am not sure that would be an effective way.

We are not going to continue to influence people for the good if we don't have enough people to be leaders in doing that. By leaders, I mean priests, brothers and sisters, and the lay leaders, for that matter, too. One of the strengths here at Saint Meinrad is the many, many lay leaders we are training to work with the Church.

I see the Ark of Peter is still on the scene, and it is being buffeted about, but so what? What is new about that? I think the future of the Church is very bright. I think there is certainly a lot of work to do, people to be brought into the fold and things to do with the structure of the Church and the community itself. I have no fears that, somehow or other, the Catholic Church is going disintegrate. I am totally convinced that will not happen and I am going to work to do my part to make sure that it doesn't.

Profile based upon: Fr. Gregory Chamberlin, OSB, to Prof. Ruth C. Engs, July 1, 2009. Interview Transcriptions, Saint Meinrad Archabbey Archives, St. Meinrad, IN.

Chapter 10: Fr. Pius Klein, OSB

Fr. Pius Klein, OSB, served in a number of positions including the tailor shop as a young brother; novice master, junior master and prior at the mission to Peru as a priest; pastor at St. Mary's Parish in Huntingburg, IN; and at present is director of pastoral assistance, refectorian and part-time chaplain to the sisters at Monastery Immaculate Conception, Ferdinand, IN.

Born May 12, 1939, in Aurora, IN, he was given the name Charles. Fr. Pius attended St. Mary's Grade School in Aurora and graduated (1957) from St. Placid Hall (a boarding school for high school boys who were considering becoming brothers). On April 19, 1959, he made his profession as a monk and made his solemn profession May 13, 1962. Since he had taken classes in Peru, the school structured for him a special four-year program prior to his ordination. He graduated from the Saint Meinrad School of Theology with a degree in theology (1974) and was ordained a priest March 31, 1974.*

Fr. Pius was appointed to San Benito Priory, Huaraz, Peru (1967-70 and 1975-1985). Here Fr. Pius was principal of the high school, served as novice and junior master and was elected prior of the monastery in 1978. He also served as pastor of a parish in Lima, Peru. Fr. Pius was at the Peruvian monastery during the devastating earthquake of 1970. He returned to Indiana after the priory closed and served as pastor of St. Mary's Parish, Huntingburg, for 21 years. In August 2008, Fr. Pius became director of pastoral assistance, refectorian, part-time commuting chaplain and "on-call" priest for the Guest House.

Prof. Ruth Clifford Engs interviewed Fr. Pius Klein, OSB, July 30, 2009.

Childhood and Early Years as a Monk

Tell me about your childhood, family life and early schooling.

Well, I was born in Aurora, Indiana, on May 12th of 1939. I have one sister and she is married and has five children; one of them has died. I grew up in Aurora, Indiana. My mother was a homemaker; my father was a part-time farmer who was originally from Kansas. He moved to Aurora because of an aunt who was his sister ... and then he met my mother. They were married on June 30th of 1938. I attended our Catholic grade school in Aurora, St. Mary's of the Immaculate Conception.

We lived in town until I was in the seventh grade and then my father, having been a farmer from a farmer family in Kansas, moved to a farm out in the country. So when we lived in town, my sister and I would just walk to school. Of course, when we lived out in the country, we took the school bus.

Did he farm then full time?

No, dad was just part time. In our family, among my aunts and uncles, we were always in some type of business venture. My mom's brother and his wife had a hotel business for a while. My mom's other brother and his wife had a bowling alley and a restaurant. My other aunt, my mom's sister, and her husband had a restaurant. It was interesting that the whole family, in a sense, was an extended family. I remember when I was growing up, before we went to the farm, my mom and dad were in the restaurant business. It was a restaurant-tavern type of business.

Did you work in the restaurant as a boy?

We helped out in the kitchen, which was upstairs. All the dirty dishes would come upstairs and we would help in washing the dishes. There was an old-type elevator – a dumbwaiter. Downstairs, they would put stuff on it and we would pull the rope and bring it upstairs. We would help with that or prepare chili. It was part-time work.

What was your religious life as a child and how did you become interested in a religious vocation?

At St. Mary's, the Franciscan Sisters from Oldenburg, Indiana, were the teachers in the school. Of course, having eight years of Franciscan influence, my first inclination was to be a Franciscan. I always felt somehow attracted to religious life and, needless to say, the sisters always encouraged it.

I remember I was particularly interested in a group of Franciscans of the poor who had a house in Cincinnati, Ohio, which is just kind of up the road from Aurora. I remember I wrote to them and they sent a very nice letter back saying they did not have the structure where they could take people who were just finishing up grade school. In other words, they had no high school program.

So at this point, you were finishing up eighth grade?

Yes, and they suggested that I finish high school and then get back in contact with them. Well, at this point, I had no desire toward the priesthood, but just religious life. So this pretty well settled the Franciscan idea for the time being. One day my mom asked me to go to our pastor, Fr. John Lynch. I later found out he was an alumnus of Saint Meinrad, and he asked me, "Well, what are you going to be doing next year?"

I had to explain to him the Franciscan experience and he said, "You know, I think where I went to seminary they have a high school, especially for those who want to enter the monastic community, but not in the role of priest but as a brother in the community."

He gave me the address and said, "Why don't you write and see?" So I did. This is when I became acquainted with what was then St. Placid Hall, the oblates who attended it and the high school. I got a letter back with all the information you would need and an invitation to come down and visit. So we did that.

How old were you?

Thirteen or 14 – somewhere around there. So we came down and visited and I thought, "Okay." We did all the necessary paperwork, but my dad was not too keen on it.

Explain your parents' feelings in more detail.

My mom was okay with it, but my dad was not too keen on it. I think the reason for this might have been the fact that I was the only son. I mean, he wasn't drastically against it, but he was saying, "I think he's maybe too young yet. Why don't you just go ahead and finish high school?" I can remember my mom saying to him, "Gene, just let him go and if it is not to be, he will get it out of his system."

When did you arrive at St. Placid Hall?

I got there in the beginning of September 1953, and at the feast of Christ the King in October we were invested as oblates with the oblate habit. That was celebrated in what used to be the Saint Meinrad Seminary Chapel and which is now the St. Thomas Aquinas Chapel for the [*Seminary and*] School of Theology. Most of our parents came down for this, so it was kind of a special celebration. In February of '55, we made our final oblation.

Tell me some more about St. Placid Hall.

There was an element of high school education but there was an emphasis on a trade, which would eventually be a service to the monastic community. I really don't know how the system worked, but I ended up in the tailor shop. The first year was pretty much academic.

What subjects did you take? What courses?

It was regular geography, history, mathematics, English, biology and some Latin. There were regular high school courses and religion over the whole four years. But then, I believe, it was in the second year we began half a day of classes and the other half day in a trade.

So at this point you were not a candidate or a novice at St. Placid Hall? You were a student?

Yes, we were just students who were thinking about the brotherhood and religious life within the Benedictine community. It was something that you were working toward, but there was no commitment. It was orientation and preparation for monastic life. For example, within the community we don't have anyone who has the same name. Everyone has a different name. When I went, for example, to Placid Hall, no two oblates had the same name. There was already an Oblate Charles, so I couldn't use it.

Well, my middle name is Edward, but there was already an Oblate Edward, so that

Fr. Pius, as a young monk

eliminated that name. My confirmation name was Joseph, well, there was already a Joseph. My next choice was Francis, but there was already a Francis. So finally Fr. Richard Hindel, the oblate director at that time, said, "Let's go through the evangelists."

He started out with, "How about Mathew?" I don't know. "Mark?" So, I thought, "Well, okay." So I ended up Oblate Mark for four years at the oblate house. Then I came up to the monastery and they went back to Charles, and then I made vows and it became Pius.

Tell me some more about your experiences in the oblate house. Describe the rooms you slept in, the facilities, etc.

The building has been torn down, but it had a basement, first floor, second floor and third floor. For a lot of the classes, we were downstairs on the first floor. The recreation room was in the basement area of the building. The classrooms and Fr. Richard's office and guest room and stuff like that were on the first floor. On the second floor were the study hall, chapel and sacristy. Those who had a specific duty, such as the sacristans, were also on that floor. On the third floor was the dormitory.

Was the dormitory divided into different rooms or was it just one big dorm?

Just two dormitories – a large and a small dormitory.

How many students in each one?

It could range from 10 to 15 in each. I can't even remember now how many of us there were at that particular time.

Were there sheets between the beds like described by some of the monks when they were novices in the monastery?

No, no, it was just a regular open dormitory. Each dorm had a prefect. One that would make sure the beds were made properly –

such as how the sheets were to be placed when you put them on the bed. On the third floor, there was a compartment with individual places where each one kept their toiletries and things like that.

Did the student have to provide them or did the community supply toiletries like soap?
Everybody had to have their own supplies. There were no supplies available, so each person had to take care of whatever they needed.

What type of clothing did you wear?
We wore what they called the "oblate habit," which was a tunic and a scapular but it didn't have a hood. So apart from recreational periods and work periods, we always wore the habit to study halls, to classes, wherever.

Were all your classes in St. Placid Hall?
Some classes, such as history and Latin, I remember we took with the seminary students. English we had apart from them, but in the seminary building. The other classes were always down at Placid Hall. Whoever was the teacher would come down there. I graduated from Placid Hall in May of '57.

Why did you decide to become a monk?
I felt comfortable with everything and, after I graduated from Placid Hall, I entered the monastery as a candidate in September of '57.

How many of the boys who graduated from Placid Hall went on to become monks?
In my class, I was the only one; nine of us entered as freshmen. Now the other ones, a lot of them in the course of the years at Placid Hall, decided that this was not what they wanted or where they

wanted to go, so I was the only one that ended up going into the monastery as a candidate.

Describe some of your early jobs as a candidate. Were you still working in the tailor shop?

I worked there periodically, but during candidacy and the novitiate you could expect to be working anywhere and doing anything. It depended on any particular need. I remember a lot of times we would be at the Abbey Press stuffing envelopes. We would work down at the chicken house [*at the bottom of the hill from the monastery*] helping Br. Donald [*Delbeke*]. We could work in the garden helping Fr. Fintan [*Baltz*]. We helped with baling hay.

How about as a novice?

You never knew where you would be working. In our novitiate quarters, every day we would see what the schedule was. Sometimes I would end up being assigned to the tailor shop, but it was just an open field. We were assigned where people needed help – working in the kitchen either peeling potatoes or snapping beans. The novice master was Fr. Claude [*Ehringer*] when I entered the monastery. Later on, he ended up being abbot at Prince of Peace [*Abbey*] in California.

Is the work different today?
Oh, much different today.

How is it different today compared to what you experienced?

When I came in the early 1950s, there was a different approach with those who were entering to be brothers and those coming into the monastery with priesthood in mind. For example, when I entered the monastery in '57, there were three different recreation rooms and a Rule of Separation. The brothers had their recreation room, the fathers had their recreation room and the clerics [*studying for the priesthood*], who were called "fraters," had their own recreation room. God forbid you would get caught in any other one, due to this Rule of Separation.

There was a completely different structure as far as the monastic system, even in the dining room. The fathers sat on one side, the clerics were always in the middle, the brothers were always on another side. When you looked back on it, you wonder how that could have ever been, but it was.

This system of separation even went for the setting of a table. The fathers always had a dinner plate, a soup bowl – if you were having soup – two glasses and the brothers only got a soup bowl. So if you were going to have soup, then you always had to have a piece of bread or something to clean out your soup bowl. The abbot's table had a full setting of nice china and a tablecloth. The abbot, prior, subprior and visiting VIP sat there.

It didn't make any difference what year you made vows. In procession [*into the church*], for example, if one of our brothers was professed 50 years, a cleric would take precedence if you processed in seniority. So in other words, in procession the order would be the fathers, the clerics and the brothers. This sounds "off the wall" now.

I can remember one incident. You see, the fathers' recreation room was right across the room from the brothers' recreation room. So you could just walk straight through. One time a sign appeared on our bulletin board in the brothers' recreation room saying we were not allowed in each other's recreation rooms – that was a no-no.

Do you have another amusing story?
One time a comic strip disappeared from the fathers' recreation room and a sign went up on our bulletin board. I don't know why our instructor felt that one of us took them, but a sign went up saying, "Please return the comic section to the fathers' recreation room, whoever took it."

The fathers always got the current newspaper. At this time, the thinking was they would go out and would need to know what was going on in the world. We never got any secular newspapers – that was forbidden. All we read were diocesan newspapers or whatever.

What else has changed over the years?
That whole system has changed so much, so dramatically. Seemingly, we have unintentionally abolished the vocation to brotherhood. The whole idea of a trade has kind of become nonexistent now.

Is this a reflection of society as a whole, where there is an emphasis for everyone to go to college?
It does seem more academically inclined. I do know that we have some that are not going on for priesthood studies, but they are not going into a trade to be a plumber, tailor, baker or to work in the kitchen. It is now more refined to be working as a writer at the Abbey Press, being an organist, musician, psychologist, computer expert, etc. That is life progressing on.

Formation was much different then. We've jokingly said that if half of us now present would have to go through all they go through now to get into the community, none of us would be here. Today you have all this psychological testing. It is interesting to look back on our day and how it has evolved.

There was another distinction between the priest monk and the brother monk. The brother monk wore a belt, and the priest monk wore the cincture with a tassel hanging down. So it was really a marked distinction. Now we all wear a belt. I remember one time when I was in temporary vows that this whole thing was really getting to me.

When was that?

I made vows on April 19, 1959, so this year [2009, *the time of the interview*] is my golden jubilee. Those temporary vows, of course, are for three years. As I mentioned, there was separation in the dining room and we couldn't talk to each other, except on Christmas when we had a community get-together and on the abbot's name day. This was called a familian feast, when everybody would get together. In the course of time, there was interaction among the different groups, but it was always based on work-related things.

I remember one Christmas when I was a junior and temporarily professed. I had become friends with one of the fraters – a cleric – and it was through work that we had gotten to know each other. We would look around to be sure nobody was watching and we would talk. It was Christmas and it was open socialization within the community.

So we were at the gathering and he said, "Well, let's go for a walk. You know we can," because the Rule of Separation was lifted for that specific event. So we did. [*The walk*] was generally called "the mile." You could leave the monastery and walk around it and come up Highway 545 and come back up [*the hill*] – that was the mile.

So we did that and we were just talking. Anyway, to make a long story short, after recreation was over, I was in our recreation room where the bulletin board was and I was looking at it. The novice instructor came in and said, "Oh, brother, are you sick?" I said, "Well, no Father." And he said, "Well, I noticed you left the familian fest."

Well, even though it was legal, I wouldn't dare tell him. The next morning I woke up and I was sicker than a dog. I had gotten the beginning of the flu, and the next morning he said, "I thought you said you weren't sick." I had a temperature of 100 and something.

Tell me the process of taking vows back then.

We – the brothers – took perpetual vows, as compared to the clerics who took solemn vows. So I am in the novitiate and you worked wherever you were assigned. Generally, with your first profession of vows, you got a stable job. When we make our first vows, we submit names to the abbot because we get a new name then. Well, my father's name was Eugene, so on my temporary list I had put Eugene and Pascal, because he has a special devotion to the Blessed Sacrament.

How about Pius?

I had those first two names. I was reading a book of Pius X and it was mentioned in the book that when he was elevated to cardinal his mother was sick and was not able to attend the consistory. When he came home to visit her, he went upstairs and put on all his cardinal robes. As he walked into her room, his mother was trying to get out of bed and he said to her, "What are you doing?"

And she says, "Well, I want to get up to kiss your ring." He went over quickly to the bed and laid her down and he knelt beside the bed and took her hand and kissed her wedding band and said, "I am the one who should kneel and kiss the ring." I thought, "That is my man," so I ended up with Pius, Pascal and Eugene on my names list. Pius was also a patron of the Eucharist.

What a beautiful story. So after you made your first vows, what did you do?

That was the time when things were beginning to change. This would be in the '60s because I made vows in '59. I got my permanent assignment to work in the tailor shop. Fr. Prosper Lindauer was at that time *custos* [*head of material items*] at the Abbey Church in the sacristy, and he got interested in vestment making. So I worked on vestments.

Most all the work was done at the tailor shop. When I came to the shop, [*the priests*] were still in "fiddleback" style chasubles [*this outer vestment had a fiddle shape and was narrow, fitted and short*]. In the late '50s –'60s, the liturgy began to evolve and so did liturgical vestments. They got fuller and longer and you began to get the "canonical" or "Gothic" cut. It was cone shape and was rounded. Then the "semi-Gothic" style was made with shorter sleeves and a rolled collar. This was followed by the "monastic style." It was a box cut and longer. We were just experimenting.

Work

So being a tailor was your primary work as a young brother?
Yes, for the rest of my years as a young professed. When I made my final vows in May of 1962, my job was changed and I became the infirmarian [*person who takes care of the sick*] for the house. It was that same year when we were beginning to establish our mission in Peru in South America. Of course, that came as a response to the invitation of Pope John XXIII asking communities to consider sending 10% of a community into the mission field. I am really not quite sure how it was finalized that we were to go to Peru into the mountains to a place called Huaraz to take over the diocese and seminary. So for the '62 mission, I volunteered to go.

Did they ask for volunteers or were people assigned?
If I remember correctly, and I don't know if it is this way now, but to go out of the country as far as our system goes, I believe we needed to volunteer. So in other words, this was not an obedience. The abbot could say, years ago, you were to go and if it was an obedience, you just took it.

Is that true today?

No. Today, there is more of a dialogue: What do you think? How do you feel? Years ago when the abbot or the superiors spoke, you did it out of obedience. So anyhow, I volunteered in '62 and was not accepted. The abbot said I was still too young to go down there.

How old were you then?

I think around 21-22. I had just made final vows. He said, "We just feel you are still too young." Well, '63 came along and again they were going to send some more people. Three were in the first group that went down there. For the next two years, they were going to send three more. When the group for '64 was going to go to South America, the abbot said, "Well, the council felt that they were going to give it a try" for me to go there. So I went to Peru in November of '64.

Did you know the language?

Almost immediately when we got there, we entered the language school specifically for religious men and women who were going to be working in South America. It was on the outskirts of Lima, Peru, itself. The area all around was kind of a desert area. They would bus out the sisters, but the men were in residence at the facility.

What it amounted to was eight hours of Spanish every day, plus Saturday morning lab work. The numbers in the classes were three, maybe four at the max, so you could really do a whole lot. It was a four-month intense course and lasted from November until February of '65.

I wasn't even halfway through the class and something in me said, "Pius, you don't belong here. You have really made a mistake to come here." It wasn't the language; it was just other factors. So I wrote the abbot and told him how I felt. And he wrote back and said, "We will take it to the Council."

Then I got a letter back and he said, "We have looked at your request and we really feel that you should stay there for a year and, if at the end of the year you still want to come home, then that is fine." Of course, now I see there was wisdom in that, but at the time I did not see the wisdom. I remember when I got that letter, I literally went out into the desert and I just cried like a Magdalen.

The Christmas of '64 was one of the worst Christmases I have ever had, and what made it worse is that we went up to our mission in Huaraz for the Christmas break. We went up 13,000 feet and then dropped down into a valley at 10,000 feet. A beautiful spot in the Andes Mountains and we were just nestled in the mountains like a little pup. However, it was one of the most god-awful Christmases I can ever remember. Then we went back to Lima after the Christmas break to finish the language school.

At the graduating ceremonies for the class, they presented a recognition to whomever had advanced most in Latin or in Spanish. However, they said, "And this year we're going to give a recognition that we have never given before, and this recognition is to the one whom we feel is most likely to succeed in missionary activities."

And I got it! Now I am thinking, "I want to get out of here and they are giving me this award as they feel I'm the one most likely to succeed!" Anyway, with that recognition in hand, we got back up to Huaraz in time to begin the new school year. The school year in Latin America goes from April to December.

What did you do there?
I was doing some tailoring, but also the situation soon took me in another position and that was teaching.

What did you teach?
Religion and English. At that time, our seminary was up on the hill close to the priory and the old seminary was down in the town.

Around 1966, we begin to think that the old seminary could be a private high school for secular students in connection with the seminary. So my whole life moved from the seminary down to the high school. So again I taught religion and English.

It was just the first year and we didn't really have a whole lot of students, but there were enough to warrant us moving on. Then around '67, the brother who was director of the school wanted out. So I became director, which back here is considered the principal. Also, at about this same time, around '66-67, I began thinking about the priesthood.

What led you to this decision?

This came as the result of seeing the dramatic need for a priestly ministry in the missions. There were some areas around us that only had Mass once a year. I thought, "I don't know if this is what I want." So I went to our superior, Fr. Bede [*Jamieson*], and I said to him, "Fr. Bede, what would you say if I told you that I am thinking of the possibility of going on into the priesthood?"

He just looked at me and said, "Pius, as far as I am concerned, you have the last word in that." Well, it took me a year to decide. One day it was, "Oh, yes," and the next was "Oh, going back to school," so I was back and forth in my thinking.

I remember one evening I was out walking. You know, like I said, our priory was about 10,000 feet above sea level and it looked like you could just reach up and grab a star and really hang on it. This particular night, it was just like the heavens were filled with fluorescents. Everything was lit up and I was walking and I was thinking about this and praying over it, of course.

I finally decided, "Yes." So before I could change my mind, I ran back to the prior's room, knocked on his door, and he said, "Come in." All I did was open the door and just say, "Yes." He said, fine, he would work on it. That night began another step or chapter in my life. I had been in Peru for four years.

So then what happened?

Well, I started doing some studying in Peru with Fr. Benedict [*Meyer*]. He was the teacher for philosophy and theology and I started taking classes with him. This led to my ordination to the diaconate [*a deacon*] December 8, 1969.

Was this about the time of the earthquake in Peru?

Yes, this devastating earthquake was in 1970 [*May 31*]. I was with Fr. Bede and we had gone to one of the schools in the town. The celebrations of birthdays in Peru, as are in most Latin countries, are something to celebrate. So they were celebrating the birthday of one of the sisters, Madre Angela. She was *directora* of the schools. Fr. Bede and I were there.

The celebration took place in the patio area of the school, which was built in a quadrangle. We were all sitting there and a little girl had just presented Madre Angela with a bouquet of flowers. As we were applauding, everything just began to move. The school was a two-story building and I looked up and, all of a sudden, I saw adobe beginning to pop out from the walls and come down into the area where we were.

We knew right away that it was an earthquake, so I started to move rather quickly – as a matter of fact, I started to run – because there was an entrance out to the street at the end of a passageway under a balcony. I thought, "Now, Pius, don't run, because people will see you run and will get panicked."

So I just kind of meandered over toward the door and, all of a sudden, I found myself right in front of a door. How I got there, I don't know, but anyway I was there. Well, there was a small entrance into a vestibule area. On one side was the principal's office and the other was a music room. I was standing there and, all of a sudden, I found myself in this vestibule and the building collapsed.

The beams over this vestibule area were still connected to one wall, and I was underneath it along with several other people. I tried to move up and I couldn't go anyplace. I tried to move off to the side and couldn't, tried to move forward and couldn't and I thought, "Okay, Pius, this is it."

The people around me were calling, "Oh, Father, Father, Father," and I said, "Don't worry we will get out, we will get out." And I was thinking to myself, "Here you are one step from eternity and you are telling these people, lying to them, telling them they are going to get out."

There was an awful lot of dust, as you can imagine. The dust started going up and, in all my efforts in trying to get out, I never once tried to move to my left. Why, I don't know, but I had been thrown right in front, or I landed, right in front of the door to the music room. In the music room, there was a piano and with the movement of the earthquake the piano had moved out into the middle of the room.

The ceiling, which was plaster over bamboo sticks tied together and mud, just kind of peeled off and the piano was holding this section. This made a perfect exit from where I was. So I crawled into that room and there were these big windows. This was typical Spanish architecture – wrought iron and decorative braiding on the windows.

I got to a window and I was pushing to see if I could push it out. I was there pushing on this grate and a gentleman in the street was pulling. Then it just kind of dawned on me. "Pius, this is not going to work because if I am able to push it out and he is out there pulling, the whole grate was going to fall out on top of him."

So I told him, "Get away from it." I kind of turned around and put my hands on either side of the wall and with my foot started kicking against it. Of course, with all the movement to loosen it up, it just popped out and I was able to get out of the building.

Of course, my first reaction was, "Where is Bede?" He was sitting right near me. So I went around and climbed up over what was left of a building and I came down and walked by a house right behind the school. From the outside, all you could see was adobe walls, even in good times. But then you would go into the house and most of them had a beautiful patio area and rooms. Well, anyway, I walked by there thinking I could kick in the back way. However, everything was collapsed.

Then I heard a woman yelling, "Help!" I looked in and here was a mother with two children. During the earthquake, they were standing in a doorframe. They always tell you to get in a doorframe and that is where they were. But the walls behind and in front of them had collapsed.

So, I was looking at three heads. A little baby she had in her arms had been knocked out and was lying at her feet and that little one was dead. She said, "Father, help us, help us. If you will help us, I will come and I will cook for you and I will take care of you." I said, "That is not the point." So I started trying to dig her out with my hands.

Well, it was almost something you would see from a Hollywood picture. There was one portion of the wall that was still standing and what was supporting it – which is not uncommon in these patios – were big columns. They were not solid, but were wood and mud. One column had cracked right in two and you could see a small piece of rock in the middle just holding it up.

So I was trying to get them out and she kept saying, "Oh, I will do this and I do that," and I said, "We have to go slow because if we don't, then everything is going to come over on top of us." So I worked and worked and finally I was getting so tired. I just said to St. Vincent de Paul, "You have to send somebody to help me. I can't get any farther."

I looked up and there stood three men, two with shovels and one with a pick axe. That is the first time I had been, and I never realized it until years later, part of a miracle. I mean, who is going to be walking around with shovels and a pick ax? I just looked up at them and said, "You are going to have to take over" and I left and tried to find Fr. Bede. If I had known where he was, I could have just turned around from where I was and touched him. Unfortunately, he had died.

There were about 250 of us in the grade school for the celebration, including a lot of students and parents. Out of those, only about 60 of us came back. As best as I can remember, there were about 70,000 who were killed in that whole earthquake.

What happened after that?

That happened in May. In July I was back home in the states. In September of '70, I was in school. I said in my prayers, "Bede, you didn't have to be this dramatic in finding me a way in getting me back." But, you know, I went back again to Peru in '74.

How did this experience affect you?

Well, as it turned out, there were several things that are kind of vivid in my mind after the earthquake. First of all, we take life for granted as we move around. This was the first time I personally saw massive death. It was just so destructive. People you had known and worked with were all gone. Death was the common denominator and life was the exception.

I remember I had never experienced it before, but I had heard how when someone dies when the process of decomposition begins, there is a sweet odor. I experienced that in a very dramatic way when one of the ladies who knew me wanted me to go to the city hall to pray for a relative who had died.

In the city hall, as you walked in, there were bodies lying all over the place and the smell was just overwhelming, it was sickening sweet. If you ever try to pray the "Our Father" without taking a breath, try it sometime because you just can't. As you walked through the town, you could identify a place where someone must still be buried under the ruble of the buildings that had fallen by the odor.

One day I was walking from our priory that sat outside of town down to the school, which was in town. A lady came up to me and we talked about the earthquake and she said, "Oh, isn't it awful poor Bishop Pius Klein died in the earthquake? Wasn't that awful?" I just looked at her and said, "Yes, it really was." I thought, I was not going to get into the fact that I am not a bishop.

So anyway Fr. Abbot Gabriel [*Verkamp*] came down and was with us for a while. In July of 1970, I returned to the states to finish up my studies. When my permission to continue to study for the priesthood first came, I dedicated it to St. Joseph. I said, "Okay, St. Joseph, let's work this out."

It was kind of uncanny that my ordination date was set for the 31st of March 1974, as March is the month of St. Joseph. So for the next four years, as well as the summers, I attended classes and took part in different work areas here within the community.

Shortly after my ordination, I was asked by Fr. Abbot Gabriel if I would be willing to accept the position of mission preacher. In other words, going around to parishes requesting help for our mission in Peru. So in May of 1974, I started going around to parishes.

Toward the end of that year – late November or early December – I was visiting with my mom in the course of traveling and I got a phone call at her house from Abbot Gabriel. He explained that one of our fathers was requesting to come home and he needed someone to go down and replace him at the parish and asked if I would be willing to go back to Peru. I said, "Yes."

Well, Mom came home from work that night and we had supper. We then visited my aunt and uncle and came home. I can still picture where I was sitting in the chair and Mom was sitting on the couch. It was around 11 o'clock and we were watching the news and she looked over at me and said, "Charles, what is wrong?"

I said, "What do you mean, Mom?" She said, "There is something wrong." So then I proceeded to tell her about the abbot's telephone call and going back to Peru. She just sat there and said, "Charles, I am going to be truthful with you. I don't want you to go back, but if that is what you feel is right, all I can say is, 'May God go with you.'"

So in February of '75, I went back to Peru. Along with our mission in Huaraz, we also had a parish in Lima. A lot of the men worked in the mountains doing missionary activities. Because of the high altitude, they were encouraged to come back down to the coast periodically. So our parish was not only a parochial center, but also a center house where the men came down to stay awhile.

I was an associate pastor at the parish. Fr. Abbot Bonaventure [*Knaebel*] also worked there. In September, I found myself being named the pastor of the parish. So I served there until 1978 when we had elections for the new prior of the monastery.

We were, until the end of our stay, a dependent house. In other words, we were dependent on the monastery, which meant that the abbot had the right to name the prior. But we were given the privilege of electing a prior and presenting the results to the abbot and he would approve or disapprove. As it turned out, I was elected prior in '78. I left the parish in Lima, of course, and took up residence at the priory. At that time, I also ended up being rector of the seminary, principal of the high school and junior/novice master, all at the same time.

Then what happened?

We began to get Peruvian vocations. But the American personnel were beginning to diminish, for various reasons. People were beginning to return to the states. The term for our prior was four years and so in '82 it was time for elections again. Well, I was re-elected, but in the following years we ended up with just two of us, myself and Br. Dominic [*Warnecke*]. It was not, I guess, an example of a professed community.

So the decision was made, back here at the monastery, to close the venture. As a result, we began to phase out the high school; we didn't accept any freshmen the next year. There was a lot of discontent from the people in Huaraz that we were in the process of leaving. We were being told, "You are important to us."

What we were doing was having an impact on the people, but this was a decision that had to be made. In fact, because of the reaction of the townspeople, we literally snuck out of Huaraz when we left. We didn't tell anybody what time or when we were going. The monastery buildings, as well as everything else, were turned over to the diocese for their use. So we came home in September of '85.

What did you do when you came back here to the monastery?

Again, I was appointed *custos* [*custodian*] of the church and I was refectorian [*head of the monks in the kitchen*]. This was also the time we were beginning to have commuting chaplains at the convent at Ferdinand. So Fr. Abbot Timothy [*Sweeney*] asked me if I would take this job to get the program moving. So in '85 we started this program.

In '86, Fr. Abbot approached me about the possibility of accepting an associate pastorate at St. Benedict's in Evansville. He said, "You think about it," so I did. When I went in and told him, "Yes, I would be delighted to go." His comment was, "Oh well, thank you, but I have already got somebody that will go."

Well, I didn't say anything and in 1987 he called me in to his office and said, "I would like for you to think about the possibility of becoming the pastor at St. Mary's in Huntingburg." By this time I was a little bit more relaxed and I said, "Now look, I want to ask you something. Are you going to pull the same thing you did the last time?"

He said, "Oh, no, no, no." "Well, I was just wondering, because if I had had a hatchet, it would have went through your desk." But anyway, we just laughed over it. So in August 1987, I went over to Huntingburg. My mom died in February of '87, so I remember this year.

I was at St. Mary's until 2008 – 21 years. They were good years. Then I was appointed refectorian and director of pastoral assistance. I am still a part-time chaplain over at Ferdinand. So that brings me up to date on my work and experiences at the monastery.

Prayer

Next, I would like to ask you about your prayer and spiritual life. If you were going to pass something on to the laity, or to a younger novice, what would you want to convey?

Just right off the top of my head would be to develop – I don't want to say "habit," because that is not the word I am looking for – but the disposition of being aware of the moment, of seeing it as a gift and God's presence in it.

This leads right into the next question: what is the most important part of the Rule of St. Benedict?

To name a favorite part would be hard, because I see the *Rule* in its entirety. In other words, I don't personally find myself seeing it in bits and pieces. I just try to see the whole picture of the *Rule* and listening – having an open ear.

St. Benedict says, "Prefer nothing to the love of Christ and may He bring us all to life everlasting." So I think it is the challenge of trying to bring to life that particular invitation that comes to us from Benedict from the scripture, not only in the structured prayer service or individual prayer, but to make it a part of our entire life.

This gets to the next question. What is your key to living Benedictine spirituality?

I think it is the tranquility of being able to see my life as a continual growth process. One of the vows we take is the conversion of life. The tranquility of knowing that at any point I don't have to be in any given situation, because our whole life is geared to the challenge of growing and learning. Life's experiences show us this.

For example, Fr. Abbot Lambert [*Reilly*], at one point, was looking for somebody to be the new prior of the house, so I was approached. Previous to that, he was going to make a change and was going to move me from Huntingburg to the parish at St. Meinrad. I told him I didn't particularly want to leave Huntingburg, but if this is what was to be....

In the format of monastic business, our abbot nominates the pastor and then the bishop approves it. The person the abbot had in mind the bishop would not accept. So in one week, I was assigned over here and then reappointed back over there at St. Mary's as pastor.

What I am getting at is that I told the abbot on both occasions – leaving Huntingburg or becoming prior – "Fr. Abbot, I will be very truthful with you. When I stop and see how God has worked in my life, I would really be afraid to say no."

This is the same thing I told Fr. Abbot Justin [*DuVall*] when he wanted to bring me home. I said, "I don't want to leave. I don't have any reason to want to, but on the other side when I see how God has worked in my life, I would fear to say no."

Is that part of the obedience?

No. Well, yes. But when I said that, I did not see obedience. It was just that I looked at my life – coming into the community, my vows, my time in Peru and how priesthood came out of that. As I looked at life situations that I thought were the most devastating thing in the world, I saw they brought blessings amidst all the uncertainties and the challenges these situations presented.

This leads to the next question. What has been your most difficult time or experience in your lifetime?

It was difficult to leave Peru. It was difficult to leave the parish. I guess the one that was most difficult, as I had mentioned earlier, was when I first went to Peru in 1964. I felt it had been a mistake and the abbot said, "Well, stay a year." Of course, at the time I had a hard time with that, but now I see the wisdom of it – the wretchedness of that Christmas, the irritability of everyone else in the community.

Knowing how I felt, they tried to be super solicitous in everything while I just wanted to tell them to shut up. Of course, going through my mom's death and leaving family was difficult. But I see all those things as a kind of natural reaction everyone goes through. But then look what God did!

Are there any other times that have been difficult?

I have been really healthy my whole life. But in May 2013, I was feeling punk, washed out, no energy, but no pain. So I went to the health services of the monastery. After an EKG, I was on my way to the emergency room at Jasper Hospital [*Jasper, IN*]. After an examination, I was told by the doctor that I needed to stay in the hospital for observation.

The following day, they tried to do a heart catheterization and found that the vein in my arm was blocked. So the next day, they took me back down and did it the old-fashioned way through the groin. After the procedure, I found out they had put in seven stents and I was in the hospital for about a week. After this procedure was done, I could tell the difference and felt much better.

What has been the most happiest or joyful time in your life?

Joyfulness has come as a result of prayer and reflecting on, and remembering, that out of situations that I thought were really difficult, God turned them into blessings. I know it sounds contradictory. Needless to say, my profession day was a day of great joy, as was my ordination day, and my role in the jubilee celebration last Sunday along with the other jubilarians. I guess joy for me is personally living out Mary's Magnificat, "My soul does magnify the Lord and he has worked wonders."

Changes in the Church

How different is the Church today compared to pre-Vatican years? In the monastery?

It's not the church I grew up in. In many ways, back then it was more authoritative and structured compared to what it is now. It was obedience for obedience's sake. "This is what you have to do," and this was reflected in the monastery when I first entered it. There was no discussion about something, and "obedience was obedience." As mentioned, the fathers ate out of a plate, a bowl and two glasses; the brothers had a bowl and broke their bread in fourths to clean out the bowl after each serving. Br. John Miller was the one I talked to when I was having problems with this. I remember once he said, "Pius, it all boils down to this: In the service of the Lord, this is what we have to accept."

How about today?

I think today the Church, as a whole, is more open and has a more invitational atmosphere, instead of things just being imposed. Now, by invitational I don't mean, "Well, you can do it, or not do it." It's just a more open atmosphere also in the monastery.

For example, before the Council, the abbot was "Lord and Abbot." Today, he is really a Fr. Abbot. But he still merits the respect of the office that he holds as father of the community. When I first came, the abbot was that figure "up there and out there," compared to today.

With all due respect to the office he holds, now he is accessible to the community. When I came home from the parish in Huntingburg, I found a note on my desk from Fr. Abbot Justin, where he said, "Welcome home. If there is anything I can do, please come or even if you just want to talk, please come and see me."

Are there other differences?

Years ago, people put priests on pedestals. As a result – looking back in hindsight, this was not healthy, because you began to act according to how people think you should act because of your vocation. There was no encouragement to develop your own personality.

Also, I remember years ago a situation when we were still living in separation between fathers, brothers and clerics. St. Benedict mentions in his *Rule* that if a monastery happens to be large, that "deans" could be appointed to govern each group. So they tried to do this with the brothers.

We had junior brothers and the senior brothers. Well, the junior brothers were underneath the novice master and the senior brothers were underneath the subprior. Talk about not knowing what we were doing. Looking back now, in reality, within the brothers we had two communities; it just didn't work.

Explain more differences between pre-Vatican Council and today in the monastery.

Now, as mentioned before, we don't have separation and this type of system doesn't even exist anymore. It is completely different. For example, as juniors we were forbidden to go to the library other than with special permission. At one point when I was a junior, I went to the junior/novice master because I was in the infirmary and I was interested in doing some reading on my illness.

So I asked him, "Could I have permission to go to the library to get this book on medicine?" His response, "Brother, you don't need that." He put the kibosh on it – so what are you going to do? Of course, today anybody can use the library. In fact, if you don't use the library, you are encouraged to. This type of growth, I think, is reflected in the entire Church.

Has society changed and does the Church reflect society?
Oh, I think so, definitely. As an example, professors aren't on pedestals anymore. Fifty years ago, we used to be on pedestals.

Yes, I think this is the same thing that has happened in the Church and monastery. After the Council of Trent in the 16th century, someone – I have forgotten who – made the observation that, after the Council, the Church stopped growing even though we went through the Industrial Revolution.

We came into the 19th and 20th centuries carrying rigid ideas while everything else in society was becoming a little bit more fluid, but the Church kept the structure of the Middle Ages. Monasticism was the same way, because it was a very integral part of the Church.

This is why Blessed John XXIII brought in a Council to open the windows and let in some fresh air. With the opening up of the windows, it wasn't a breeze that came in through, however; it was the winds of a hurricane, which really turned everything around.

Now, like anything else, from a human nature standpoint, there was a natural reaction – it was like letting a little child loose in a candy shop. The pendulum after the Council went all the way from the left and swung with a vengeance over to the right.

Then, of course, letting a child loose in the candy shop means he is going to get sick. I now see the pendulum beginning to come back. This post-Vatican influence has also occurred in our monastic life. Having lived in both the pre- and post-Vatican worlds, however, is a blessing.

Even if the Mass is now to be celebrated in the vernacular, was eliminating Latin from the academic curriculum a good idea?

There again, I think that when the pendulum swung from the left to the right, there were some aspects of the liturgy that were dismissed because the Council felt it was a freeing process. As far as the use of the Latin language, who speaks Latin? The whole business of going to the vernacular was discussed centuries ago.

So this is where the Church is really being challenged by individuals who can't see the differences between reality and romantic ideas. For example, when I gave my first Mass, my mom said, "Oh Charles, why don't you say your first Mass in Latin?" I said, "Well, Mom, I just really don't think that would go over."

So we have our older generation carrying the nostalgia of how it used to be. In a certain sense, it is a natural reaction and I think it can be a healthy one, too. I am not saying that it is negative, but a challenging situation that was brought about by changes in the Church.

I wonder what the hierarchy of the Church is now thinking sometimes. It almost seems like they want to recapture the past. Some of the things that you do, you do because this is what Rome has said to do. But you just think, "Hey, these guys are sitting behind their desks and they may be thinking up things for us to do."

There is an old saying in German, *Spitzfindingkeit,* little things. And seemingly, now the hierarchy seems to be overly protective. Really, I think we are growing into a new Church and I think changes in society are a big part of it.

What have been positive and what have been negative changes, not just in the Church but in the parishes?

I think the faithful taking part in the life of the parish is very positive. But this is very hard because the majority of your people in the parish are not accustomed to this. Before, it was the priests and sisters who ran the parish. Then we began to say to parishioners, "Okay, you can be Eucharistic ministers and lectors."

Women before were never allowed in the sanctuary; now they take part. Rome is now coming up with a new format to celebrate the Mass, changing the kiss of peace and new translations. They are just now getting comfortable with what happened with Vatican II and the changes that resulted from that. As far as reluctance from going from Latin to English – something so simple – tells me people are trying to recapture something that they feel was lost.

You know, we have our Eucharistic ministers now. The Eucharistic minister can distribute the bread and the wine. The Eucharistic minister, if there is any bread or any wine leftover, can consume it. But they cannot purify the chalices; a priest or deacon has to do that.

Now you are thinking, "Okay, what is Rome trying?" Since people were not accustomed to many of the changes and taking active part in the parish, it is really a challenge to get them involved and make the parish theirs. The majority of them haven't the faintest idea what to do or how to react, because this has never been part of their life because it was structured to such an extent.

Then you have the younger people, and they don't bring anything with them except what is new in society. So it's a challenge to instill in them some sense of the sacred from the past. Well, you are the pastor and you try to say, "We are a parish," and try to get that concept across.

[*Editor's note: This interview was conducted in 2009 and many of the changes mentioned are now accepted practices in most parishes.*]

Are these issues leading to positive or negative changes?

If you stop and look at it and say, "Negative," you could, but again it is an opportunity to take something seemingly negative and try to bring positive out of it.

There has been a decline in religious vocations. What effect has this had on the monastery and the Church as a whole?

Needless to say, it has greatly affected the ministerial presence of priests or consecrated religious and it is projecting a sense of sheep-without-a-shepherd attitude. Despite change, there is something in all of us that still wants structure.

The reduction of priests is proving rather difficult for many of our parishioners. It's trying for them when we start talking about priestless Sundays, and for them to get used to Eucharistic ministers, lay lectors and lay ministers taking communion to the homebound.

I remember when I was at the parish, everyone would say, "Well, Father, why can't we look at what the Methodist Church does, look at what the United Church of Christ is doing?" from the point of view of social outreach, community involvement and things like that. I don't know how many times in reference to this I have had to say, "Well, look, first of all, our structure is a lot different."

For example, we have four Masses— the 6 o'clock, the 8 and the 10 on Sunday and the 5 o'clock on Saturday. Really, within St. Mary's we have four communities that attend Mass at specific times. We have the community of 5 o'clock on Saturday who wouldn't be caught dead at the 6, 8 or 10 o'clock Masses on Sunday and so on.

When you just have one Sunday service and your whole congregation is there, it is a lot different. You can draw the community together. In our parish, this is difficult because we have four communities. For example, 10 o'clock Mass was our main Sunday Mass and God forbid that singing would be going at any of these other Masses.

This is why, as pastors, we have to be slow in bringing about changes without disrupting everything. I looked at the parish and saw where it was at, and my desire was to try and meet them where they are, and not where I think they should be or where I want them or hope they would be.

How are we going to get things to work without causing all kinds of havoc among the congregation? So with the lack of, for example, a pastoral director or pastoral assistant, I have had the opportunity to be at many parishes. I had two parishes that were combined together.

At one parish, I had the Saturday evening Mass at 5:30. Then at that same parish, a 7:30 morning Mass on Sunday. You have to keep that Mass short so you can be at the other parish at 10 for their Mass, but you have to keep that one short so you can go back to the other parish for the 11:30 Mass, and it can be confusing.

This is all because of the lack of vocations?

Yeah, because of the lack of priests. Fortunately, there are people who are starting to rise up and take responsibility. It is not working apart, but of working with them.

Is this a positive change?

I think this is positive and it frees the ordained minister. So often the priest gets saddled, or the sister or the DRE [*Director of Religious Education*] or the religious or whatever with everything from business administration to being overseer of the property. Years ago, that is the way it was. There are people out there in the pew who are capable of taking on that type of activity and I think it will just take time to encourage them.

I guess one of the things we did not do in pre-Vatican was to empower the laity. We kept them on the other side of the communion rail. With the hurricane winds that came in when John

XXIII opened the window, that was one of the positive opportunities that the Council brought in and it will only happen in time.

Who knows? Maybe somehow the lack of priests in parishes will end up being that empowering factor for the laity to realize, "Hey, we are Church. It is not the priest, it is not the religious, but it is us."

How about here in the monastery, with the lack of vocations, what kind of changes have you seen?

Well, one of the things we are faced with is there are certain ministries outside of the monastery that we are not able to be of service because of the lack of manpower.

How about within the monastery? Has the lack of manpower caused issues within the monastery?

When I first came here, we had brothers in the bakery and we had brothers in the kitchen. Now we have no one in the kitchen. We have one brother who does go down to the bakery in the morning. We had a slaughterhouse and brothers were involved with that.

I say brothers, because at that time they were the ones who did these jobs – tailor shop, shoe shop, art shop. We had brothers in plumbing and the electrical shop. We were just involved in all of these types of works, which was a part of the community life. This situation no longer exists and these particular vocations have been inadvertently lost.

Do you see that changing?

I don't see any trend right now going back to the way it was before. Some of them might have hobbies for this or that, but as far as making it full-time work, no. The problem is that, at present, we only have two novices; they take classes. If I am not mistaken, there are just four juniors and one of them is making solemn vows, so we only have three. So right there, we are limited in terms of the number of people to do things.

One of the fathers put it this way after a meeting. He said, "You know, Pius, we are getting to a point where they want more bricks, but are not giving us straw." It is nice to be able to say, "Okay, we do our own dishes, we do this or that." I am not speaking negatively about it, but sometimes I think we need to look at who we have. One of the brothers the other day at lunch mentioned that the average age for the community is about 65. What is that saying?

Because the community is aging, what do you see as the future of the monastery?

I guess if this situation was particular to this monastery, then it would be viewed in a different way. But we are one of hundreds of communities who have the same challenge. So taking it to another level, where is the value of the monastic life in society as a whole? What have we done or what has happened to lose that vision? Was it Vatican II? I don't know.

Will monastic institutions regenerate?

Yes, I see it slowly coming back, but I won't live to see it. There are many of our young people who are not as liberal as we might think in their approach to things. Where they will take this, I am not quite sure. Just a personal observation, but one of the detriments was with the closing of so many parochial schools. I really believe in having the presence of religious there.

I know it sounds simplistic, because in our educational program at the parish, we had close to 500 students. They ranged from kindergarten through high school. Classes are once a week. The little ones come from 3:30 to 4:30, the middle school students come from 6:00 to 7:00, and then you have students in high school from the freshmen to the seniors from 7:30 to 8:30 at night. I constantly felt obliged to encourage our catechists.

We had 50 volunteer catechists in the parish. I know it was frustrating with what you could do with those kids in just one hour a week, especially with the group that comes in from 7:30 to 8:30 at night. They have gone through a whole day of school. The young ones get out at 3:00 and they are bussed to St. Mary's for religious ed classes at 3:30 to 4:30. Personally, I feel that we really lost a lot when the religious communities of women pulled out of education.

I keep trying to tell the catechists, "Do what you can. It is God's work. Just do what you can." I know there are a lot of challenges to it. They want to start a Catholic high school; well, they kind of got it off the ground now. The only way that a Catholic high school is going to work here in our area is to have a Catholic presence. Having Sister Gloria Day as principal and 40 lay teachers and Father coming in periodically to give a spiritual nosegay, for example, is not going to do it.

What are your hopes for the future of the Church? How about the monastery?

Personally, I have great hopes that things are going to turn out well if we're convinced that the Lord is involved in the Church that He has founded. I have great hope. I just don't think all the dust of Vatican II has settled yet. Right now the Church is trying to recapture particles to bring some things back together.

I would like to give a quote from St. Teresa of Avila, "Let nothing disturb you; let nothing frighten you; all things pass; only God remains." In our monastic community, our abbot takes the place of Christ within the community. Although many things have changed at Saint Meinrad over the years, it is still, and will be, Saint Meinrad.

Profile based upon: Fr. Pius Klein, OSB, to Prof. Ruth C. Engs, July 30, 2009, Interview Transcriptions, Saint Meinrad Archabbey Archives, St. Meinrad, IN; additional information from Fr. Pius, September 2015.

Chapter 11: Fr. C.G., OSB+

Fr. C.G. has had several occupations over his lifetime, including being a teacher of doctrinal theology in Saint Meinrad School of Theology, spiritual and retreat director, organist for the community, lecturer on the Rule *of* St. Benedict *for many Benedictine communities and, in later years, and currently, keeper of the monastery vegetable garden. He is an example of someone who has come up out of the depths of alcoholism through Alcoholics Anonymous (AA), Benedictine humility and prayer.*

Fr. C.G. was born August 4, 1939, in Evansville, Indiana, and given the name Glynn Allen. He attended St. Benedict and Christ the King Catholic grade schools in Evansville and graduated from Saint Meinrad Minor Seminary (1957) and the School of Theology (1965). He made his first profession August 15, 1960, professed solemn vows in 1963 and was ordained a priest September 5, 1965. After ordination, Fr. C.G. studied at Sant' Anselmo Benedictine College in Rome (1965-67) and received the licentiate in sacred theology (1967).

Father C.G. lived for some years away from the community under permission of a Decree of Exclaustration and returned to the monastery in 2011.

Dr. Ruth C. Engs interviewed Fr. C G., OSB, December 19, 2012. Other material was added October 2015.

[*+Editor's note: Only the first and last initials for Fr. C.G. are used due to the AA tradition of maintaining anonymity in public venues such as the press, media, books or other publications*].

Childhood and Early Years as a Monk

Tell me about your childhood, where you lived, early schooling, etc.

I was born August 4, 1939. My parents' hometown was the small southern Indiana town of Mount Vernon, southwest of Evansville, and the first year of my life we lived there. My parents moved to Evansville because of opportunities for working in defense plants.

The Evansville shipyards were building the LST [*troop landing ship*]. Republic Aviation, as it was called then, was building some of the fighter planes (P-38) used in the Second World War. My father worked in the shipyards and my mother worked as "Rosie the Riveter" at Republic Aviation.

In Mount Vernon, my mother was from a prominent, well-known Catholic family. Their name was Thompson. My father was from an evangelical Lutheran family. His family was fairly prosperous because of farms and a general store with a saloon attached.

My father had been married once and divorced. And he and my mother married when she was 19 and my father was 36 or 37, so it was a sizable age difference between the two. There also was a difficulty in that their marriage was not canonical, because she had married a divorced Protestant.

Of course, by the time I came along, 10 years after their marriage, I really didn't know much about this. I came in subsequent years to know firsthand the suffering my mother felt through all the years and the tensions the situation caused. All of the discussions in the current Synod on the Family about such situations are things I feel very strongly about.

Did you have brothers or sisters?

I have one brother, who died a year and a half ago, and he was five years younger than I. His name was Duane. I was named Glynn Allen. Both these names always struck me as strange for the time and place in which we were named, but my mother had no recollection of how they thought of these names for us.

There's a humorous story about my given name. When I was to be baptized, my mother was still in bed, and a younger aunt and uncle took me for baptism at the old local Mount Vernon church, St. Matthew's. An old priest, Fr. John Rapp, was the pastor, and everything was done in Latin, of course. Well, they brought me in, and announced that I was supposed to be baptized Glynn Allen.

And he told them, apparently with some blustery impatience, that Glynn wasn't a saint's name, and proceeded with the baptism anyway. Well, when I was to go into the first year of grade school, we pulled out the baptismal certificate only to discover that I had been baptized John Allen, which was my grandfather's name! He had baptized me by my grandfather's name.

To leap ahead some years later, when I came to the monastery, I couldn't use Glynn, and I couldn't use John, and I couldn't use Allen, so I chose Julian and registered to vote. Then, I made profession and became C. So, at some point, all those names had to be combined under the one name Glynn – or C.G. Gxxxxx – for a passport. So, now I'm C.G. Gxxxxx.

Tell me about your early family and religious life as a child.

My parents both worked. After the war, my mother got a job as a furniture saleswoman at a time when to have a woman on the sales force in a furniture store was not at all a usual thing. She was signed on by a gentleman that owned the furniture store, and so she became a furniture salesperson.

My father was, by trade, an electrician, and he did electrical work under different contractors. He was a strong union member with the International Brotherhood of Electrical Workers and worked on, over the years, some very, very large projects, like the nuclear power plant at Oak Ridge, Tennessee, and things like that.

We lived in a small, four-room house of the kind that was built during the war and right at the beginning of entry into the war. I think those houses probably cost $3,000 when they were first built, which was a sizable sum in those days, but quite manageable for a working family.

The age difference was a feature in my family life, I think. As I noted, I was born 10 years after they married, which means that my father was 46 when I was born. So, by the time I was moving up into my teens, my father was well into his 50s and early 60s. I never thought much of that at the time, but, in retrospect, I can see what sort of differences the age gap made.

I've said something about how the non-canonical marriage introduced great tension in my mother's personal and family relationships. I joke sometimes that, by way of a kind of compensation, she became a black belt in Catholicism. Although she could not receive the sacraments herself, she made extra effort to see to it that we were good Catholics. She made sure that we were thoroughly catechized, went to Catholic schools, were altar boys and choir members, and that we got into whatever else you could get into in the Catholic institutions of those days.

Tell something about your schooling.

My schooling was Catholic grade school at the large Evansville Catholic parish, St. Benedict, and I went there for four years. Then, the parish we actually lived in, Christ the King, expanded and opened its grade school. Evansville was then expanding to the east side of the town as part of the suburban development. So the last four years of the grade school, I attended Christ the King. I was active in Boy Scouts. I was in the choir. I was always a fairly decent student – got good grades and was a quick learner.

How about high school?

I came to the minor seminary [*high school and first two years of college*] at Saint Meinrad September of '53. We were part of the post-war boom of Catholic kids. It seemed at times that if one of us could say the "Our Father," make the sign of the cross and genuflect in a relatively decent way, they were candidates for the seminary. A lot of boys came to the Minor Sem and then were winnowed out through the years. So, from around the Midwest and East Coast, there were a hundred kids in my entering high school class – the minor seminary.

The high school had pretty much a kind of classical academy education with lots of Latin, some Greek, lots of reading of history and literature. It had less involvement in the sciences and mathematics, but enough to be credible, and it was a disciplined way of life. In those days, the school was under monastic sponsorship. All of the faculty members and administrators were monks. There were no laymen teaching.

Before we discuss your experiences in high school, while at home when you were young, what was the healthcare like then? Did the doctor come to you or did you go to the doctor's office?

We went to the doctor. I had to have an eye doctor, and I had, of course, a dentist. I don't recall anything like regular childhood visits to a doctor, but surely had them for yearly checkup for school or sports. It seems that everybody in the southern Indiana river valleys generally suffers from some brand of sinus trouble, and I had my share of it. And so, I did go to an eye or nose/throat man periodically to get sinuses disinfected. I would have to go for these treatments in which they put an antibiotic on a very long flexible wire Q-tip up into my sinuses and I would sit in front of a heat lamp to get it to absorb.

Did you smoke or drink when you were a youth?

I remember playing with cigarettes. My father smoked cigars and eventually pipes. My mother did not smoke. I remember messing around with cigarettes in, like, fourth or fifth grade. There were woods down at the end of a street, and a buddy of mine and I would go down there and play like we were smoking.

Were you allowed to smoke in the minor seminary?

No. There was no smoking during the school year for the underclassmen up through senior year of high school. Smoking was one of the great policing things for disciplinarians to roust offenders out. I had begun to smoke during the summers when I was about maybe 15.

Was this typical? Did a lot of your friends also smoke?

Yes, in the neighborhood that I came from.

How about when you entered the monastery?

Well, we couldn't smoke when we were novices and juniors [*generally the first four years in the monastic community*]. We could only smoke when we got ordained. And so, on the day of ordination, you could ask the abbot for permission to smoke, and he generally would give it. A lot of people smoked in those days. The older men generally smoked cigars. Younger men smoked cigarettes, and that was typical through, I would say, the '80s.

Then smoking began to taper off under outside influences and was only allowed in some areas. You couldn't smoke in the faculty area or in your faculty room and so on. And then, a no smoking ban was started under Abbot Lambert [*Reilly*] around 1995. As to drinking, no. My family weren't drinkers – that is, my immediate family.

I had two rogue uncles on my mother's side who were both alcoholic, and one was married and the other one was many times married. In my immediate family, there might be a bottle of bourbon for holidays and special occasions, but it would sit on the shelf for a whole year. And my father would drink beer every once in a while and especially in the summers.

I don't remember feeling that alcohol was a kind of a ritual, an adult kind of a rite of passage. When I was 18 or 19 and older, my father might offer me a beer. If I were with classmates on an outing someplace, we might arrange to have a cooler of beer of some kind or another, but it wasn't much of a big deal, really.

How about hobbies and activities when you were young?

I was a musician. I swam a lot. During the summers a couple of years, I had a job as a lifeguard and swimming instructor in a private club pool, Central Turners. A sound mind in a sound body makes a good citizen.

Describe your interest in music.

Well, my mother loved Benny Goodman and was desperate that I play the clarinet, so I was put onto the clarinet, which I never liked and was never good at, but she insisted. Then we struck a bargain. I would stay with the clarinet if I could take piano lessons. I wanted to play the piano, but I had a couple of teachers who weren't very useful.

Then I latched onto a sister who taught in the Christ the King grade school and she was very good. She put me onto really good stuff and I sort of took off from there. I eventually switched over to playing the organ and played the organ for a very long time here in the Abbey.

When you first came to the minor seminary, what was your daily routine?

The schedule in the minor seminary was a kind of modified monastic schedule. I believe there was a 5:30 rising and then morning prayers. Then, we'd have Communion Mass (there was the Eucharistic fast), and then breakfast, and then you were off to classes right away. Then lunch, and you were off to classes again. There was a dinner in the evening and recreation.

So it was like a huge boys prep school, except it was very much a monastic environment. My recollection of it was that it was a fantastic education.

What led you to come here?
Well, I'd been my mother's son. Certainly, one early motivation was tied to the importance of Catholicism in my mother's eyes. I'm certain that was part of it. But I was also reasonably religious and an intelligent, thoughtful kind of religious kid. I had been in all the Catholic activities so I was sort of targeted by the nuns and the priest in the local parish. They thought, "This might be a good candidate," and my folks, especially my mother, was very much in agreement with that.

Fr. C.G., as a young monk

So, it was not a difficult thing. We had visited up here in the eighth grade on school trips, and I rather liked what I saw. I found it a great adventure.

How did you see the Church in your early years?

I think my most memorable sense of the Church in the late '40s and through the '50s was the period in which the Church was sort of going through a kind of renaissance in the United States. There were lots of Catholics around, and we had been around long enough so that we were gradually showing up in social positions, in government, education, the arts and in literature.

There was even a literary journal in those days called *Renaissance,* and a great flowering of Catholic aesthetic, artistic and intellectual ferment in the '50s. It was Catholicism coming of age with a very strong Catholic identity that was not defensive. Before, Catholics, I think, had always been in a sort of a defensive position with regard to the large, overwhelming Protestant culture. But in the '50s, a more confident Catholicism emerged and it was characterized by a flowering of just all sorts of stuff, including a liturgical renewal and social justice movements.

Catholicism in the United States had a huge, strong infrastructure, both in terms of the amount of real estate and the location of parishes, schools and universities, and a great abundance of personnel – sisters and priests were coming out of the woodwork.

I certainly did feel both confident and proud of it. You sort of stood up as a Catholic in those days. And the education I got was, in a way, a kind of further immersion with a very strong historical background in addition to classical languages, especially Latin, which put you in touch with the main body of the Catholic tradition.

What was the tone and nature of the discipline when you were a young monk?

Well, I came to the monastery in '59 in the novitiate. The most influential aspect of the monastery at that time was simply the monastery building itself. It was within huge sandstone walls that had been there since about 1889. So, by 1959 when I came, that building was almost a hundred years old. It was dark; it was creaky;

it was drafty. Walls between cells were paper thin. It had common bathrooms, common showers, wooden stairwells that went from basement to the third floor, and sort of dim lighting.

There were no frills, and it was not a comfortable home environment. The regimen was Spartan and demanding. Junior monks, during the formation and novice years, cleaned toilets and bathrooms. There were lots of instructions on being a monk and lots of stuff on the history of the monastery and the monastic order. We were under the direction of the novice master and he was the same person as the junior master – Fr. Damasus Langan. Visits from family were rare.

Fr. Damasus was always assisted by a second-in-charge called a *socius*, or companion. The novice/junior master was the man responsible for formation, teaching, discipline. And the *socius* was a little bit more of the companion sort of man. He was the buddy, if I can put it that way, who recreated and played sports with the young monks.

You were put to lots of tests, abandoning your own plans and projects to the common direction of the whole place, whatever you were assigned to do. I very much remember getting in trouble over that one time. We were coming up on the Feast of All Saints, and it fell to the novice class to provide the decorations for a party for the rest of the juniorate.

We had acquired a whole bunch of army surplus parachutes with true parachute silk. And I came up with the idea of creating these banners on which we would paint the figure of a saint that was patron to each one of the juniors. Well, as I was inclined to do, I bit off more than I could chew.

The party was supposed to be on a Saturday afternoon, and on that Saturday morning, we weren't quite finished with painting all the banners. We were assigned to some sort of housework on that morning. So I successfully seduced a classmate into thinking that, "Well, surely, everybody could see, including the novice master, that finishing work for the party far outweighed the importance of getting the floors clean."

So, on our own, we shifted priorities and went up to the room where we were working on the banners. Well, it came to the novice master's attention that we were not cleaning the rooms on the floors as assigned. Right before noon prayer that day, the boom got lowered. We got the banners up, but Novice Edward and I had to clean the floors in the afternoon and couldn't go to the party.

I guess that's your amusing story from your early years in the monastery.

Well, that's one of them ....

Work

The next area of questions concerns work. What assignments were you hoping for, what did you want to do and what did you do?

Well, that's fairly straightforward. A junior monk really didn't have any kind of work assignment until after ordination to the priesthood. Nor did you really have any kind of discussion about where you might want to go and what you were interested in doing for professional involvement. You didn't have that discussion prior to solemn vows.

I was due for solemn vows in 1963. After solemn vows, and when I was going on to priesthood, discussions were raised largely by people from the schools expressing interest in people who would follow a particular field of study to fill a position in one of the schools. I always assumed that I would be in the schools and would be a teacher.

I had an avocation as a musician, but it was still relatively amateur. So the pursuit of a direction was really a matter of choosing between what options were suggested or proposed. Two came along: one from the college level, who wanted me to be interested in English literature, which I was; and one from the School of Theology, which wanted me to be interested in theology, which I was. So, eventually, I opted for theology and was sent off to Rome for two years to acquire a degree suitable to teaching in a seminary, at Sant' Anselmo, the Benedictine college in Rome.

Tell me more about being in Rome.

I was in Rome from 1965 to '67. I got there in September of the year where the formal closing of the Council that took place on December 8th in the piazza of St. Peter's Square. A bunch of us Americans from Sant' Anselmo went down for the afternoon on the day of the closing.

I didn't much like Rome. Sant' Anselmo, as an institution, has always been torn between being a monastery responsible with the formation of its monks, and a graduate house of studies, in the sense of a *collegio*. These two never rested quite well with each other. There was an internal ambivalence that made some of us wonder, "What in the world are we doing here?" Still, the education was good, by and large, and there were two or three people, one especially, whom I was utterly enthralled by as a teacher of theology. He could've recited the phone book and I would've taken notes on it.

But there was just too much church in Rome – everywhere you turned. It was very hard to get outside of this enormous Catholic culture. It was almost oppressive. Now, other conferees and colleagues just drank it all up with the attitude of, "Good heavens, show me another church, and I can die in peace." I just couldn't do that.

What degree did you get from Sant' Anselmo and then what did you do?

I got the STL – the licentiate in sacred theology in 1967 – and came back here. The summer I got back, I was in a parish for six weeks. I was assigned to teaching, starting in September, and I had two courses during that semester and then three in the next semester. I began teaching with great success.

I was the new kid on the block and sort of a breath of fresh air in this period after the Council. I was a participant in the effort to reconstruct Catholic theology in a way that would accommodate the times and the needs. It was really a very heady and a very wonderful period. We didn't know much about what we were doing, but we did it with enthusiasm.

It was stressful, but it was engaging. But then, it got more and more difficult. We had all been educated in things that you could rely on as your context, background or resources. This included the knowledge of Latin and Greek. When I first started teaching, my students had that background. I could tell them, "Go to the library and look up this or that text," and they could do it. I could come into class and read a bit of a scripture passage from the Greek and they would follow along and make notes and so on. After five years, that was no longer the case.

This meant that what you thought you were able to do gradually disappeared. You couldn't presuppose anymore. The way of teaching which I had been doing for years – the standard lecture – became almost impossible. Teaching became more of a dialogue, more discussion, more roundtable kind of stuff. So, it became increasingly frustrating.

I could remember, from time to time, thinking, "I don't know what I'm doing." We tried what was then called "team teaching," and we had several courses in which there were three or four disciplines in a given class. And we would interact among ourselves, but, for the most part, there were sort of glassy-eyed stares, rather like people watching a circus act.

How many years did you teach?
From 1967 to 1993 and then I left teaching.

What happened then?

Well, after 1993, I left teaching because I had relapsed badly in drinking. I've already mentioned that when I came to the monastery, I was not particularly inclined to drink. It just wasn't a large feature in our house. When I got to the monastery, the daily amount of wine that you could have was an eight-ounce water glass at the main meal, and that was my first introduction to alcohol on a daily basis.

The wine was a brutal sort of red wine that was made locally out of Concord grapes with stems and leaves pressed in with it. So it had a bitter edge to it and it was fairly strong. The rule or custom was that people could have eight ounces – one water glass.

You could, if you were devious – I'd had an inclination to be so – try to wiggle an extra glass up to the end of the table to make sure that the guy who was filling them from the pitcher would overlook the fact that there were five glasses and four people, to get more for yourself. Also, there were occasional familian fests or *Gaudeamus* [*celebrations*].

You could get beer at those gatherings and, generally, it was limited to two beers. I think, in retrospect, that I had become at least an excessive drinker – problem drinker – or maybe even had moved over the line into alcoholism by the time I was 23 in the monastery. It was not a noticeable thing at that point, but I was doing all the things that subsequently I recognized would be alcoholic behavior.

I know that by the time I went off to Rome in '65, especially the second half of the first year over there, having something to drink in the room had become pretty much the norm. Very often I would drink myself to sleep at night, but I was functioning, highly functioning, as a matter of fact.

The same was true when I came back. I was still sort of that uninhibited drinker, but without conspicuous consequences, other than people raising an eyebrow from time to time. And I think my parents, my mother especially, had some concern. She was very sensitive to the alcoholism because of her brothers. There was more than one time that she cocked her eyebrow. I came to know later that she was much more involved in her concern than I knew at the time.

When I started teaching in '67, the atmosphere of the School of Theology was very much akin to a graduate residence. There was a great deal of socializing – open bars, beer busts and things like that, of which I was an enthusiast. Well, it finally caught up with me because I became non-functioning.

When was that?

1969. The first of forced treatments occurred in 1969 and that was followed – I counted them up the other day – by six different interventions. I had a pattern, which I subsequently discovered, that was a disaster. There were things about my personality that inclined me to feel any expressed concerns about my drinking as "getting caught."

I felt the intervention was a kind of condemnation. Treatment didn't get very deep because I was almost irrationally driven on return from treatment to "get back to normal." After every return from an intervention and a period of treatment, I would come back and make every effort that I could to get things back to normal and to raise the stakes.

What do you mean by "raise the stakes"?

I would get into what I had always done – teaching, music and any of the talents I thought to have; but I would try to do these more impressively, better and with greater projects. Inherent in it was wishing that we could all just forget about the past and just go forward. Well, in doing it that way, (a) I never got to any kind of underlying issues in my life; (b) I was setting myself up, really, for another eventual crash because it was just too much of a burden to bear because it involved a lot of playacting.

I was trying to reassure and impress others that everything was "going to be okay," and that's an enormous burden to carry to try to make everybody comfortable and that everything's going to be all right. So I would crash. This happened in '72, '76, '93, 2000.

Then what happened?

Fr. Lambert became a kind of advisor/spiritual director for me in 1993. And then he was elected abbot, and I became his social and administrative secretary. I became house prefect and returned to playing the organ again. I did a lot of retreats, some in faraway places for the Missionaries of Charity.

I was eventually invited to be a commuting spiritual director for priests of the Diocese of Tulsa and then of Oklahoma City, which I did between '95 to around 2000. Father, then Abbot, Lambert had kindly undertaken to foster sanity and sobriety in my life. But the obstacles to that were still in me. I crashed again. That was my last crash.

My crashes, by the way, always had a certain spectacular quality about them. The most spectacular, probably, was 1993. It was supposed to be the beginning of the second semester. It was the end of January and I was slated to teach.

I started drinking again, and I was sitting up in my office in the school drinking all through that weekend, wondering how I was going to put together a syllabus for the second semester, which was supposed to start on Monday.

I was up there all day Saturday and Saturday night and then through Sunday. It suddenly dawned on me about 4:30 in the afternoon on Sunday that I was supposed to play the organ. Well, I was loaded. I was really loaded. I'd been drinking bourbon all weekend. So I threw on the blacks and ran down to get onto the console of the mighty Wurlitzer [*organ*] and pulled the stops, turned it on and it was ready to go. I started playing some sort of entry only to discover that my hands didn't work.

I was paralyzed practically. Well, I tried to make it through Vespers, of course, and a drunk alcoholic always thinks he's done wonderfully. He pulled it off. Well, I didn't pull it off. A friend of mine said it sounded like I was playing the organ with boxing gloves on. So that was one of the great crashes of all time.

In 2000, when you had your last crash, then what?

I was sent off to a treatment place in Virginia, which did not deal with alcoholics specifically, but purported to deal with cleaning up developmental issues in one's past and moving forward in a purposeful way. I just hoped to comply with it long enough to get out of there. I hated being there. I didn't like the setup. I'd begun drinking again at this treatment place. I endured it for about a year and three or four months, and then I ran. I just left.

I decided that I was going to throw over everything – monastic life, priesthood, everything. I was going to get a train from Washington, D.C., and come back to southern Indiana and start over. Not a particularly bright plan. Chuck everything and start over? A really grand plan at age 63, of course.

I landed in a little downscale motel in Warrenton, Virginia, and stayed there about six or seven days over Fourth of July weekend. I realized I had nowhere to go. I was just done for. So I called back to the monastery. Interestingly enough, that's the first time I ever asked for help. All the other times, I had been sort of packaged and sent off. But I asked for help that time and I think that made all the difference.

So I flew back to Evansville and was met in Evansville by two of the brothers who took me over to St. Louis to a place run by the Servants of the Paraclete. I was in their program for about a year. Then I stayed in residence for about six months and got a job. I worked at Dillard's department store in the men's section.

And then, it became clear to me that if I was really going to make it, and make the necessary interior changes that I needed to, it would be inviting another round of this senseless cycle to come back here and say, "Okay, I'm ready to teach, or play the organ or whatever."

I talked to the abbot a lot and I leveled with him. I said, "I don't hate monasteries. I don't hate the Church. I don't hate priesthood. I don't blame any of those for anything. It's just that if I come back and try to do the same thing over, it's likely to produce the same result."

So I asked for and got a Decree of Exclaustration, which means permission to live outside of the monastery and be responsible for one's own well-being and living. I finished up at Dillard's and then got a job with Enterprise Rent-A-Car in a division that took care of managing the rental accounts that were being paid for by insurance companies during the course of repairs on a vehicle. That involved dealing with body shops and monitoring repairs, taking care of the customer and being a contact with the local Enterprise leasing offices. I did that for five years and then came back here in 2011.

And what has helped you to be successful this time?

Certainly AA was a part of it, but there were also things that I discovered over the period of nine or so years that I was on my own. All during that time, I had a regular therapist who had been with me at the St. Michael Treatment Center. I had a very, very good AA sponsor and a really splendid AA men's group, who shared among themselves a degree of openness and intimacy and willingness to talk about, or hear others talk about, almost anything that you could imagine in their lives.

I think that among the most important things I discovered had to do with my state of mind back in the 1960s when I was on the verge of making solemn profession. At that time, I told my family and some confidants here that I was feeling a great deal of unease, that something was gnawing at me, but that I didn't know what it was. All I could say was, "There's something that doesn't seem right."

The people I turned to reckoned it a case of nerves, something like butterflies before the wedding. From the family side, my mother especially – remember the black-belt Catholicism – there came a kind of full-court press. Here, confidants were reassuring.

Only much later (45 years!) did I gain some insight into what was going on in me. I came to think of the great difference between motives and reasons, a good reason. At 20, I was drawn to the monastery by a whole range of motives – things that moved me, that determined what I was really after in focusing on the monastic community.

Very many of these motives were not at all healthy – dependency needs, some escapist aspirations, and so on – and I was feeling, I now think, a lot of internal confusion. I understood practically nothing at all of what they were. From the much later point, I could understand that my vague sense that "something wasn't right" had to do with the immaturity and craziness, really, of these conflictual motives. And it seemed to be that I had missed out deciding for the right thing and for the right reason.

A very good therapist I had during my years out of the community suggested that I'd not really made a decision back then, but instead simply allowed profession and what followed to go forward. I've come to think that I made decisions, but they were in pursuit of what the motives aimed for and what, of course, life in a monastery and all the work of the house could never deliver. Although alcoholism as a disease-condition has its own beginnings, development, etc., it is also the case that alcohol went a long way to fitting in with the conflicts in my own personality. To put it another way, it's quite probable that I would have become an active alcoholic even had I learned differently in growing up, even had I not aspired to the monastery and to priesthood and all the rest. But I can know only of what I actually became, and did, and what followed.

Why did you come back to the monastery?

Believe me, I agonized over that for two years before I actually reached some solution. Well, I had options. It was either come back to the monastery or strike out on one's own. That was it. I was living on my own, but the simple fact of the matter was that if I severed all ties and started to live completely on my own – heck! I was 71 years old, with no equity.

I would've had to work another four or five years just to get to minimum Social Security payments. On the other hand, to come back to the monastery just because there was financial security was equally bankrupt. So, it was two impossible things.

When I finally came to an insight as to what was missing all along, I knew there was a solution. It was a matter of decision. Did I really want to do what I had set out to do in the first place, but now with a clear sight and a clear vision? And when I worked with that question in prayer, in therapy, in spiritual direction, AA and all the supportive elements I could find, then I said, "Yes." I eventually just said, "Yes, that's what I want to be. I just want to go back and, for the first time in my life, to be a monk."

And so, I have come back and, God love them, the brethren are just absolutely astonishingly charitable and kind. There wasn't an eyebrow raised and I slid back in just as if I had left the day before. It was like, "Welcome back." However, I've purposefully asked the abbot, "Let me just lay low for the time being."

I don't want any high-profile stuff that I used to rely on so much to prove myself. I don't want to play the organ. I don't want to get involved in the music. Maybe I can do retreats and be useful there. I don't want to teach unless it's some little informal thing that I can draw on cumulative wisdom, if there is anything to draw on, but I don't want to do classes and lectures and stuff like that. He agreed to that. In time, I've been able to return to familiar uses of my talents, but it's very different now.

Prayer

What's your most favorite part of the Rule?
I think the chapter on humility – Chapter 7 – is just a masterpiece of spiritual wisdom. I've studied it many, many years. I always say, "I studied what I really needed in my life, but couldn't manage to get a hold of it." C.S. Lewis said one time to an aspiring doctoral student, "You should never write about what you need in order to survive." So, yeah, I think it's Chapter 7.

What is your key to living Benedictine spirituality as a monk?
I think it's a combination of four things. It's obedience, which means the effort to overcome one's self-will by consenting again and again and again to abide by the directives of the Rule, an abbot and the customs of the house. The issue is not subservience; the issue is overcoming one's own self-will that calls the shots on everything. So, that's one part.

The second part is prayer. Our seven hours of common prayer throughout the day plus the nighttime prayer are meant to be educative. They are a different kind of liturgy from the Eucharist and are meant to instill constant praying, not in the sense of yammering, but in the sense of attitude or disposition of prayer, so that when you don't have anything else to do, you just immediately revert to an inner praise of God.

The third thing is overcoming one's desires. It's putting one's desires in their place – all kinds of desires, some of them good, some of them not so good. The issue is to subdue them. It starts with simple things: comfort, fasting and not possessing. Just have what you need to get by with whatever you have to do. And then, it goes to deeper renunciation stuff, such as monitoring inner thoughts.

The last one is the charity of the brotherhood. Everyone in the monastery is an invitation for self-giving – for charity – and that's an invitation a hundred million times a day.

What would you, in terms of prayer and spiritual life, want the laity and younger novices and juniors to know?
Well, depending on what they come with, I would say, in terms of prayer, engage with the discipline of the life, which includes the daily times of prayer and the times of personal prayerful reading. Do what you're given to do and just open yourself to it. Don't worry about outcomes. Just do it. Long for a habit of praying. That is, hope for that. It's not going to be something you can make happen on your own, but long for it.

The third thing is make your prayer utterly personal to you, as it's an expression of yourself to God – good and bad. It's all that. So it doesn't need formal words. No. In fact, it probably doesn't need words at all. You just open yourself. It's like pouring out your heart without words. So the Office becomes the Divine Office – the *Opus Dei* – something entirely different for you because it's surcharged by what's going on in your heart.

You have already discussed the most negative times in your life, so could you discuss some more about AA?
Sure. From about '75 onward, I was introduced to AA. Because of a peculiar distortion in my personality – that is, having to project a personality that is competent, effective, productive and so on, without really knowing what was going on – I would tend to incorporate AA into that persona. I became knowledgeable about AA. I was able to speak about it, even convincingly, but it wasn't getting into me.

It was St. Paul's "I can preach to others, and myself become a castaway." It was really only when I had lost and shoved away everything in 2003 that I finally said, "I'm done." I was utterly – talk about bottoms – there. I was asking for something that gave me a reason to live. And so, I was ready finally to embrace the AA way of life.

Now, why is it that AA and monastic life can go together? Well, one would think that the monastic life ought to be enough to sustain a life of sobriety, and maybe it is. I never really tried it that way, but in the AA fellowship, one key feature is the constant recognition of the precise and particular character of one's powerlessness in relationship to alcohol.

That's a particular kind of powerlessness, but that sense of powerlessness, of poverty of spirit, can ramify through everything else in the monastic life. It's always a matter of being able to say, "It's not me by myself. It's God assisting me in doing whatever I do, and I need God's help in whatever I do."

Other people can get that through the monastic life. The alcoholic, I think, ordinarily has to get it and renew it in the context of the AA community, because that community is the collective fellowship of those who have been there. So that kind of powerlessness, which brings you to acknowledge that you need God and that this need is never absent, is something learned peculiarly by the alcoholic in AA but then transferable to everything else.

Then everything else takes on the character of what it's supposed to be, that is, involvement in the life of God by accepting his blessings. This handing oneself over to God is the AA way of life and it becomes, then, a new wellspring.

What's been the happiest or the most joyful experience in your lifetime?

I think coming back here. Yeah, I think it's coming back to the monastery after having discovered what I needed in order to be able to do it right. It is really a great joy to feel that I am, finally, doing what so many years ago I promised.

Changes in the Church

As you know, St. Benedict himself became discouraged by a general disregard of spiritual ideas in his time, and today, some observers are of the opinion that society is once again falling into indifference to the meaning of a virtuous life and lack of spirituality. How has this affected Benedictine spirituality found within the Abbey and within the Church?

I think you'd have to go back to the '50s and '60s to get a hold of that question. Abbot Timothy [*Sweeney*] recently remarked that people in the 1960s and early '70s constitute a kind of lost generation. I'm in that group. It wasn't just the upheaval in Catholicism – the [*Second Vatican*] Council and all that's after it. But from 1961 or so onward, you had the counter-cultural movements; you had the drug culture emerging; you had the sexual revolution; you had the student riots in Europe; you had the Stonewall riots in New York; you had the emergence of all sorts of protest groups and demands for change and recognition.

It was a cultural upheaval on an enormous scale, and people came into the monastery when this was happening all around us. There was an opening up of things that hadn't ever even been talked about in a monastery. If you talked about them, it was in hushed tones in a dark room someplace under the seal of confession. This openness came in with the people and then, of course, we're not a closed place.

We have lots of avenues of egress and return and inward/outward stuff all the time. So the upheavals in the culture and the society had their effect within the monastery. It is a marvel, in a sense, and a great testimony that successive abbots managed to hold the thing together. There was a palpable sort of anxiety in all those years about, "Are we going to be able to hold this together?"

We had an abbot resign in '66. We had never had an abbot resign the first hundred years. They died with their boots on, for heaven's sake. "What, an abbot resign?!" Unthinkable kinds of things were happening. We had four abbots in the first hundred years. I think we're working on our fifth now in the second hundred years—Bonaventure, Gabriel, Timothy, Lambert and Justin, and we're not even 2054 yet.

Well, why is that? Well, it's because we acknowledge that we were now in a period of great, enormous upheaval. The people in administration have given what they can, and now somebody has to take it up and go forward with it, and I think that's what's happening. We've had remarkable people in place and we've been wise enough to elect them. They have carried the whole thing forward, but it's been an enormous trial and difficult to do so. I think it's not over yet.

How different is the Church today compared to when you first came here?

Enormously different. The style, the tone, the shape of the liturgy, the language of the liturgy, revision of the rites. Compare the before and after with the rites in the Latin and the Tridentine forms of the liturgy. Sure, the substance is the same. The essential structures are there, but all of the way in which it is conducted is completely different. The sensibility of it is different.

The old Catholic culture was about 450 years old, if you want to count it from the Council of Trent. If you want to count it from Gregory the Great, then it's about 1,200 or 1,500 years old. It was characterized by an enormous sense of permanence. And there were things that were always and everywhere the case, and those essential, basic things never changed. So change was the unthinkable, but it has become a constant experience.

People point to the collapse of social institutions, the customs and things like that, and that's true. A lot of things collapsed – a lot of the institutions. By institutions, by the way, I just mean regular and recurring ways of responding to the same situation. You have two people together. They regularly eat dinner together in this way at this time. That's an institution. And they divvy up the washing dishes and cooking and stuff like that. That's an institution.

So there were a number of institutions that were customs of the house. Many of these fell by the wayside. So we are in a kind of minimalist monasticism these days. We feel a little naked, I think. On the other hand, it's pretty nifty because you can do pretty much what you want. That's the sense of things. Do we want to structure this a little more, or do we want to just do the customary practices?

That gets right into the next question. Compare the morale of the monastery today to the past.

I think the morale is fairly upbeat. People are certainly conscious and aware of each other, by and large, and there's an enormous amount of attentiveness to each other, in a good sense. There is a pitch in and willing to cooperate. There's a lot of helping going on, such as picking up on tasks, jobs and responsibilities.

How has the decline in vocations impacted the Church and the monastery?

It's worrisome. It's hard to know what to make of it. Historically, if you did a demographic study over the last 150 years, you'd see a slow progression upward. Then in the late '30s and the '40s through the '50s, was a huge bulge.

Of seminarians?

Seminarians, nuns, priests. Then it begins to level off and decline, and then it went into a more severe decline. Now there is sort of an upward trend again. But in my age group, we think of the 220 monks connected to the community and the 160 that were here when I came in. What's happening is, of course, that the attrition among the older men is faster than young men coming in. How long will it take for that to even out? We don't know. Of course, you can't just go out and beat monastic vocation into somebody's head.

It is, in the admirable words of AA, a matter of attraction and not promotion. You can't go out and say, "You should be a monk because you're Catholic, healthy, talented and bright, so why don't you come visit for a while, see the place?" You can't do that. It's stupid and it invites disaster. So you put your sign out in a discreet, unobtrusive and non-manipulative way. You let people know that this is a kind of life that's available if you'd like to try it. You use normal, prudent screening processes to do that, and for the rest, you rely on God.

I don't know any other way to do it, but the fact remains, in the next 10 years, we'll probably experience a still sharper decline in total population. I hope, I pray, that we'll progress back up to a level of 120. During the '40s and '50s, on the basis of the large population we had, we found things to do because we had people to do various things. Now we don't have the people, so we're having to pull back from the things that we found them to do and that feels like a retreat, a giving up and a loss of vigor.

Perhaps one of the most important changes in the seminary curriculum occurred with the de-emphasis on Latin. Even if the Mass were to be celebrated in English, was elimination of Latin from the academic curriculum a good idea?

No, but I don't see how it could've been otherwise. I don't know what's going to happen there. I think that seminarians should learn sufficient Latin to handle ecclesiastical Latin, but I also think that, coincidentally, that's not going to happen. This is because aptitude for priesthood and ministry does not necessarily include linguistic skills and abilities. I think it's a good idea for everybody to learn Spanish.

In terms of changes in the Church, what do you consider positive and what are negative since the days of the Council?

I would say it this way. I think the directions of the reconstitution of theology and the Church are proceeding forward and they're good. Some changes are going to be okay; some are going to be troublesome; and some are going to be difficult to deal with. They are just contributions to a larger movement. How they winnow out, God only knows. I trust that they'll winnow out okay. That's why I don't like to engage in a heavy-duty battle with any given emergence of this or that or the other thing. You can examine it. You can ask about it. You may even want to critique it, but I won't go to the mat for it because it's a single element.

It will eventually get worked into a whole or it'll have some impact. If you find yourself opposing it, you may be opposing the will of God. On the other hand, if you're in there fighting and espousing something and it turns out to be merely the self-willed interest of the group, well what are you accomplishing by that? So keep your eyes open. Keep your ears open. And if asked about something, say it, but otherwise, pray.

Now, following up on that, what has been lost and what has been gained, assuming that you agree there's no going back to pre-Council days?

Well, I suppose the greatest thing that's been lost is an enormous sense of permanence and stability. That's been lost. It's neither good nor bad. It's uncomfortable, because it means having to get used to development or progress or movement that is unfamiliar.

I'm concerned that one of the things that has been lost is a lessening of doctrinal affirmation in favor of religious studies. We live in an era of empirical observation and nose counting, and that's not amenable to affirming what is firmly held and known and believed, or what can reliably be said as a normative order of things.

That kind of thing is a question that is answerable by philosophy and theology, but if you ask people today to settle on it in some way or another, they don't think philosophically. And if they do think philosophically, they don't know what philosophy to embrace in order to think. And when it comes to theology and doctrine, most people these days are saying, "Well, that's just what the Pope thinks." So we're in a kind of a reductionist time. It's a kind of supermarket of ideas without any clear affirmations.

The eclectic, formless mentalities of what is named "post-modernist culture" is really difficult for a deeply religious person, for monks. A world without boundaries, natures, forms, categories is really antipathetic to Catholic and monastic living.

Comment on your hopes for the future for the Church and the Abbey.

In my view, the Church and this reformation was a great blessing. God is bringing something worthwhile and what's coming up as worthwhile is this: the Church cannot, as an institution, aspire to have the global clout that governments can aspire to or United Nations or the EU or the mega-institutions. So, it is forced, per necessity, to become leaven in all cultures and societies. It can't do anything else. It cannot compete with governments or societal institutions or business structures.

How about monastic life?

Well, I just think monastic life is a kind of compact Christian living. It's like the distillation of an essence. It's the savor of what the gospel calls us to do. Monasteries are not about comfortable living in a situation where there's not much discomfort. Monasteries are about taking on the gospel and renunciation of the goods of this world, because we're convinced that the goods of this world are to be transformed into the consummation of "all things in Christ."

And so we renounce things of the world, not because they're evil. We're not world-hating people. We renounce them because they are destined to be something more and we try to cultivate, in our dimwitted way, what that more is and try to manifest it to some degree or another. And it is a kind of foretaste of what the heavenly Jerusalem is all about. It's sort of unbridled union in the charity of God of all peoples, all nations, all countries and all languages, summating into its final homecoming of everything.

People will begin to catch on that the ephemeral nature of living these days – moving from one thing to another, looking for this, looking for that – is not producing anything. It's not getting them anywhere, and I think that's a fertile field for both the attraction of the monastic life and the inspiration of God to say, "Yeah, well, why don't you think about this? Come and see and try it out."

Profile based upon: Fr. C.G., OSB, to Prof. Ruth C. Engs, December 19, 2012. Interview Transcriptions, Saint Meinrad Archabbey Archives, St. Meinrad, IN; additional comments from, Fr. C.G. September-October 2015.

Bibliography

Engs, Ruth Clifford, Editor. *Conversations in the Abbey: Senior monks of Saint Meinrad reflect on their lives*. St. Meinrad, IN: Saint Meinrad Archabbey, 2008.

Fry, Timothy, OSB, Translator. *RB 1980: The Rule of St. Benedict*. Collegeville, MN: Liturgical Press, 1981.

ORDO 2009. St. Meinrad, IN: Abbey Press, 2009.

Appendix: Angel Bread Recipe[*]

Yield: 1 regular-size bread pan for 8 people
Time: About 1½ hours, including baking

Ingredients:

1 packet of active dry yeast

2½ cups regular flour

¼ cup white sugar

2 tsp. baking powder

½ tsp. salt

½ tsp. baking soda

½ cup butter

1 cup buttermilk

Directions:

1. Heat the oven to 350°F. Combine the yeast with ¼ cup warm water and pinch of salt in a small bowl. Let sit for 5 minutes.

2. Mix together the flour, sugar, baking powder, baking soda and salt, in a large bowl. Add ½ cup of butter. Blend with your fingers until the mixture resembles coarse crumbs. Add the yeast mixture, buttermilk and stir just until combined.

3. Place the dough on a floured surface and knead about 5 minutes.

4. Place in an ungreased bread pan. Cover the pan with a kitchen towel and let the dough rest for about 20 minutes in a warm area or until dough has risen.

5. Bake until the top is firm and a straw or toothpick comes out clean, 40-45 minutes.

6. Slice and serve hot or warm with butter and/or molasses.

*Although the exact recipe for Angel Bread made by the brothers is unknown, this is similar in taste to what some of the older monks remembered. As an alternative, it can also be rolled out and cut into individual biscuits.

Index

CPSIA information can be obtained
at www.ICGtesting.com
Printed in the USA
BVOW10s0223011217

501667BV00015B/487/P